Quantitative Techniques for Financial Analysis

C.F.A. SERIES

Quantitative Techniques for Financial Analysis

JEROME L. VALENTINE, C.F.A.
Trust Officer, Manager of Computer Research — Investments
Republic National Bank of Dallas

and

EDMUND A. MENNIS, C.F.A.
Senior Vice President and Chairman, Trust Investment Committee
Republic National Bank of Dallas

1971

RICHARD D. IRWIN, INC.
HOMEWOOD, ILLINOIS 60430
IRWIN-DORSEY LIMITED, GEORGETOWN, ONTARIO

First Printing, August, 1971

Library of Congress Catalog Card No. 77–158045

Printed in the United States of America

Foreword

The increasing infusion of sophisticated mathematical and statistical tools and techniques in general business literature has created an awareness by the financial analyst of the need to acquire a better understanding of the applicability of quantitative techniques to his own professional skills. Books on the mechanics of quantitative techniques exist in abundance, as do publications dealing with the quantitative analysis of specialized financial topics. What appears to be needed in the field of securities investment, however, is a comprehensive treatment of quantitative tools of practical application to the techniques of professional financial analysis or portfolio management. Generally the analyst is expected to be concerned more with what goes into and comes out of the technique, rather than with the detailed mechanics of a particular technique. The modern tool-kit of the analyst, then, requires a set of quantitative techniques which will enable him to measure precisely concepts which he may already express verbally in his research reports or portfolio reviews.

The C.F.A. Research Foundation, in its continuing efforts to furnish literature of significance to the practitioner of financial analysis, has attempted in this publication to meet the needs of the younger analyst who is in the process of acquiring professional skills, together with those of the more experienced analyst who wishes to refurbish his tool-kit.

The sources of financial support for this publication may be of interest. In 1968 the Financial Analysts Federation created the Nicholas Molodovsky Award, the highest honor that can be bestowed by the Federation. It is presented only to those individuals who have made an outstanding contribution of such significance as to change the direction of the profession and to raise it to higher standards of accomplishment. This award was established to honor Dr. Nicholas Molodovsky, one of the profession's outstanding scholars and the first recipient of the award. Primarily in his capacity as Editor of the *Financial Analysts Journal,* but also as a writer and critic, Dr. Molodovsky labored long and hard to bridge the gap between the academic and professional worlds and struggled to make the growing use of quantitative techniques in financial analysis more palatable. The Nicholas Molodovsky Award consists of a financial contribution in the recipient's name to a research project of special personal interest. Thus, the initial financial support for this study was received from the Financial Analysts Federation in recognition of the significant professional contributions of the late Dr. Nicholas Molodovsky to quantitative financial analysis. Additional financial support was provided by the Nicholas Molodovsky Fund, representing the contributions of a large number of financial analysts who wished to be identified with a publication dedicated to a major leader in their industry.

The problem of finding an author to write a book to meet the objectives outlined above presented unusual difficulties. The Foundation needed someone who was not only familiar with quantitative techniques and the computer, but who had also a practical background and long experience in financial analysis and investment management. In order to get the best of both these worlds, a joint authorship was decided upon. Jerome L. Valentine is a Trust Officer in charge of the Computer Applications Section of the Trust Investment Division of the Republic National Bank of Dallas. A graduate of Drury College, he has done graduate work at Vanderbilt University and New York University and is completing his doctoral studies at North Texas State University. He joined the Republic National Bank in 1967, and he has been a practicing financial analyst since 1964. In his present position, he is responsible for all computer work used in the Trust Investment Division.

Edmund A. Mennis is a Senior Vice President and Chairman of the Trust Investment Committee of the Republic National Bank of Dallas. A graduate of The College of The City of New York, he received his M.A. degree from Columbia University and his Ph.D. from New York University. A practicing financial analyst since 1945, he has also been an Associate Editor of the *Financial Analysts Journal* since 1960 and has been active on the Research and Publications Committee of The Institute of Chartered Financial Analysts in reviewing material to be used as part of the C.F.A. examination program.

Ordinarily a joint authorship involves a division of responsibility, with each of the authors assuming the task of writing a part of the book and reviewing the work of his coauthor. In this instance, however, Mr. Valentine assumed the responsibility of organizing and writing the text. Dr. Mennis reviewed the innumerable drafts of the manuscript from the viewpoint of a practicing analyst who was some years removed from academic exposure to quantitative techniques and who had only a nodding acquaintance with the computer. The resulting text hopefully has combined the talents of both authors to produce a book that is both theoretically sound and practically oriented.

Upon completion of the earlier drafts of the manuscript, the authors benefited considerably from critical appraisals by a special Review Committee established by the C.F.A. Research Foundation. Members of the Review Committee were: Frank E. Block, C.F.A., Senior Vice President, Girard Bank, Philadelphia, Pennsylvania; Robert D. Milne, C.F.A., Partner, Boyd, Watterson & Co., Cleveland, Ohio; M. Dutton Morehouse, C.F.A., Manager, Brown Brothers, Harriman & Company, Chicago, Illinois; Jack L. Treynor, Editor, the *Financial Analysts Journal,* New York City, New York; and Peter F. Way, C.F.A., Vice President, First National City Bank, New York City, New York.

In addition to the contributions of the Review Committee, the authors gratefully acknowledge the constructive suggestions received from many individuals who responded to an inquiry from the Foundation. The manuscript was not submitted to the Trustees of the C.F.A. Research Foundation for approval prior to publication, and the authors would wish to assume all responsibility for the content of this study.

The authors are also indebted to the Literary Executor of the late Sir Ronald A. Fisher, F.R.S., and to Oliver & Boyd, Edinburgh, for their permission to reprint Table III from their book *Statistical Methods for Research Workers;* and to the Literary Executor of the late Sir Ronald A. Fisher, F.R.S., to Dr. Frank Yates, F.R.S., and to Oliver & Boyd, Edinburgh, for permission to reprint Tables III and V from their book *Statistical Tables for Biological, Agricultural, and Medical Research.*

This approach to quantitative analysis is somewhat novel, and the C.F.A. Research Foundation would welcome suggestions for any improvement.

Monroe Hall
University of Virginia
Charlottesville, Virginia
June, 1971

C. Stewart Sheppard
Executive Director
C.F.A. Research Foundation

Contents

xi

Chapter
1   What This Book Is About

As the world has become more complex, the quantitative techniques of statistics and mathematics have been used with increasing success to simplify analysis and to solve problems in many fields. In recent years the proliferation of quantitative techniques in the field of financial analysis has been enormous, but the busy analyst has found it difficult to acquire an understanding of the necessary tools because of the special language in which they have been presented. Assuming only an understanding of elementary algebra, this book will attempt to bridge the gap between the practitioner and the quantitative theorist, with emphasis on understanding the functions of the tools rather than describing elaborate computations and proofs. Thus, the practitioner will know what to use and when, and what it can do for him, with the "how" in most instances being accomplished by a statistician or a computer.

The Growth in Quantitative Technique

The quantitative techniques of statistics and mathematics have been applied with success to a large number of disciplines. They form the backbone of the scientific approach to problem solving, and it has become fairly obvious that the scientific method has provided the more significant successes in man's attempt to probe the objective world. The successes of the quantitative approach occurred first in the natural sciences, but in recent decades the social sciences have moved rapidly toward the use of mathematical analysis as more powerful techniques have been developed, as the computer has made practical the computations which these techniques require, and as the demands for precision and objectivity rose in these newly developed disciplines. Psychometrics now stands beside psychology, just as econometrics has joined economics. Sociology and anthropology have developed quantitative applications, and a number of techniques have been used in political science. Although these developments do not yet rival the constructs of physics or chemistry, man is now beginning to apply the methodology which has explained the behavior of falling apples and atomic energy to the problems that he faces in the socio-economic world in which he lives.

Finance and economics have hardly been immune to this trend. Journal articles now bristle with equations, and the output of models of the national economy is an influence upon national policy. The financial analyst, responsible for a critical appraisal and projection of developments in these two fields, is directly challenged by this trend. The quantitative method can provide tools for probing problems which can only remain guesswork on the intuitive level. Without an understanding of how these tools work, the analyst is left to attack a modernized army of problems with only the sniper's rifle of isolated intuitive insight. That a rifle is an excellent weapon cannot be denied, but it cannot be expected to stop a tank. In the growing complexity of the world and the growing sophistication of the investment profession, problems are now so imposing that it is appropriate for the analyst to begin to develop weapons in defense. Quantitative weapons are the most logical choice because of the precision with which they consider the structure of the data and also because their objectivity permits results to be used by different analysts. In addition, quantitative techniques permit existing theory to be subjected to tests of validity, and the results of various quantitative studies can be used as the basis upon which more sophisticated theories can be built. This cumulative property of scientific knowledge can produce a complex theoretical structure that would only be speculation if built by intuition.

Problems in Learning Quantitative Tools

Unfortunately, it is extremely difficult for the practicing financial analyst to acquire the tools of mathematics and statistics. The demands on the average analyst's time are too severe to permit formal academic course work, and in most regions of the country such courses are available only during business hours and are rarely directed toward the specific needs of the financial analyst. Conversations of any duration with quantitative specialists are difficult because of the shortage of trained personnel in this area, the demands upon their time, and the presence of a language barrier. The literature of mathematics and statistics is voluminous and of very high quality but suffers from several drawbacks. It is oriented either toward trained specialists or toward course work where a professor is available to explain techniques. In the former case, decoding is virtually impossible; in the latter case, the material which relates the description of the technique to the concrete problems of the real world is omitted under the assumption that the instructor will provide motivation. The literature which describes techniques in verbal terms invariably deals only with the simplest of tools and does little in expanding understanding of the more complex aspects of the subject.

Actually, there are solid institutional reasons for this problem. Traditionally, mathematical tools have been used by individuals in certain specialized functions—academic mathematicians, physicists, chemists, professional statisticians, and the like. These individuals undertook formal training in quantitative techniques before beginning their careers and then continued their professional development after receiving their degrees. This meant that the market for literature in the area was fragmented into three basic divisions. Textbooks trained the initiate under the direction of a master craftsman, journals informed the experienced technician of new developments and assumed a high level of expertise, and elementary works provided youth with the basic material necessary before initiation.

This system served its purpose quite well, but when new disciplines began to require information concerning certain aspects of quantitative theory, the institutional framework was slow to adjust. A quite similar problem has developed in the less easily described realm of professional values. The standards of value in quantitative work were developed under the specialized system. As a result, the literature in the field is considered to be worthwhile if: (1) it is as brief as possible; (2) it omits "trivial" intermediate steps in reasoning; (3) it emphasizes proofs instead of intuitive justification; (4) it contains a high degree of theoretical generality and a minimum of practical application; (5) it deletes "unnecessary" verbal rephrasing of mathematical formulations. As a result, work by professional academicians is considered to be significant for almost exactly the same reasons that it is unintelligible to the uninitiated.

A reaction to this traditional approach has developed, and a number of business schools and economics departments have started their own quantitative departments. Although this is a helpful move toward broadening the usage of these tools, the same forces which created the older mathematical institutional and value structure appear to be operating now in these new social structures. Once again access to the techniques requires formal preparation and once again the literature appears to be dropping into the three basic market fragments. Only this time the apprentice is initiated into the cult of econometrics or management science instead of math or physics. An intelligent verbal description of the uses of the more advanced techniques for those who may wish to apply the tools without having to present a mathematical proof of their internal structure is once again beginning to acquire an aura of intellectual unacceptability.

In addition to the problems stemming from the specialized nature of the literature and the values motivating the style of presentation, the financial analyst attempting to begin explorations in the field will soon discover that those applications which are presented do not directly relate to the particular problems which he encounters daily. This too is quite natural, for the applications in general texts will relate to disciplines having an established tradition of quantitative methodology simply because most readers will be oriented toward this type of work (examples might be quality control, inventory management, scientific experiments, or physics). The general nature of those illustrations is unfortunate because the techniques can most easily be understood in terms of a particular, practical example from which the analyst can generalize to other, more complicated applications.

Approach Used in This Book

When The Institute of Chartered Financial Analysts decided to include quantitative methods in the C. F. A. program, these considerations presented a more than usually difficult problem. The material used for the candidate's preparation needed to assume a level of professional competence equivalent to the MBA, but a quantitative orientation at the beginning of the program could not be required. The use of the techniques should be presented, but without any emphasis upon the actual computations required and without any proofs whatsoever. The material would be more valuable if it were application-oriented and if the applications were directly related to the normal work of the analyst (although possibly simplified for ease in presentation). The shortage of material having these unusual characteristics explains the presence of this book.

An attempt has been made through all of the chapters to conform (as rigidly as the authors' capability permits) to the following basic principles. The verbal text is written on a level which should not insult the intelligence of the practicing analyst, but the mathematical development assumes no training beyond a long-forgotten course in high school algebra. The presentation is essentially verbal, with the mathematical formulation presented only insofar as it is necessary. The emphasis throughout is upon an intuitive understanding of the various techniques as practical tools which can and should be used in everyday situations. Each quantitative tool is considered to be a "black box" requiring a certain type of input, solving a certain type of problem, and producing output which possesses certain clearly defined characteristics. The phrase "black box" used throughout the book is not used in its precise mathematical sense. Instead, it refers to any tool which need not be subjected to intellectual dissection to be useful in practical analysis. A telephone is the most obvious example. This book is not intended to provide the analyst with a knowledge of the computational aspects of the tools which are described, for this information is available in numerous texts for reference when needed and ordinarily can be handled by a technician. Instead, a conscious attempt has been made to provide the reader with a working knowledge of the basic quantitative concepts, the approach which is implied in the method and the manner in which the quantitative techniques can be effectively used.

The choice of techniques to be included in the book has been based upon the ease with which the tools can be applied to the investment function but an effort has been made to include the tools which are basic to an entire area of research or which help to illuminate fundamental quantitative concepts.

The first chapter is on notation and attempts to show why the apparently abstruse language of mathematics is actually quite valuable. In addition, this arrangement allows the majority of notational problems to be eliminated before new concepts are introduced.

The chapters on algebra and elementary statistics are included as a refresher for those who have forgotten basic material. An attempt has been made, however, to show the intuitive basis for a number of the simple operations upon numbers.

Probability theory is treated from the standpoint of subjective probabilities simply because this approach permits practical applications without complex theoretical developments.

Linear regression is treated on an elementary level in order to show a basic but valuable statistical technique before more subtle statistical concepts are introduced.

The chapters covering the more advanced techniques begin with the calculus. The presentation of this chapter is extremely elementary and is intended only to provide the analyst with a knowledge of the manner in which calculus can attack problems. If an attempt were made to provide an insight into the actual techniques of the calculus, even the most cursory treatment would require more pages than can be devoted to any five chapters in this book.

The chapter on hypothesis testing introduces the basic concepts of statistical inference and is the first chapter which provides some of the flavor of the statistical method.

The analysis of variance develops the concepts of inference in terms of certain types of applications.

Multiple regression develops the basic ideas of the chapter on simple regression in light of the material contained in hypothesis testing.

Elementary matrix algebra is discussed because it is the basis for a very high percentage of the work currently being published and also gives an insight into the structure of such diverse problems as elementary accounting and linear programming.

Linear programming is the basis upon which a larger literature in the area of maximization techniques has been built. It provides practical results in itself and also can serve as a cornerstone in the analyst's understanding of the nature of any problem in which maximum or minimum values are desired.

The two chapters treating the computer are included because this tool, while not necessarily quantitative, has been the fundamental reason why the other techniques have become economically practical in investment work. The first chapter on computers discusses the nature of the machine and how programmers provide it with instructions. The second chapter discusses the much more complex problems of project control and systems development.

A number of tables have been included as appendixes to the book. Although the various chapters can be read without reference to these tables, a deeper understanding of a number of the examples in the text can be gained if the tables are referred to by the reader.

A list of additional readings which will permit the analyst to explore models in some detail has been included at the end of a number of the chapters. A brief description of the books is provided in order to permit the reader to select readings which are most likely to satisfy his personal objectives. The particular works chosen in these lists are, quite naturally, the result of the authors' personal background and biases. It would be absurd to maintain that the works which have been included are the only valuable material in their particular field, and it is probably impossible to find a set of readings that are clearly superior to alternatives. It is hoped, however, that the reader will find that the material selected emphasizes the aspects of the techniques which are meaningful to an analyst and provides a substantial broadening of intellectual horizons.

Simplifying the Problem of Reading Quantitative Material

A few comments concerning how this material can most effectively be used in self-study may prove beneficial. The most important point in reading any quantitative material is to remember that one of the main advantages of mathematics is that it is concise. As a result, even when the techniques are described verbally in some detail, one page of material has the same information content as a large number of pages covering qualitative subjects. This implies that a reading rate $\frac{1}{5}$ to $\frac{1}{10}$ of the reader's regular rate is quite normal—the information content is really being digested at normal speed. If the material is read at a normal reading rate, unless the reader is very familiar with both the content and the authors' syntax, comprehension will be extremely low.

Another feature unique to quantitative subjects is the importance of equations and graphs. In verbal subjects, such scribblings serve to amplify and illuminate the text; however, in this type of material, they *constitute* the text, and the verbal description serves to amplify and illuminate. As a result, an abnormally serious consideration of numbers and graphs is needed. The reader should therefore accept without discouragement the likelihood that he will cover only a few pages of text in some normal study periods. Other sections will tend to go much faster simply because the same number of concepts is expressed in a larger number of pages.

A great deal of time can be saved if each chapter is skimmed before it is read carefully. Mathematical developments tend to move methodically from point to point, and comprehension is greatly simplified if a preliminary scan of the chapter has shown the reader roughly where the development is leading. This tendency toward point-by-point development produces an additional reading problem, for it is difficult to proceed if an earlier step in the analysis is not understood. For this reason, it is important to attempt to reread and rethink each point within a chapter before continuing to the next concept. The chapters are largely independent, and a failure to understand the material in one chapter should not greatly affect the others, although the chapters should be read in order if possible. Each chapter is preceded by a brief summary describing the material that follows, so that the reader will have an overview of the tools and their applications before their more detailed presentation. The chapters on notation and algebra are the backbone of all other chapters and should be read until thoroughly mastered. Hypothesis testing contains concepts which are important in almost all of the advanced techniques and which are vital to the understanding of the quantitative methodology.

No claim is made that the content of this book exhausts the set of quantitative techniques which have value in financial analysis or that this is an exhaustive treatment of the subjects covered. The approach that has been taken is that an understanding of the functions of the various tools is more important than an understanding of either the computations or the related proofs. As a result, the function of the technique should be presented first in order to deepen the understanding of more technical material which may be encountered by the analyst at a later time.

The dual purposes of the book are to assist the analyst in his attempt to acquire more powerful methods for research and to assist the profession in its attempt to move toward a more scientific methodology. Academic rigor has been avoided in order to create a simple presentation. It is hoped that as a result of this material the analyst will be motivated to continue reading in the quantitative area and that this material will provide him with the intuitive foundation upon which a solid understanding of these techniques can be built. If any such analyst should develop the mathematical sophistication eventually to return to this book and consider it to be a naïve presentation, the highest aims of the authors will have been achieved.

Models, Their Nature and Value

Having completed an introduction to the book, it seems reasonable to provide an introduction to the nature of the tools which will later be discussed individually. Each quantitative tool can be regarded as a model of reality, and the most fundamental characteristic which is common to all models is that they inevitably are an abstraction from the real world. As an example, a child's airplane model is an abstraction of a real airplane which portrays the plane's shape and color but does not bother to reproduce the unwanted characteristics — its size, weight, expense, and so forth. On the other hand, an accounting model of the same airplane would abstract a picture of its expense very accurately but would disregard its shape and color as well as its size and weight. As can be seen by these simple examples, models definitely have a common feature. They do not give a *complete* picture of reality; they only give a good picture of certain *important aspects* of reality. The particular aspect which is seen as important has nothing to do with the model; it depends on whether the user is a schoolboy or an accountant. As a result, there is no such thing as a *good* model, only an appropriate one — a model which adequately abstracts from the real world those aspects which may be needed by the particular user at that time. A model, then, stands in direct relation to a need, and a model satisfying many diverse needs is said (at least by mathematicians) to be *powerful*.

In the above example, the accounting model is powerful because it can be applied to an airplane, or to a car, a diversified business, or anything which has financial aspects which need to be pictured. The accounting system represents, or "abstracts" those financial aspects and disregards the rest of the plane, car, etc. If this abstraction did not take place, the investment analyst would have an impossible job in comparing General Dynamics to General Motors. The accounting model is powerful *because* it is abstract; and mathematics, being the most abstract of all disciplines, could naturally be expected to provide the most powerful models. The usefulness, precision, and generality of the quantitative technique have become so accepted in the exact sciences that at the present time a theory is not regarded as completely formulated unless it is stated mathematically.

Mathematical models are abstract techniques, or procedures, which are known to yield the correct (or approximately correct) answers. A simple example of a mathematical model is the compound interest table used by the analyst to calculate the growth rate of, say, the earnings per share of IBM over the past ten years. Another model is the arithmetic mean or "average" used many times each day by almost all businessmen. The advantage of these and more complicated models is that they solve real problems, that is, they satisfy real needs, which is, of course, the only justification for any model. The "quantitative model" is broken down into a large set of smaller tools, so that it is possible to regard basic arithmetic, algebra, the calculus, multivariate statistics, and the like as more specific models used to solve more specific and unique problems. Each of these vague areas, of course, is broken down into a number of smaller tools. Each technique is designed to provide an accurate solution to a very specific type of problem, and as a result the most significant problem in the use of the quantitative model as a whole is the selection of the appropriate tool for any given problem.

The major advantage to using these mathematical techniques is that they make it possible to draw upon a "storehouse" of knowledge which has required several thousands of years and no small number of geniuses to develop. By using a mathematical model to solve the particular investment problem at hand, the solution technique is provided by, say, Newton — leaving the analyst free to select techniques and to cast problems into a form solvable by some established procedure. In effect, the analyst is using the thoughts of Pythagorus, Newton, and others to solve certain technical problems defined by the senior analyst. Using this approach, the researcher is able greatly to extend his power to analyze his problems, and superior investment results might reasonably be expected.

It is important to emphasize that the use of any technique or model is possible only if a particular problem is molded into a form which the model can accept. Because this molding of the problem into available solution patterns can only be done by a man who understands the real nature of the problem and the characteristics of the available tools, the techniques of mathematics must be understood by the analyst or it will be impossible for these models to be effectively applied.

It is interesting to note that mathematics has its models too. The use of graphs to show the relationships between variables which are implied by various equations, as well as the analogy of "space" to represent the variables being considered, illustrate the fact that mathematics itself utilizes the abstractions and the molding patterns which are common to all models.

One very interesting point which may be regarded as basic to all that follows is that the English language, like all languages, is in itself a model of reality. It has its own notation, its rules of punctuation and syntax, and a very complex set of symbols (words) which are manipulated within the given set of rules. By using the alphabet and building words and then sentences, paragraphs, and books, English is capable of expressing virtually any set of concepts. As a result, it is one of the most powerful of all of the models. But *the language of mathematics* is a very complex model which closely parallels the verbal language of English in function. Using mathematical notation, it is possible to build "expressions" which are permitted by the mathematical rules and then manipulate them by the established grammar in the system. It is the notation of math that "communicates," and its disadvantage of complexity is more than offset by its precision. In addition, the structure of the permissible expressions of mathematics, although more unfamiliar than the grammar of English, permits greater accuracy in portraying the problem and also allows greater generality. One of the main advantages of the use of all mathematical models is their ability to communicate meaning without the possibility of misinterpretation.

Chapter
2 Notation or the Language of Symbols and What They Mean

In order to use quantitative techniques, some method must be used to represent real world relationships in a simple and precise form. Mathematical symbols, which on the surface appear unintelligible, are merely conventional notations to permit the statement of complex relationships in a clear and readily understandable manner. As the letters of the alphabet became inadequate, mathematicians used letters of the Greek alphabet as a supplement. This chapter provides an explanation of simple and more complicated mathematical expressions, and explains the use of subscripts, exponents, and the important summation symbol, the Greek letter Σ. At the end of the chapter, a table describes the implied or conventional usage of a number of symbols that can help decode many apparently complicated formulas.

ELEMENTARY NOTATION

From the introduction, mathematics can be seen to be a system of models which can be used to represent the real world in purely quantitative terms. Although this representation must necessarily involve some abstraction and as a result some distortion of reality, the precision and manipulative power of the system more than offset its inability to consider problems from a qualitative standpoint. But the precision which has been emphasized stems largely from the notation of mathematics, and this notation is in itself a model expressing mathematical concepts. Over the course of the development of mathematics, a number of conventions have gradually evolved which permit mathematical ideas to be easily conveyed, and the most useful of these have been gradually consolidated into the quantitative notation which we now use.

11

As a matter of fact, the initial use of Arabic numerals is considered by many to be the greatest single advance ever made in the entire history of quantitative methods. The use of this system of numbers in arithmetic was expanded when, in the Middle Ages, algebra was first introduced in Europe. This development, in turn, established the need for a symbol which could be used to represent some unknown quantity, some number which was known to have a value but whose value was as yet concealed from the researcher. This quantity, which we now refer to as a *variable,* was expressed as the letter x. The manipulation of numbers and variables progressed rapidly, with symbols used to express even the operations which were being performed upon these values. The *Encyclopaedia Britannica,* in its article on mathematical notations, indicates that the use of two parallel lines ($=$) to express equality began in the 16th century, with Robert Recorde: ". . . bicause noe .2. thynges, can be moare equalle." The "+" and "−" signs were apparently introduced in the 15th century as a result of a system of recording warehouse weights. Later, "×" for multiplication and "÷" for division were added. Modern algebraic notation tends to rely heavily upon the use of parentheses to indicate both the order in which operations are to be performed and also to imply multiplication. As a result:

$5 \times x$ or $5 \cdot x$ or $(5)(x)$ means "5" times "x," and can be written simply as "$5x$."

$(5)(x)(x)$ means "5" times "x" times "x."

In addition, x, y, and z were pressed into service as symbols to permit problems involving more than one variable to be analyzed. Eventually, letters were even used to stand for unchanging quantities. These "constants" were represented by the earlier letters of the alphabet such as "a," "b," or "c." Notation at this point permitted people to write such statements as:

1. $4 = 2 + 2$
2. $4x = 16$
3. $y = a + b + c$
4. $y = ax$
5. $y = a + bx$

These examples show several types of important mathematical quantities. The most fundamental quantity, of course, is simply a number such as "2" or "4." When mathematical thought moved beyond simple arithmetic by introducing letters such as "x" or "y," it was really introducing a new type of quantity. This quantity, a variable, was a number as real as the numbers 2 or 4, but it had the new characteristic of having a value which was unknown. This unknown value could be 2, 4, or any other number, but the variable could be manipulated exactly as if its value were known. This discovery was the foundation for the development of algebra. Viewed another way, a variable was a number which could assume any value, a number whose value could be allowed to vary. The older type of quantity exemplified by 2 and 4 therefore became known as "constants" to distinguish their fixed character from the more flexible variable.

Letters such as "a" or "b" were used to denote constants in mathematical expressions to show that the quantities being represented had these constant, unchanging qualities even though the expression did not specify their numerical value. The quantity represented by "a" was not specified as being either "2" or "4," but it was shown to be a value which would be known whenever the expression was evaluated and which did not vary in value during the course of the analysis.

In this new notational framework, the value of one variable could be expressed in terms of another variable. For example, y could be said to equal $a + bx$, meaning that the actual numerical value of y was known only indirectly through a knowledge of the numerical value of x. The relationship between unknowns could be specified, defining variables in terms of other variables. Such a definition is called a "function," and in this particular case y is expressed as a function of x. This indirect assignment of value is the cornerstone of mathematics, and all quantitative techniques are merely the reshuffling of these assignments or (stated another way) the manipulation of functions.

Recalling for a moment the "word problems" of high school days, it would be possible to translate the statements 1 through 5 above into the following English sentences:

1. Two added to two equals four.
2. Four times an unknown quantity (x) equals sixteen.
3. There is a quantity (y) which is equal to the sum of three other quantities (a, b, and c).
4. There is a variable (y) which is equal to the product of a constant quantity (a) times another variable (x) . . . or . . . there are two quantities which are proportional to each other.
5. There is a variable (y) equal to the sum of a constant factor (a) and a proportional quantity (bx).

As can be seen, mathematical notation is substantially simpler than English.

In effect, comparing the relationship between mathematical equations and their corresponding English statements in a way similar to that used above is an attempt to compare the relative merits of two different models of the same item. When the models deal with quantitative relationships and become even moderately complex, the advantage of the symbolic notation of mathematics over the verbal model increases very rapidly.

As mathematical applications were expanded beyond the simple basic algebra used in the above statements, additional notational requirements were rapidly encountered. First, problems which were realistic enough to serve some practical purpose quickly began to involve more symbols than the alphabet could accommodate, and as a result the Greek alphabet was added. When even this became inadequate, subscripts were added to the letters to permit a distinction between variables. As expressions became more complicated, parentheses were introduced to indicate the order in which calculations were to be performed, with all operations within parentheses performed before other calculations were begun. Another problem stemmed from the development of completely new models by which additional problems could be subjected to quantitative manipulation. Examples of this are the calculus, differential equations, probability theory, and more recently the development of statistics. In each of these disciplines, specialized operations and frequently used numbers had to be represented, and new symbols were quickly developed to give precision to the advanced approaches. By examining a few of these streamlining techniques at this point, it is possible to introduce symbols which can be used to simplify the later discussion of more complicated mathematical tools. The following sections are therefore not an exhaustive treatment of the notation used throughout this book but can be regarded as an introduction to a few basic symbols frequently encountered in almost all quantitative work.

Special jargon has been developed to allow mathematical quantities to be referenced in English format. Some of the most basic terms are shown in Figure 2–1.

A number of relations other than equality are treated in mathematics and have been given special symbols. The notation for the most common "relational operators" is shown in Table 2–1.

Several other frequently encountered symbols are described in passing at this point. $|x|$ means "the absolute value of x." This is the value of x without regard to the sign. For example, $|\pm5| = 5$. The symbol "$\pm$" means "plus or minus"; in everyday language, it could be translated as "give or

FIGURE 2–1

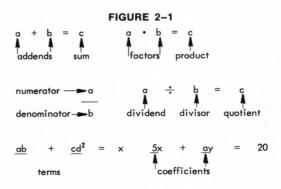

TABLE 2–1

Symbol	Description
$=$	equals
$>$	is greater than
$<$	is less than
$\leq$	is less than or equal to
$\geq$	is greater than or equal to
$\neq$	is not equal to

take" some amount. An example might be 4,376 feet $\pm$ 20 feet, meaning "4,376 feet, give or take 20 feet as an allowance for errors in measurement." The symbol ". . ." means "and so forth" or "etc." The dots stand for the missing numbers which are not shown for convenience in notation. An example is 1, 2, 3 . . . n, which simply means 1, 2, 3, and so forth until the number n is reached. The symbol "$\therefore$" means "therefore."

EXPONENTS

One of the most useful additions to the notation which has so far been introduced is the use of exponents. Recall from earlier days that x^2 is another way of writing $(x)(x)$, or x times x. Obviously, x^3 is a simpler way of writing $(x)(x)(x)$. But it is relatively simple to expand the use of exponents well beyond this extremely simple application. For example, mathematicians have used x^{-1} as a symbol for $\frac{1}{x}$ for quite some time.

Using this approach, it is possible to write:

$$\frac{10x + 5}{5y + 50} \quad \text{as} \quad (10x + 5)(5y + 50)^{-1}$$

and keep the formula in a more convenient form by writing it on only one line. The approach can be expanded somewhat by writing x^{-2} for $\frac{1}{x^2}$. Using this extension, we can write:

$$\frac{10x + 5}{(5y + 50)^2} \quad \text{as} \quad (10x + 5)(5y + 50)^{-2}$$

and keep the relationships in the formula from appearing to be more difficult than is the case.

A number of the formulas in statistics use the radical sign $\sqrt{}$ to express the operation of taking the square root of a number. An exponent can easily be used to accomplish this same purpose by defining $x^{1/2}$ as being simply another way of stating $\sqrt{x}$. By using this approach, $x^{1/3} = \sqrt[3]{x}$, which is the cube root of x. From this it is relatively simple to regard $x^{2/3}$ as simply another way of writing $\sqrt[3]{x^2}$.

SUBSCRIPTS

Unfortunately, there are not enough letters in the alphabet to permit a reasonably complicated mathematical argument to be presented without a great deal of confusion. As a result of this problem, subscripts have been used to allow the reader to differentiate between variables. For example x_1 is not the same as x_2. Similarly, $y = a + bx$ could easily be expressed as $x_1 = a + bx_2$. Since any number can obviously be used as a subscript, it is simple within this notational system to create as many variables as are needed in the statement of the mathematical problem. Although the flexibility of the system virtually eliminates the problem of precisely representing numerous variables, a major notational advantage of a completely different sort has made subscripts even more valuable. Because both x and y were available for subscripts, it became possible to have x_1, x_2, and x_3 as three separate and distinct variables which nevertheless had something in common — the quality of "x"ness. Each of the x's or the group of all x's could then be related to, say, y_1, y_2, and y_3, which were similar to each other with respect to "y"ness but nevertheless were three separate and distinct variables. The three y's could be regarded as different from each other but *very* different from the three x's.

As an example of this notational scheme, consider x and y as two men each owning a personal portfolio. The portfolio manager for both men typically analyzes portfolios by dividing the stocks in the account into three categories — basic industrial, moderate growth, and high growth. He then takes the total market value of the portfolio in each category as a percentage of the total market value of the entire portfolio in order to derive an account's diversification. By using subscripts, the portfolio manager can call the percentage of x's portfolio which is invested in basic industrial stocks by the symbol "x_1." Similarly, x_2 equals the exposure of account x in moderate growth stocks, and x_3 indicates participation in the high growth issues. Naturally, $x_1 + x_2 + x_3 = 100\%$ if 100% of the portfolio is invested. Since the account executive also does the same thing for y's account, $y_1 + y_2 + y_3 = 100\%$. And certainly it is possible to say $x_1 + x_2 + x_3 = y_1 + y_2 + y_3$ simply because 100% = 100% even if the two portfolios differ substantially in composition and size.

If all of this seems to be somewhat academic, the problem is probably that this particular example is an extremely simple situation. Real business problems involve many more variables, making the advantages of subscripts more obvious. However, even in this somewhat artificial situation, the expression using subscripts is substantially more meaningful than the equivalent statement without subscripts: $u + v + w = x + y + z$. If the different groups in the two portfolios are to be analyzed, the portfolio manager is able to refer to the same group in both portfolios by simply using the same subscript for both x and y. For example, both x_1 and y_1

analyst's nightmare, but the senior analyst could take great pride in the precision of the statement of the assignment. His assistant may not *understand* the assignment, but he could never *misinterpret* it. And if the junior analyst is sufficiently familiar with statistics, the correct calculations will always be performed.

This is not always the case when the assignment is given as: "Get me the average of the stock's average price for the last ten years." In fact, a rigorous senior analyst with a good junior might even write in June, 1968:

$$\frac{\sum_{i=1958}^{1967} \frac{(x+y)_i}{2}}{10}$$

where:

$x = $ high price
$y = $ low price
$i \ = $ year

and be certain that the junior man does not use the mean price *to date* for the year 1968 as one of the ten items being totaled. In fact, if both men were familiar with both subscripts and exponents, he may well write:

$$\frac{\sum_{i=1958}^{1967} (x_i + y_i)(2)^{-1}}{10}$$

where:

$x = $ high price
$y = $ low price
$i \ = $ year

which is, as can be seen from what has been said before, a brief and also a precise statement of the particular number which he wishes. Once a familiarity with the notation has been gained, this expression can be written as rapidly as an English description of comparable accuracy.

MORE SUBSCRIPTS

With a knowledge of the advantages obtained from a subscript, the most natural development, of course, is the use of two or more subscripts. This apparently complex application is actually no more difficult than the tables which investment men have always used, such as Table 2–2 which can be set into subscript form very easily if we let $i = $ the number of the row and $j = $ the number of the column. If the analyst is discussing Gulf in a meeting of the Investment Committee, he is talking about the first row, and as a result, $i = 1$. If he is dealing with Standard Oil of New Jersey, the fourth row is being used, and $i = 4$. Now if he considers

TABLE 2–2
Average Annual Price/Earnings Ratio of
Industry X (International Oils)

Name	1967	1966	1965	1964	1963
Gulf	12.6	11.3	13.5	14.4	12.4
Royal Dutch..................	10.2	9.3	11.2	12.8	10.6
Standard (California)	11.7	12.9	14.3	14.2	14.1
Standard (New Jersey).....	12.1	14.2	17.3	17.2	14.3
Texaco	13.7	13.8	17.1	18.4	15.6

Gulf's *P/E* in 1966, he is dealing with a particular column; in this particular case it is the second column that is important, making $j = 2$. If he considers 1967, $j = 1$.

If the analyst would bother to rewrite the table with all of the subscript values entered, it would look like Table 2–3.

TABLE 2–3
Industry X

$i = 1$ $j = 1$	$i = 1$ $j = 2$	$i = 1$ $j = 3$	$i = 1$ $j = 4$	$i = 1$ $j = 5$
$i = 2$ $j = 1$	$i = 2$ $j = 2$	$i = 2$ $j = 3$	$i = 2$ $j = 4$	$i = 2$ $j = 5$
$i = 3$ $j = 1$	$i = 3$ $j = 2$	$i = 3$ $j = 3$	$i = 3$ $j = 4$	$i = 3$ $j = 5$
$i = 4$ $j = 1$	$i = 4$ $j = 2$	$i = 4$ $j = 3$	$i = 4$ $j = 4$	$i = 4$ $j = 5$
$i = 5$ $j = 1$	$i = 5$ $j = 2$	$i = 5$ $j = 3$	$i = 5$ $j = 4$	$i = 5$ $j = 5$

Each "element" in the table obviously has a unique set of subscripts, so that the analyst can easily refer to each element by its subscript values, as shown in Table 2–4.

TABLE 2–4

$x_{1,1}$	$x_{1,2}$	$x_{1,3}$	$x_{1,4}$	$x_{1,5}$
$x_{2,1}$	$x_{2,2}$	$x_{2,3}$	$x_{2,4}$	$x_{2,5}$
$x_{3,1}$	$x_{3,2}$	$x_{3,3}$	$x_{3,4}$	$x_{3,5}$
$x_{4,1}$	$x_{4,2}$	$x_{4,3}$	$x_{4,4}$	$x_{4,5}$
$x_{5,1}$	$x_{5,2}$	$x_{5,3}$	$x_{5,4}$	$x_{5,5}$

First subscript $= i =$ row
Second subscript $= j =$ column

Using this approach, $x_{5,5} =$ the price/earnings ratio of Texaco in 1963.

The notation permits us to identify each number, but it does much more than that. It gives each and every number in the entire table the basic name "x," indicating that it is an element in industry **X**. All of the numbers have something in common: they are from the "**X**" table, dealing with P/E's in the oil industry. In fact, it is now possible to refer to the entire block, or "matrix" of numbers by simply referring to **X** as opposed to, say, **Y**. What could **Y** stand for? The oil industry's sales figures, or possibly the chemical industry's P/E's.

Two additional advantages to this extremely valuable approach need to be described before passing on to new material. First, we can now talk about *all five* years of Gulf by referring to one symbol; that symbol is $x_{1,j}$ meaning the first row and any column. (The j, instead of a specific number as a column subscript, means "any column.") $x_{2,j}$ can therefore be seen to mean the *second* row and any column. In the notation, it is just as simple to discuss the results of all companies in 1965 by saying $x_{i,3}$, meaning any row and the third column. This is because the "i," instead of a number in the *row* subscript's position, means "any row." $x_{i,1} =$ any row in the first column $=$ the P/E of any of the companies in 1967. Now it is possible to write the symbol for the average P/E for Gulf for the five years which we are considering:

$x_{1,j} =$ Gulf, any column, as we already know.

Therefore,

$\sum_{j=1}^{5} (x_{1,j}) =$ The total of the columns for Gulf, using notation that we have already developed.

Therefore,

$\sum_{j=1}^{5} (x_{1,j})(5^{-1}) =$ The average of the individual annual P/E's of Gulf for the five years.

In the same way, we can find the expression for the average P/E of all companies in industry **X** in 1967, which we need, let's say, in order to compare the market's valuation of the industry relative to the S&P 425 at the close of 1967:

$x_{i,1} =$ Any company in 1967, because 1967 is the first column.

Therefore,

$\sum_{i=1}^{5} (x_{i,1}) =$ The total of all of the 1967 P/E's of the companies.

Therefore,

$$\sum_{i=1}^{5} (x_{i,1})(5^{-1}) = \text{The average 1967 } P/E \text{ of the companies in industry } \mathbf{X}.$$

Placing the two averages in the table (and showing the notation for several other averages as well) we have Table 2–5.

TABLE 2–5

Name	1967	1966	1965	1964	1963	Average for Each Company
Gulf	$x_{1.1}$	$x_{1.2}$	$x_{1.3}$	$x_{1.4}$	$x_{1.5}$	$\dfrac{\Sigma_j(x_{i,j})}{5}$
Royal Dutch	$x_{2.1}$	$x_{2.2}$	$x_{2.3}$	$x_{2.4}$	$x_{2.5}$	$\dfrac{\Sigma_j(x_{2,j})}{5}$
Standard (California)	$x_{3.1}$	$x_{3.2}$	$x_{3.3}$	$x_{3.4}$	$x_{3.5}$	$\dfrac{\Sigma_j(x_{3,j})}{5}$
Standard (New Jersey)	$x_{4.1}$	$x_{4.2}$	$x_{4.3}$	$x_{4.4}$	$x_{4.5}$	$\dfrac{\Sigma_j(x_{4,j})}{5}$
Texaco	$x_{5.1}$	$x_{5.2}$	$x_{5.3}$	$x_{5.4}$	$x_{5.5}$	$\dfrac{\Sigma_j(x_{5,j})}{5}$
Average for Each Year	$\dfrac{\Sigma_i(x_{i1})}{5}$	$\dfrac{\Sigma_i(x_{i2})}{5}$	$\dfrac{\Sigma_i(x_{i3})}{5}$	$\dfrac{\Sigma_i(x_{i4})}{5}$	$\dfrac{\Sigma_i(x_{i5})}{5}$	

Note: The Σ does not need the "1 to 5" symbols because the meaning is obvious from the table. It is useful to specify whether the meaning is "sum over i" or "sum over j" only because this technique is being presented for the first time. Once the material becomes more familiar, the meaning of the subscript can also be inferred from the table.

This table shows the actual calculations that the analyst already makes when he creates an average "spread sheet." Going one small step further, how would the analyst have his statistical assistant calculate the number in the lower right corner of the table — the average of "the average P/E's in each particular year"?

He would want to average the expression which covers each year's average:

$$\frac{\sum_{i=1}^{5} (x_{i,1})}{5} = \text{The first year's average.}$$

Therefore, this is needed for every year:

$$\frac{\sum_{i=1}^{5} (x_{i,j})}{5} = \text{The year's average for } \textit{any} \text{ year; for the } j\text{th year.}$$

This expression must be totaled for all five years (all five values for j):

$$\sum_{j=1}^{5} \left[\frac{\sum_{i=1}^{5} (x_{i,j})}{5} \right]$$

And in order to find the average, we must divide the total by five:

$$\frac{\sum_{j=1}^{5} \left[\dfrac{\sum_{i=1}^{5} (x_{i,j})}{5} \right]}{5}$$

Although the final statement of the average appears to be a little forbidding, it is an accurate statement of what is to be done — of what the number is. The expression in this notation could be given to a junior analyst familiar with elementary statistics, and the precise answer desired as well as the procedure for computing that answer would be fully defined.

The symbol Π, called pi, can be used instead of the symbol Σ for some types of applications. The usage is exactly the same, except that instead of *summing* $x_1, x_2, x_3 \ldots x_n$, the *product* is taken. In other words, if the symbol is Σ, the numbers are added together; if the symbol is Π, the numbers are multiplied together.

ALPHABETS

Earlier in this chapter, the use of Greek letters was said to have originated in the shortage of letters in the "normal" alphabet. Since the early stages of notation development, however, a number of conventions have been added to the use of Greek symbols. Although the usage has never been strictly formalized, writers frequently assume that the reader will be able to infer the meaning of symbols from a knowledge of these general rules and the context in which the symbol appears. As a result, a brief description of the implied usage of the alphabets can be of great value in a reader's attempt to "decode" apparently abstruse mathematical formulations, as outlined in Table 2–6.

In statistical usage, notational problems become even more unwieldy. Statistics is a discipline that deals with the description of a *population*. A population is a clearly defined group. Alternative definitions are "class" or "set." Examples are the set of all C.F.A. candidates, the set of all financial analysts, the set of all stocks, and the like. Any population has

TABLE 2–6
Mathematical Usage

Greek Alphabet	English Alphabet	Description
α alpha β beta γ gamma	a b c	Used as constants in mathematical expressions.
δ delta Δ U.C.* delta	d D	Used to denote small changes in the value of variables.
ϕ phi Φ U.C. phi ψ psi Ψ U.C. psi	f F g G	Used to indicate a particular function. (Functions are discussed in the chapter on algebra, but can be briefly defined as numbers whose values are indirectly defined; numbers that are defined in terms of other variables.)
	i j	Index numbers used to show the value of subscripts. The maximum value which may be assumed by the subscript is usually denoted by m or n.
κ kappa λ lambda μ mu	k l m n	Used as constants or parameters. Parameters are artificial or relational quantities used to tie together real variables in mathematical expressions.
ξ xi η ēta ζ zēta	x y z	Used to denote a variable being described in mathematical terms.
Π U.C. pi		Used to indicate that the product of a number of quantities is to be taken.
Σ U.C. sigma		Used to indicate that the sum of a number of quantities is to be taken.

* Note: U.C. stands for upper case.

one or more characteristics which may be treated quantitatively. Unfortunately, the characteristics usually are amenable only to estimation. For example, it is not practical to find the average intelligence of all financial analysts—this value must be estimated. Statistics calls the actual characteristics of the population being studied *parameters,* and these parameters are denoted by Greek letters. The estimate which is found for the value of the parameter (the estimated intelligence of financial analysts) is denoted by an English letter or by a Greek letter with a carat. An example of such an estimate might be $\hat{\sigma}$ (read "Sigma hat"), which means the estimate for the population characteristic σ regardless of what kind of characteristic that might be. More complex distinctions than this are basic to mathematical literature, but this book is designed for an introductory level and will avoid wherever possible the introduction of notational complexity. The statistical notation actually used will be developed as needed in the later chapters.

All of the advantages of any type of mathematical notation, however, can be utilized only when the symbols are used together to form expressions, and these expressions are manipulated in order to provide a meaning more useful to the researcher. The most basic rules for changing mathematical statements are found in elementary algebra.

Chapter
3 A Review of Elementary Algebra

Algebra provides a set of rules for the manipulation of mathematical expressions, and an understanding of these rules is essential to a comprehension of the material in the chapters that follow. The elementary operations of addition, subtraction, division, and multiplication are explained, and then more complex combinations are considered. Fractions and exponent treatment are reviewed, and a description of the "how" may make logarithms more comprehensible. Finally, functions and equations are introduced to prepare for more detailed treatment later.

INTRODUCTION

The system for manipulating numbers and variables known as basic algebra has gained an unwarranted reputation for difficulty. Actually, it is only a system for manipulating quantitative expressions as a means of improving their understandability. The fundamental problem of algebra is the solution of equations, i.e., finding the hidden numbers defined by mathematical statements of "screens." The set of rules involved in the process of algebraic simplification is actually much less complex than, say, the rules for playing contract bridge. If algebra has also gained a reputation for being dull, there are understandable reasons for this attitude. Learning algebra is equivalent to learning the rules of bridge, and the enjoyment of the game is not in the memorized rules. Nevertheless, without rules there could be no game.

This section will hopefully serve as a refresher to readers who are already familiar with the elementary aspect of algebra but who have not used it since school days. An intuitive "feel" for the operations is emphasized. Fortunately, the subject is actually very limited, and it is only necessary to cover:

1. The elementary operations
2. Fractions
3. Exponents
4. Logarithms
5. Equations and functions.

THE ELEMENTARY OPERATIONS

The simplest mathematical results are achieved through the use of addition, subtraction, multiplication, and division. Although every analyst is familiar with these operations, a few words are used here to place them into the context of the other sections.

Addition is the simplest operation of mathematics, but it nevertheless took the human race millenia to develop it as a useful tool. The technique probably developed from a situation like this: A shepherd would pick up a stone when each sheep would leave the pen in the morning. In the evening, when each sheep was returned to the pen, he would throw one pebble away. If, after the sheep were in the pen, he had a pebble remaining, one sheep would be lost. If, instead of one pebble remaining at the end of the day, he found that he had the following number of pebbles:

he would realize that he had a real problem!

If two herds were placed together, the pebbles could be "pooled" in one pouch, and the system could continue with the result of this "addition."

The next step was probably the use of symbols less cumbersome than stones, and then came the attempt to "predict" the outcome of the changes in the stones. For example, if three stones were added to four stones, the result was always the same, seven stones. As a result, the following table of "predicted" results could be built. Modern man, of course, is quite familiar with the sum of any two numbers, and it is difficult to realize that the entries in Table 3–1 had to be gradually developed by practical experience of what happened when two groups were placed together.

By using this table, or by memorizing it, anyone could predict the number of pebbles which would result from adding two pouches together. Why is the entry in the fourth row and the fifth column equal to seven? Simply because it *works* — it agrees with what would happen in the real world.

TABLE 3–1
Additions

	0	1	2	3	4	5	6	7	8	9
0	0	1	2	3	4	5	6	7	8	9
1		2	3	4	5	6	7	8	9	10
2			4	5	6	7	8	9	10	11
3				6	7	8	9	10	11	12
4					8	9	10	11	12	13
5						10	11	12	13	14
6							12	13	14	15
7								14	15	16
8									16	17
9										18

From this, it can be seen that addition is a model, and it is valid only because it agrees with the reality that it represents.

If the shepherd sold eight sheep, he would throw away eight stones in order to keep his "books" in balance. Eventually, this technique gave way to subtraction. Using the subtraction table, the results of the manipulation of the stones can be "simulated," and since the stones simulated the sheep, the table is a model of the sheep. In Table 3–2, the entry in the table is equal to the value at the left of each row subtracted from the value at the top of the column.

TABLE 3–2
Subtractions

	1	2	3	4	5	6	7	8	9
0	1	2	3	4	5	6	7	8	9
1	0	1	2	3	4	5	6	7	8
2		0	1	2	3	4	5	6	7
3			0	1	2	3	4	5	6
4				0	1	2	3	4	5
5					0	1	2	3	4
6						0	1	2	3
7							0	1	2
8								0	1
9									0

In the addition table, the unentered elements were blank because they were not needed. $3 + 2$ is not in the table because it equals $2 + 3$ and this value *is* entered, etc.; but in the subtraction table the unentered elements do not stem from $3 - 2$ equalling $2 - 3$; they stem from the fact that the entry cannot be expressed in terms of pebbles because it is a negative number. In prehistory, the shepherd would have a severe problem if a stray sheep were accidentally mixed into his herd. When the sheep entered the pen, he would run out of pebbles and still have one sheep left.

Intuitively, he would know that this was the opposite of what he was trying to avoid, and, since he would have been unhappy if he had been "long" pebbles, he would be happy being "short." This is the fundamental idea of the negative, the idea of "opposite." But it was not until the Middle Ages that rudimentary definitions for the use of negative numbers were developed. Table 3–3 and following tables therefore go beyond the mathematical capabilities of the ancient Greeks.

TABLE 3–3
Negatives

	1	2	3	4	5	6	7	8	9
0	1	2	3	4	5	6	7	8	9
1	0	1	2	3	4	5	6	7	8
2	−1	0	1	2	3	4	5	6	7
3	−2	−1	0	1	2	3	4	5	6
4	−3	−2	−1	0	1	2	3	4	5
5	−4	−3	−2	−1	0	1	2	3	4
6	−5	−4	−3	−2	−1	0	1	2	3
7	−6	−5	−4	−3	−2	−1	0	1	2
8	−7	−6	−5	−4	−3	−2	−1	0	1
9	−8	−7	−6	−5	−4	−3	−2	−1	0

Division, as used by financial analysts, is a process by which numbers can be made more comparable through the use of a common "base." The net income available to common of two companies cannot be usefully compared from the standpoint of a stockholder unless it is changed to net income per common share. Division, then, is the technique by which a researcher can remove an unwanted weighting — a bias which "loads" the data in a disadvantageous way. The dollars of dividends declared for one fiscal year of a company is "biased" from the standpoint of an individual shareholder because it is implicitly "weighted" by the number of shares outstanding. In order to discover the "meaning" of total dividends, the stockholder needs to divide by shares outstanding. In other words, since the implicit weighting by shares outstanding is unwanted in this case, it should be removed or the study will have to allow for the bias at every step. The weighting can, of course, be removed by division. Division, then, is a model which eliminates unwanted weights from base data.

The usefulness of division in analysis stems from the fact that the fundamental function of the investment analyst is to relate many diverse facts and trends. This diversity in large part stems from undesirable weights which must be removed before comparisons are possible. The entire system of ratio analysis is based upon improving the comparability of company data. *Company-relative* data, comparing companies to their industry, the market, or the economy, are based on division. Indexes are a series of numbers set to a common base in order to follow the same principle of improved comparability. A few financial items, their unwanted "bias," and the ratio resulting from adjustment are listed in Table 3–4 as examples:

TABLE 3–4

Item	Weight (Unwanted bias)	Result (Desired item)
$ net to common	Shares outstanding	Earnings per share
Long term debt	Size of company's capital	L.T. debt as % of total capitalization
Pretax income	Sales volume	Pretax margin
Income tax	Pretax income	Effective tax rate
$ investment in IBM	$ size of portfolio	% diversification in IBM

Multiplication, of course, introduces weights to numbers which should be made either more or less important in a study. For example, suppose an account is 50% IBM, 25% AT&T, and 25% GM. The portfolio manager wishes to compute the average P/E for stocks in the account. Assume the following P/E's:

$$IBM = 40$$
$$AT\&T = 15$$
$$GM = 15$$

Then in order to represent the average, the manager should *weight* each stock by the size of the holding in the portfolio — he must *introduce* a needed weight which is not present in the data, as follows:

Average P/E Ratio $= .50(40) + .25(15) + .25(15) = 27.5$

FUNDAMENTAL MANIPULATIONS

Working with combined operations is very simple but requires the introduction of a few additional rules. The first set of such rules deals with signs:

$(+2) + (+2) = +4$ To add numbers of like signs, add
their absolute values and attach
$(-2) + (-2) = -4$ their common sign.

As an example of the intuitive justification which lies behind the treatment of the signs, assume that a company has two divisions and that each division earns $2,000. The company obviously earns $4,000. If each has a $2,000 deficit, the company has a $4,000 deficit:

$(+2) + (-4) = -2$ To add numbers of unlike signs, subtract the smaller absolute value from the
$(+4) + (-2) = +2$ larger and attach the sign of the number having the greater absolute value.

The practical meaning of this rule can be clearly seen if a hypothetical company has only one of its two divisions operating at a deficit. The results of the two divisions will tend to offset each other in this case, but the company (which is the sum of the two divisions) will have a profit or loss depending upon whether the profitable or the deficit division shows the operating results having the largest absolute value. If one division earns +$2,000 and the other earns − $4,000, the result of adding the divisions into the company is a −$2,000, a $2,000 deficit:

$(+4) - (+2) = +2$ To subtract two numbers, change the sign of the number being subtracted
$(+4) - (-2) = +6$ and then use the rules for addition.

$(+4) - (+2) = +2$ therefore becomes $(+4) + (-2) = +2$

$(+4) - (-2) = +6$ therefore becomes $(+4) + (+2) = +6$

Since addition indicated the "pooling" of divisions, subtraction can be regarded as the "removal" of a division. For example, assume that the hypothetical company decides to sell one of its divisions. The earnings of that division will be subtracted from the total. Assume:

Company earnings	+$2,000	
Division A	+$4,000	(operating at a profit)
Division B	−$2,000	(operating at a deficit)

Now if division B is sold, the new total earnings of the company will be equal to the $2,000 company earnings minus division A's earnings of −$2,000, producing the earnings of the "new" company of $4,000. This, naturally, equals the profits of division A because this is the only division left in the company. This shows that minus a minus equals a plus because selling a deficit division raises profits.

Multiplication and division follow these rules:

(1) + by + produces +
(2) + by − produces −
(3) − by + produces −
(4) − by − produces +.

In terms of the hypothetical company:

(1) If the company in the example decides to expand division A to

four times its present size, its divisional earnings will be ($4,000)
(4) = $16,000.

(2) If it expands division B to four times its present size, the impact
on the company's profits will be (−$2,000)(4) = −$8,000.

(3) If it sells two operations identical to the profitable division A,
we have (−2)($4,000) = −$8,000 benefit to the company (showing
that "minusing out" a plus to the company is obviously a disadvantage).

(4) If it sells two operations identical to the unprofitable division B,
we have (−2)(−$2,000) = $4,000 benefit to the company (showing
that "minusing out" a negative to the company is beneficial).

The order in which operations are to be performed is indicated by
parentheses or brackets. All operations inside parentheses are to be
performed first. For example:

$$(4 + 7)(8) \quad = $$
$$(11)(8) \quad = 88$$

or:

$$(4 + 7)(8) + 7 = $$
$$(11)(8) + 7 = $$
$$88 + 7 = 95$$

If there are parentheses enclosed within parentheses, such as $((3 + 4)(2 + 2) + 2)$, the calculations in the innermost parentheses must be performed first:

$$((3 + 4)(2 + 2) + 2) = ((7)(4) + 2) = 30$$

In the absence of parentheses, it is assumed that the following priority
for operations will be used:

First: Exponents
Second: Multiplication
Third: Division
Fourth: Addition and Subtraction

Illustrations:

$$(2)(8) + 7 \quad = 16 + 7 \quad = 23$$
$$8 + 7 - (6)(2) = 15 - 12 \quad = 3$$
$$8 \div 2 - 4 \quad = 4 - 4 \quad = 0$$
$$8 \div (2 - 4) \quad = 8 \div -2 \quad = -4$$
$$4^2 \div 2 - 4 \quad = (16 \div 2) - 4 = 4$$
$$4^2 \div (2 - 4) \quad = 16 \div -2 \quad = -8$$

$$(2^3)(2) \div (4)(1) \quad = (8)(2) \div (4)(1) \quad = 16 \div 4 = 4$$
$$(2^4 \div 4)^2 \div 2 \quad = (16 \div 4)^2 \div 2 \quad = 4^2 \div 2 = 8$$

$$(3^2 + 4^2)(2) - 20 = (9 + 16)(2) - 20 = 50 - 20 = 30$$
$$75 - (3 + 2)^2(2) = 75 - (5^2)(2) \quad = 75 - 50 = 25$$

An important warning is necessary at this point: Never divide by zero or by a symbol which is later discovered to have a zero value.

FRACTIONS

Only a very small number of operations dealing with fractions need to be remembered: addition, subtraction, multiplication, division, and simplification.

If two fractions have the same denominator, the numerators can simply be added. The same principle holds true for subtraction:

$$\frac{a}{c} + \frac{b}{c} = \frac{a + b}{c} \qquad \frac{a}{c} - \frac{b}{c} = \frac{a - b}{c}$$

If, however, the two fractions do not have identical denominators, they cannot be directly added. It is necessary to first perform an "adjustment," converting the fractions into equivalent fractions which *do* have the same, or common denominator. This is done by multiplying the fraction by $\frac{2}{2}$, or $\frac{3}{3}$, or $\frac{4}{4}$, etc. This, of course, is the same as multiplying by one and the operation leaves the value of the fraction unchanged:

Add:

$$\frac{1}{2} \text{ and } \frac{1}{3}$$

$$\frac{1}{2} \cdot \frac{3}{3} = \frac{3}{6} \qquad \frac{1}{3} \cdot \frac{2}{2} = \frac{2}{6}$$

Therefore:

$$\frac{1}{2} = \frac{3}{6} \qquad \frac{1}{3} = \frac{2}{6}$$

And:

$$\frac{1}{2} + \frac{1}{3} = \frac{3}{6} + \frac{2}{6} = \frac{5}{6}$$

This technique of finding a common denominator can be used in the subtraction of fractions as well. For example,

$$\frac{1}{2} - \frac{1}{3} = \frac{3}{6} - \frac{2}{6} = \frac{3 - 2}{6} = \frac{1}{6}$$

Multiplication and division of fractions are less complicated. To multiply, simply multiply the numerators and then multiply the denominators:

$$\frac{a}{b} \cdot \frac{c}{d} = \frac{ac}{bd} \qquad \text{or} \qquad \frac{1}{2} \cdot \frac{2}{3} = \frac{1 \cdot 2}{2 \cdot 3} = \frac{2}{6}$$

In order to divide, invert the divisor (simply turn the fraction upside down, making the numerator the denominator and vice versa) and then multiply the resulting fractions:

$$\frac{a}{b} \div \frac{c}{d} = \frac{a}{b} \cdot \frac{d}{c} = \frac{ad}{bc} \qquad \text{or} \qquad \frac{1}{3} \div \frac{1}{2} = \frac{1}{3} \cdot \frac{2}{1} = \frac{2}{3}$$

the
divisor

the
divisor inverted

In order to simplify fractions, virtually all of the previous techniques may be used, but two tools are very important. The first is cancellation. If the same factor appears in both the numerator and the denominator, they can be removed from the fraction:

$$\frac{\cancel{2}\,(a + b)}{\cancel{2}\,(c + d)} = \frac{a + b}{c + d}$$

This can only be done to factors, not to terms. The reason that cancellation is legal is self-evident in the following illustration:

$$\frac{2(a + b)}{2(c + d)} = \frac{2}{2} \cdot \frac{(a + b)}{(c + d)}$$

$$= \frac{1}{1} \cdot \frac{a + b}{c + d}$$

$$= \frac{a + b}{c + d}$$

Cancellation can be used when two fractions are being multiplied just as easily as when considering only one fraction:

$$\frac{c(4 + d)}{2(a + b)} \cdot \frac{2(a + b)}{c^2 + d^2} = \frac{c(4 + d)}{2\cancel{(a + b)}} \cdot \frac{2\cancel{(a + b)}}{c^2 + d^2} = \frac{c(4 + d)}{c^2 + d^2}$$

This is legal because:

$$\frac{c(4 + d)}{2(a + b)} \cdot \frac{2(a + b)}{c^2 + d^2} = \frac{c(4 + d) \cdot 2(a + b)}{2(a + b) \cdot c^2 + d^2}$$

$$= \frac{2(a + b) \cdot c(4 + d)}{2(a + b) \cdot c^2 + d^2}$$

$$= \frac{1}{1} \cdot \frac{c(4 + d)}{c^2 + d^2}$$

The second important device in simplification deals with complex fractions — fractions which have fractional numerators or denominators.

When a complex fraction is encountered, it is often useful to eliminate the less important fraction by simply removing its denominator and multiplying it by the nonfractional number:

<table>
<tr><td align="center">Example with
Fractional Denominator</td><td align="center">Example with
Fractional Numerator</td></tr>
<tr><td align="center">$\dfrac{2}{1/3} = \dfrac{2 \cdot 3}{1} = 6$</td><td align="center">$\dfrac{1/3}{2} = \dfrac{1}{2 \cdot 3} = \dfrac{1}{6}$</td></tr>
</table>

This device is permitted because it is a short method for performing the following manipulation:

<table>
<tr><td align="center">Fractional Denominator</td><td align="center">Fractional Numerator</td></tr>
<tr><td align="center">$\dfrac{2}{1/3} \cdot \dfrac{3}{3} = \dfrac{6}{3/3} = \dfrac{6}{1} = 6$</td><td align="center">$\dfrac{1/3}{2} \cdot \dfrac{3}{3} = \dfrac{3/3}{6} = \dfrac{1}{6}$</td></tr>
</table>

EXPONENTS

In the section on notation, the advantages of exponents were indicated. In this section, the rules governing the manipulation of these exponents need to be covered.

First, $a^m \cdot a^n = a^{m+n}$. This can be seen from the simple illustration:

$$2^3 \cdot 2^4 = 2^7$$

or:

$$(2 \cdot 2 \cdot 2)(2 \cdot 2 \cdot 2 \cdot 2) = 2^7 \quad \text{since there are seven 2's multiplied.}$$

Next, if we raise a number with an exponent to a power:

$$(a^m)^n = a^{mn}$$

because:

$$(2^3)^2 = 2^6$$

or:

$$(2 \cdot 2 \cdot 2)(2 \cdot 2 \cdot 2) = 2^6$$

Next, if a product is raised to a power:

$$(ab)^n = a^n b^n$$

because:

$$(2 \cdot 3)^2 = 2^2 \cdot 3^2 = 36$$

or:

$$(2 \cdot 3)(2 \cdot 3) = 2 \cdot 2 \cdot 3 \cdot 3 = 2^2 \cdot 3^2 = 36$$

Next, if a fraction is raised to a power:

$$\left(\frac{a}{b}\right)^n = \frac{a^n}{b^n}$$

because:

$$\left(\frac{2}{3}\right)^2 = \frac{2^2}{3^2}$$

or:

$$\frac{2}{3} \cdot \frac{2}{3} = \frac{2 \cdot 2}{3 \cdot 3} = \frac{2^2}{3^2}$$

Next, if a fraction has the same numerator and denominator except for the fact that they are raised to different powers:

$$\frac{a^m}{a^n} = a^{m-n}$$

because:

$$\frac{2^3}{2^2} = 2^{3-2} = 2^1$$

or:

$$\frac{2 \cdot \cancel{2} \cdot \cancel{2}}{\cancel{2} \cdot \cancel{2}} = 2^1$$

Fortunately, these same laws apply to fractional exponents as well as to integer exponents. Since it has already been shown that square roots, cube roots, and so on, can be expressed as fractional exponents, the rules for exponents apply to taking roots as well.

LOGARITHMS

Introduction

Logarithms have developed a formidable reputation over the years, largely because it is difficult to grasp intuitively the meaning of calculations regarding their use. Nevertheless, logs, as they are commonly called, are extremely useful in both basic calculations and in advanced mathematical theory. They present the following advantages: (1) they make multiplication and division a simple process when a desk calculator is not available; (2) they provide the basis for all of the compound interest, annuity, and present value calculations used daily by all analysts; (3) they are the fundamental reason why a slide rule works; and (4) they are used in the theory which makes virtually all of the advanced statistical models available to the business community.

FIGURE 3–1

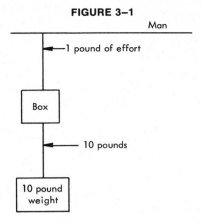

In order to gain a feel for the nature of a logarithm, consider the following analogy: A man must prevent a ten-pound weight (which he is holding with a rope) from falling. In order to do this, he must exert ten "pounds" of effort. Now, in order to assist him, he hooks a "black box" to the rope which will increase his "power" tenfold. By exerting one pound of effort, he can hold the ten-pound weight as in Figure 3–1.

It is possible to extend this analogy still further by considering the case of a 100-pound weight. The black box already used by the man had an "input" of one pound of force and an output of 10 pounds, and so the man can simply purchase another box identical to the first and hook it to his rope. This second box will receive the power output by the first one. It will therefore have an input of ten and an output of 100, a tenfold increase. As a result, the man will still need to exert only one pound of effort to hold a 100-pound weight. This can be diagrammed as in Figure 3–2.

This system is getting somewhat cumbersome; in order to keep things simple, the man trades in his two boxes and buys a single deluxe unit which has a dial on it. If set at "one," it puts out the power of one box; a "two" setting gives "two boxpower," and so forth. Now his system looks like Figure 3–3.

At this point, if someone puts a 1,000-pound weight on the rope, the man can simply throw the switch to "three" and still maintain control. As a matter of fact, if he encounters a weight of, say, 500 pounds, he is still all right because he can set his dial at some number between two and three which will handle this particular weight. Actually, this "deluxe model" has a "governor" on it which automatically sets the dial at the proper number (fractional or not) which will balance the weight regardless of how heavy it might be. For any weight, there is an index setting which matches it, and for any index setting, there is a weight which it will balance.

FIGURE 3–2

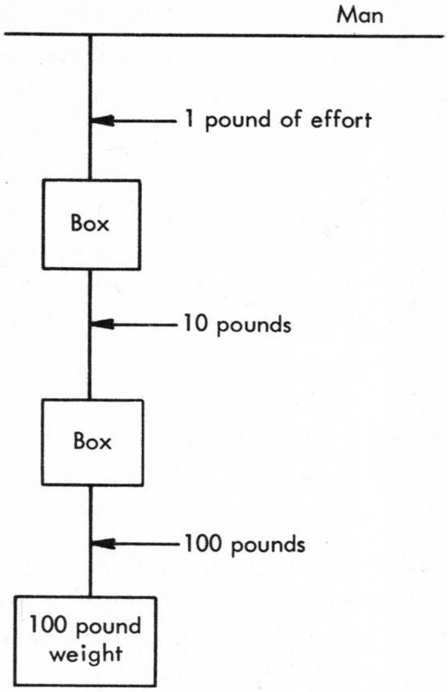

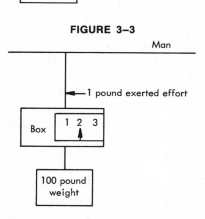

FIGURE 3–3

The obvious question now is what all of this has to do with logarithms. The answer is that the weight which can take on any value actually stands for any positive number in the number system, and the index setting necessary to balance the weight (number) is the logarithm of that weight (number). There is nothing more mysterious about logs than the use of this index setting on the box instead of the use of the number itself.

This may not be complex, but it would certainly be superfluous if it didn't assist the analyst in solving practical problems. Two simple properties of logs will point out their usefulness: (1) adding logs is the same as multiplying the numbers; (2) subtracting logs is the same as dividing the numbers. This means that the index numbers do not have the same behavior in mathematical operations as do the numbers that they represent. On the positive side, this means that an analyst can work either with a number or its index setting (log), whichever will make the calculations easiest. On the negative side, this fact seems to throw logs back into the realm of the mysterious.

Actually, the difference in the behavior of logs and numbers could have been anticipated from the analogy. If someone had inserted a 1,000-pound weight in place of the 100 pounder, the man would have thrown the switch from "2" to "3" and kept everything in balance. Multiplying the weight by 10 is certainly not the same as adding 1 to the index setting. Nevertheless, the setting *did* remain in balance, and if we simply knew how the index numbers behaved relative to the numbers, we could use them without having to refer back to ropes and boxes (although we could always do so with valid results if we wished). Mathematicians have worked out the behavior patterns of the index settings, and it is possible to use their findings instead of working them out for ourselves. Incidentally, if the fact that adding logs is equivalent to multiplying numbers is still confusing, notice that the man's *adding* one to the index setting offset someone *multiplying* the 100-pound weight by 10.

In mathematical notation, the index setting is represented as $\log_a N =$ the logarithm of the number N to the base a. N stands for the weight, and the base a is simply the "power" of the box with its basic setting of one. In our analogy, this number was 10 (a tenfold increase in output over input), and the use of the base 10 is the system of common logarithms. Assuming common logs, the index setting is written as $\log N$. The fundamental fact about logarithms is that:

if:

$$\log N = X \text{ (where } X \text{ stands for some "index" setting)}$$

then:

$$N = 10^x \quad \text{(which means that the "index" setting is the exponent of 10 that will "bring the number 10 into balance" with the weight } N)$$

It is this simple mathematical identity that makes the analogy of the weight work. The index setting "adjusts" the number 10 to bring it into balance with N, and it adjusts it by acting as an exponent. Only four fundamental properties of logarithms need to be pointed out at this point:

1. $\log (AB) = \log A + \log B$

   This simply says that adding two index numbers will produce another index number — and the new index is the setting that will balance a weight equal to the product of the two weights associated with the first two indices. In other words, adding indices equals multiplying numbers.

2. $\log \dfrac{A}{B} = \log A - \log B$

To divide numbers, subtract indices.

3. $\log A^k = (k) \log A$

Raising a number to a given power is the same thing as multiplying its index setting by the given number.

4. $\log \sqrt[k]{A} = \dfrac{(\log A)}{k}$

Taking the kth root of a number is the same thing as dividing its index number by k.

Two important practical points need to be mentioned. First, if an analyst wishes to add or subtract numbers, logarithms cannot be effectively used. This is no great loss, for resorting to logs would be a waste of time on these simple operations, anyway. Second, if an analyst wishes to use logarithms instead of the numbers, he must convert from "weights" to "index numbers" using tables, perform the simplified calculations, and then *convert back* from indices to numbers. If the log isn't converted back into the number that it represents, the user may make the mistake of thinking that the power setting *is* the number that it represents. This is the same as maintaining that log N *is* N. The process of getting back to the number from a log is called taking the antilogarithm (usually called antilog). Mathematically, antilog (log N) $= N$, which means that if the log of a number is found and then the antilog of the log is found, the result will be the original number.

Determining Logarithms

In order to find the log (or, logarithm) of a number, a table of logarithms is used. Any log to base ten is divided into two parts: characteristic and mantissa. The characteristic of the log is the whole number portion of the log. In 1.17609, for example, the characteristic is the number 1. The mantissa is the fractional portion of a log. In 1.17609, the mantissa is .17609. If an analyst wishes to convert a number to a log, he first must determine what the characteristic of the log will be. This is quite simple, for the characteristic is one less than the number of digits in the number (whole number portion only) for which the log is desired. Examples: log 10 = 1, log 100 = 2, log 10,000 = 4. If the number is less than one, it is written 0.xxxx and the rule still holds (using the entire number), but in this case the characteristic is negative. Examples: log 0.1 $= -1$, log 0.0001 $= -4$, log 0.000001 $= -6$.

The analyst next needs to locate the mantissa, or fractional part of the log. The mantissa is found in a logarithm table using the number for which the log is needed without regard for the decimal point. The characteristic and the mantissa are then added to find the log. If the characteristic is negative, it is more useful to keep the mantissa and the characteristic separated. This is especially important when using a logarithm table in connection with a mantissa.

In order to find the mantissa of 12.5, the analyst would disregard the decimal and go down the rows to 12, then across the columns to 5.

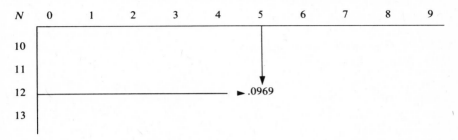

The mantissa of the log of 12.5 therefore equals .0969. Because the location of the decimal point in the number does not affect the mantissa, this is also the mantissa of the log of 125 and 1250. Adding the characteristic to the mantissa for various numbers, we find that:

$$\begin{aligned}
\log 1.25 &= 0.0969 \\
\log 12.5 &= 1.0969 \\
\log 125 &= 2.0969 \\
\log 1250 &= 3.0969 \\
\log 12500 &= 4.0969
\end{aligned}$$

To find the antilog of a number, an analyst can use the log's mantissa to find the number in the table and then place the decimal point in the location indicated by the characteristic. For example, if the analyst had performed several calculations using logs and had ended with 4.0969, he would desire the antilog of 4.0969, the number which this log represented. In order to find this number, he would locate the mantissa in the log table.

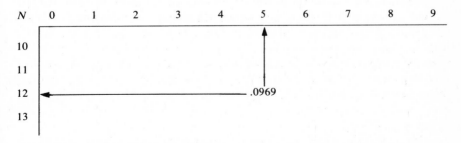

As can be seen, .0969 is the mantissa of 125. But this does not indicate anything about the location of the decimal point in the number. Its value could be 1.25, 12.5, 125, etc. Referring to the characteristic of the log

(4, in this case) the analyst moves the decimal four digits to the right of its "base" position at 1.2500 and has the answer of 12500. If the characteristic had been negative, he would have moved the decimal to the left instead of the right (the number would have been made smaller rather than larger).

If the number whose log is desired is less than one, the characteristic will be negative, as has already been mentioned. When using the log table to find the mantissa of such a number, nothing unusual is encountered. For example, the mantissa of .125 is .0969. Since the characteristic is negative, however, adding it to this mantissa will produce a negative number having a fractional part which is different from .0969. When the antilog would be taken, the mantissa (.0969) necessary to find the antilog would not be immediately obvious from an inspection of such a logarithm. For this reason, it is standard practice to state the mantissa and characteristic separately when the characteristic is negative. For example, $\log (.125) = .0969 - 1.0$. By following this rule, the fractional portion of the log will always be the mantissa used in the log tables.

Natural Logarithms

In closing this section, return once again to the original analogy. If a base other than 10 were used, the analogy still holds. Changing bases is the same as trading the box which multiplied the man's power by ten for a box which would increase his power by, say, about 2.71828 as an example. The settings on the index pointer would need to be adjusted, but this is a simple matter—they need only be multiplied by some number that will keep everything in balance (.43429 in this case). This is true for any shift in base, but our particular example shows the system of *natural* logarithms (or logs to the base *e,* which is approximately equal to 2.71828) and their simple connection to *common* logs (or logarithms to the base 10). Because logarithms to any base have the same general nature, the analogy always holds. Changing the base is equivalent to changing the power capacity of the box and hence the index setting needed, but the structure of the problem remains essentially unchanged. As a result of this fact, any base may be chosen which might be convenient to the user. Common logarithms (base 10) are commonly used for basic calculations, while natural logarithms (base *e* approximately equal to 2.71828) are most natural in advanced mathematical theory.

Behavior of Logarithms

In the system of common logarithms, note once again that the characteristic of the logarithm is the "whole number" part of the log (the "1" of "1.17609"). This characteristic is the whole number on the index setting in the analogy, and while a setting of "1" balanced 10 pounds, the characteristic of 10 is two digits minus one, or "1." A setting of "2" balances 100 pounds, which has three minus one = "2" digits, and so on. This is why the "rule of thumb" using the number of digits to determine the characteristic of common logs produces the correct result. Moving one step further, a weight of less than 10 pounds would give the box some trouble, because even with the basic setting of "1" it would still have an output of 10 pounds and this would be too much power. The solution is to use a fractional setting, so that only a fraction of the total power output of one box will be used to hold the weight. This is the reason that numbers from 1 to 10 have a log with the form 0.xxx. If the weight is less than one, the black box must actually subtract a portion of the one unit of power which was supplied by the man. This can only be done if the log is negative, which is the reason why all numbers less than one have a negative characteristic. The negative characteristic will get larger and larger as the numbers get closer and closer to zero. Finally, since it is absurd to think of a negative weight, a negative number cannot have a logarithm.

FUNCTIONS AND EQUATIONS

Single Equations

The other aspects of algebra are usually viewed as being supplementary tools which facilitate the solution of equations by simplifying the basic equation. Dealing with equations is essentially a matter of performing these preliminary simplifications and then manipulating the data by the use of a basic rule:

*Whatever is done to one side of the
equation must also be done to the other
side for the statement to remain equal.*

This rule is grounded in simple logic, for equals plus equals are equal, equals times equals are equal, and so on.

Illustrations:

$$\text{Given } 5x + 12 = 20$$
$$\text{and subtracting } -12 = -12$$
$$\text{we find that } 5x = 8 \text{ is a true equality.}$$

$$\text{Given } 5x = 8$$
$$\text{and dividing by } 5 = 5$$

$$\text{we find that } \frac{5x}{5} = \frac{8}{5} \text{ is a true equality}$$

$$\text{and that } x = \frac{8}{5} \text{ when we simplify.}$$

Notice that throughout all of the operations used to simplify the equation, x had a value of 8/5 and substituting this value into any of the equations would produce a true equality. The value of x was always 8/5, but its value was not known until the equation was simplified. "Solving" for x is merely this process of simplifying until the unknown value of x becomes obvious.

If an equation is to be solved for, say, x, then the solution requires that x be placed alone on one side of the equation. The other side is then usually stated in the simplest possible way as a matter of convenience. As the first step in accomplishing this, all terms involving x are moved to one side of the equation and all terms not involving x are moved to the other side. This is done by subtracting terms from both sides as shown in the examples above. A short cut accomplishing the same thing is called "transposing," where the term is simply rewritten on the other side with the sign changed:

$$5x + 12 = 20$$
$$5x = 20 - 12$$
$$5x = 8$$
$$x = 8/5$$

Transposing will always move an unwanted term from one side of the equation to the other. Once all of the terms involving x are on one side and all of the other terms are on the other, the equation may still need to be simplified by adding terms or removing a coefficient from x. For example:

$$3x + 4x = 5 + 9$$
$$7x = 14$$
$$x = 2$$

Systems of Equations

Using the techniques already described will permit the analyst to isolate x when x is the only unknown value which is to be discovered, i.e., if x is the only variable in the equation. But if both x and y are to be discovered, it will be impossible to find the value of x unless the value of y is already known. On the other hand, the value of y cannot be found unless the value of x is already known. The problem is that although one equation provides enough information to permit the value of one variable to be found, it is inadequate when two variables are present. If two unknowns are to be discovered, two equations are needed; if three unknowns are present, three equations are needed, and so forth. The set of equations is called a "system" which must be solved "simultaneously." A system of equations requires two or more different equations, and the equations are not different if they "reduce" to the same equation. For example, $x + y = 1$ is the "same" equation as $2x + 2y = 2$, in that it provides no additional information about the relationship of x to y.

This section considers only linear equations, i.e., equations in which each variable is not raised to a power and enters the equation as a simple addition. Quite naturally, the problem is called the simultaneous solution of a system of linear equations. Only the two variable case is considered in the chapter.

The following equations show an explicit example of a system of two linear equations in two unknowns as well as the algebraic structure of all such equations:

$$5x + 10y = 50 \text{ has the general form } a_1x + b_1y = c_1$$
$$2x + y = 25 \text{ has the general form } a_2x + b_2y = c_2$$

In order to solve any such system, the following formulas can be used by the analyst, although the derivation is not presented here:

$$x = \frac{b_2c_1 - b_1c_2}{a_1b_2 - a_2b_1} \qquad y = \frac{a_1c_2 - a_2c_1}{a_1b_2 - a_2b_1}$$

In this particular case, the solution is as follows:

$$x = \frac{1 \cdot 50 - 10 \cdot 25}{5 \cdot 1 - 2 \cdot 10} \qquad y = \frac{5 \cdot 25 - 2 \cdot 50}{5 \cdot 1 - 2 \cdot 10}$$

$$x = \frac{-200}{-15} \qquad y = \frac{25}{-15}$$

$$x = \frac{40}{3} \qquad y = \frac{-5}{3}$$

This technique does nothing for the development of an intuitive "feel" of what is happening. An analogy and the use of graphs may make the significance of the simultaneous solution of equations somewhat clearer.

An Application of a System of Equations

When the computer was first applied to the problems of investment analysis, a technique known as "screening" or "filtering" became very popular. Using this approach, the computer user could specify, for example, all stocks having a P/E below 10, a yield above 4%, and a positive earnings growth rate. The computer would supply the names of all companies which satisfied the user's requirements. This approach of "pulling" certain companies from a larger set of companies according to some user-specified criterion is a precise parallel to what mathematics and statistics do for the quantitative analyst. One of the best examples of mathematics as a "retrieval system" for numbers is the use of equations.

Suppose that an analyst knows that a company has fixed costs of $10 million and that additional costs of $0.8 million are incurred as each additional million units of its product are manufactured. He could then say that the cost of production of the company is equal to:

$$\text{Cost} = 10 + 0.8P$$

Where:

P = the number of units produced, expressed in millions.

If the company has no production, its cost will equal $10 + (0.8)(0)$, or 10. This is the level of fixed costs. In addition, for each additional million units produced, an additional $0.8 million will be added to the $10 million cost level. The equation, then, is a model which eliminates many unwanted pairs of values for Cost and P. For example, ($P = 10$, $\text{Cost} = 25$) is not a reasonable pair of values for the analyst to select if he believes his equation. It is easy to see that the model has "filtered" out many unacceptable pairs of numbers, that is, many unacceptable combinations of production and cost. Since the analyst has not indicated what the actual level of production is, he still has an infinite number of pairs left; but then again, he has removed an infinite number of possibilities as well. At any rate, he has screened out enough numbers to allow himself to find the "normal" cost level for the company as soon as he knows the company's production level.

Now assume that the company under consideration has $8 million of investment income before taxes and that it is assured of the sale of all production at $1.10 per unit. The total dollar inflow to the company from both sources follows the rule:

$$\text{Inflow} = 8 + 1.10(P)$$

It is now possible for the analyst to use the information in those two rules to develop additional knowledge by using the technique of solving a system of two simultaneous equations. At some level of production, the dollar inflow will exactly equal the cost, permitting the company to break even. This break-even point will occur, obviously, at the point where "Inflow" equals "Cost." This means that "Cost" can be substituted into the second equation, producing the following system:

$$\text{Cost} = 10 + 0.8P$$
$$\text{Cost} = 8 + 1.10P$$

when the company operates at break even. The implied level of production can be found using these equations. Each of these two equations constitutes a "screen" which the company must pass. Each equation screens out a number of inadmissible combinations of production and cost. The company must pass not only the first screen, but the second as well. How many values for "cost" pass the requirement Cost $= 10+0.8P$ *and still pass* the requirement Cost $= 8 + 1.1P$? Only one number for cost (and for production) survives the "double screening." As it happens, the surviving value for cost (and for production) can be retrieved by applying a model. This model, of course, is the simultaneous solution of a set of linear equations. Using the formulas already developed, we can apply this model to solve the problem. The general form of the equation is:

$$a_1x + b_1y = c_1$$
$$a_2x + b_2y = c_2$$

Our particular equations are:

As already stated	In "normal" form
Cost $= 10 + 0.8P$	$0.8P - \text{Cost} = -10$
Cost $= 8 + 1.1P$	$1.1P - \text{Cost} = - 8$

The general form of solution is:

$$x = \frac{b_2c_1 - b_1c_2}{a_1b_2 - a_2b_1}$$

$$y = \frac{a_1c_2 - a_2c_1}{a_1b_2 - a_2b_1}$$

In this case, the form is:

$$P = \frac{(-1)(-10) - (-1)(-8)}{(0.8)(-1) - (1.1)(-1)}$$

$$\text{Cost} = \frac{(0.8)(-8) - (1.1)(-10)}{(0.8)(-1) - (1.1)(-1)}$$

At this point, the problem is reduced to simple numerical calculation. We know that:

$$P = \frac{(-1)(-10) - (-1)(-8)}{(0.8)(-1) - (1.1)(-1)} \qquad \text{Cost} = \frac{(0.8)(-8) - (1.1)(-10)}{(0.8)(-1) - (1.1)(-1)}$$

It follows by algebra that:

$$P = \frac{+10 - 8}{-0.8 + 1.1} \qquad \text{Cost} = \frac{-6.4 + 11}{-0.8 + 1.1}$$

$$= \frac{2}{0.3} \qquad = \frac{4.6}{0.3}$$

$$= 6.66 \qquad = 15.33$$

We can see from this that the sales plus investment income at the break-even point for the company as indicated by the criteria set up by the analyst is $15.33 million and the break-even production level is 6.66 million units.

It is possible to graph the arguments in the preceding analysis by applying a model frequently used by mathematicians as a "display device" for their logical manipulations. Setting up two perpendicular coordinates, we will give the horizontal axis the name "*P*" and the vertical axis "*I*" for dollar inflow, as in Figure 3–4.

FIGURE 3–4

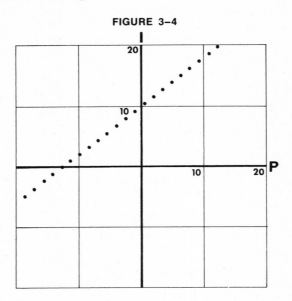

Several possible pairs of values for *P* and *I* have been plotted for reference. If we choose a specific value for *P*, chances are that it would not yet have been plotted, but we could enter it by going "over" to the value on the *P* axis and then "up" to the proper value on the *I* axis. Since *P* can be given any value, let's examine Figure 3–5 where 500,000 values have been plotted. This looks like a straight line because the points are so "dense" on the page. Actually, if *all* of the pairs of values were plotted, the graph *would* be a straight line, and there would be an infinite number of points because there are an infinite number of possible pairs of *P* and *I*.

If we plotted the second equation on the same graph, we would have Figure 3–6. Each line is the set of values "permitted" by that equation; that is, each line portrays only those pairs of values which "passed" one "screen" or equation. Only one point is "permitted" by both equations, as can be seen by the fact that only one point is on both lines; that

FIGURE 3-5

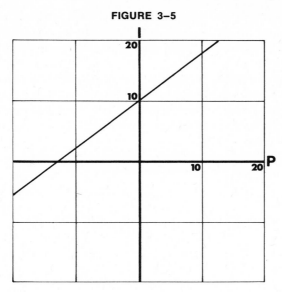

FIGURE 3-6

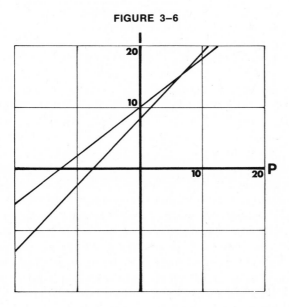

is, if we screen either line by using the other equation, only one point will pass this second screen. This is seen on the graph as *one point which is on both lines,* as one pair of values which is *in both sets of acceptable solutions.* Obviously, this "uncommon point" is the point of intersection of the two lines, and this point is the only (*P, I*) pair permitted by both equations. Naturally, the value of I at that point of "intersection" is 15.33.

In economic theory, the use of simultaneous equations to find the values of economic variables constitutes a major branch of econometrics. From the standpoint of the analyst, this particular type of application is the most important example of the theory of simultaneous equations.

Probably the simplest possible way of looking at the economy is to break the National Income (Y) into two components, Consumption and Investment. This means that:

$$Y = C + I$$

Since this rule is true by definition, it would be impossible to have Consumption at 10, Investment at 1, and the National Income at 15. This means that the equation, like all equations, has screened out a large number of combinations of values. If economists maintain in addition that in this economy consumers save 5% of their income and that this is a rule which is never violated, this means that:

$$C = .95Y$$

This equation screens out still more combinations of values. For example, it would now be impossible to have Consumption at 10 and National Income at 15.

Obviously, if enough equations can be found which accurately describe the nature of the economy, at some point all of the combinations of values will have been screened out except one value per variable. If all of the equations used are correct, the values for the variables would necessarily be correct. In order to complete this screening, it would be necessary to have one equation for every variable in the model. This is reasonable, because it took two equations to solve for two unknowns, and three unknowns would naturally produce more combinations of values which would require a third equation to screen, four unknowns would require a fourth "screening" equation, and so on.

The quality of any economic model, however, is dependent on the accuracy of the rules (equations) which are used, not on the number of equations that are involved. An increase in the number of equations would have a direct benefit only because the number of economic variables being predicted by the model would increase. The reason realistic models are always fairly large is the unfortunate fact that accurate "rules" cannot be found using the more highly aggregated economic variables, so that the equations must relate various lower level components in the economy. This necessarily produces a system having a large number of variables, and it is the large number of variables that forces the use of a large number of equations.

Functions

Actually, what the analyst was saying by an equation and what the graph was saying by a line was simply that two variables have a relationship—that one is a function of the other. In the particular case of the example used in the preceding section, the mathematical statement, or equation, asserted that dollar inflow was a function of P (of production).

Since a function asserts that there is a definite relationship between two different items being analyzed, the function indicates that it is possible to *find* one variable given the size of the other. In the example of the preceding section, if the dollar inflow of the company is a function of production, it is possible for the financial analyst to find I given P. More generally, if any y is a function of any x, it is possible to find the value of y given x. Once x is known, for all practical purposes, y is known also. As a result, if y is a function of x, it is reasonable to say: "You tell me x and I'll tell you y." In effect, what the function does is to tie x and y together in an established mathematical relationship. Because this relationship may in many cases be known by the analyst, once x is known y is simple to find. In our example, once P was known, I was easy to locate because the function (the equation) was clearly defined by the research analyst. Even if the exact function is *not* known, quite often the analyst can find it by the use of statistical techniques.

From this, it is easy to see that any equation involving two or more variables expresses a function just as does an English sentence which relates two items. If, however, a mathematician wishes to express that "y is a function of x" without specifying *how* they are related, he can write:

$$y = f(x) \quad \text{(pronounced "} f \text{ of } x \text{")}$$

where "f" obviously stands for "function" and does not mean "f" times "x."

This notation is useful, especially when the precise form of the relationship is unknown. Another use of $f(x)$ is as an abbreviation of the *actual* relationship. In the example used earlier, $I = 10 + 0.8P$ could have been written more simply as $I = f(P)$ if the *form* of the relationship was not a matter of interest. This same type of notation can easily be extended to include many variables instead of the two which have been examined in this simple example. If, for example, the research department maintains that P/E is a function of the growth in earnings (G), the quality of the company (Q), and the stability of earnings (S), we have:

$$P/E = f(G, Q, S)$$

The functional notation can be expanded by the use of subscripts. This means that f_1 can refer to one function and f_2 to another. For example, if P/E is a function of growth, $P/E = f_1(G)$ and if growth is a function of rate of return (R), $G = f_2(R)$. In the example:

$$P/E = f(G, Q, S)$$

it may be possible to establish that $G, Q,$ and S are not related to each other in any way, in which case the relation could be rewritten as:

$$P/E = f_1(G) + f_2(Q) + f_3(S)$$

From this discussion, it can be seen that functions (definite quantitative relationships) are the main "screening" mechanisms in the mathematical approach. Through a function, it is possible to "transform" a given value for G into a value for P/E. In effect, knowledge of G becomes a "roadmap" by which we can locate the corresponding P/E. The advantage of using this approach in investment work is obvious because the large number of relationships which exist between different items being analyzed can easily be regarded as functions. This permits the analyst to arrive at a conclusion concerning one or two items and then "automatically" deduce his implied conclusions concerning a large number of additional variables. An example of this approach would be to arrive at a conclusion concerning the percentage change in Gross National Product and then deduce the level of Gross Corporate Product in the nonfinancial sector.

Functions, when known by the analyst, are expressed as equations, and as a result equations can be regarded as the basic sentences of the quantitative language. From this, it is possible to argue by analogy that since success in the English-speaking countries is a function of an individual's use of "English" sentences, success in quantitative problems tends to be a function of the use of "mathematical sentences" — of equations. The basic manipulation of equations and their component parts is, of course, the material that has been covered in this chapter on algebra.

Chapter
4 The Mathematics of Compound
Growth Explained

Compound growth or compound interest, when a quantity increases at a constant rate rather than a constant amount, is one of the most frequently used techniques in financial analysis. The four major types of compound growth problems are analyzed: (1) the future value of a quantity subject to compound growth; (2) the present value of a future quantity subject to compound growth; (3) the future value of an annuity, that is, a fixed sum paid or received at regular time intervals; and (4) the present value of an annuity. The use of tables in determining these types of values is described and formulas are given for use when tables are not available.

INTRODUCTION

One of the most important portions of algebra for the financial analyst is, quite naturally, the mathematics of finance, which is based upon the principle of compound interest. If a man borrows money, he must eventually repay both principal and interest. If he repays the entire obligation at the maturity of the loan, then during the term of the loan he obviously had some interest accrued against him. If he is charged *interest on the interest* due, then the debt is said to be subject to compound interest.

Another example of a compounding process is the growth in the net income of a company. If a company begins with per share earnings of $1.00 and this figure increases by 10% in the first year, the result is $1.10. But the $0.10 of additional earnings gained during the year is used to provide additional earning power. If the company's per share earnings grow by 10% in the second year, the earnings per share will be $1.21. This represents an additional $0.10 on the original $1.00 plus $0.01 gained as a result of the $0.10 earned in the first year. The act of including increases in computing new values for EPS (earnings per share) forces the process to be treated as an example of compound growth.

Compound growth is actually a very simple process where each new value is a stated constant percentage increase over the preceding value. An example might be EPS growth at 10% per year, producing the series: ($1.00, $1.10, $1.21, $1.33 . . .). Another example might be the 8% per day growth of the number of germs in a culture, producing the series: (1.00, 1.08, 1.17, 1.26, . . .). Another example is the increase of $1.00 deposited in a 5% per year savings account, producing: ($1.00, $1.05, $1.10, $1.16, $1.22, . . .). Obviously, if more than $1.00 is invested, the series is simply multiplied by the initial amount invested to find the value of total wealth after any given number of periods.

Compound growth can be seen to be the second simplest kind of growth. The simplest way for numbers to increase is to add a constant value to the preceding value, producing, say: (1.00, 1.10, 1.20, 1.30, . . .). This is called linear growth, and the series is called an arithmetic progression. An example of linear growth might be the behavior in the P/E (the ratio of price to earnings per share) of a stock when the growth rate in EPS increases by 1%. Assume, for example, that an analyst believes that the P/E of a stock can be found by the equation $P/E = 10 + 0.8G$. As additional units of G are added, the P/E will increase from 10 by the constant amount 0.8, producing: (10, 10.8, 11.6, 12.4, . . .). Compound growth is only slightly more complex than this, stating that the increase is a constant *percentage* of the preceding value instead of a constant *absolute* amount. Since almost all quantities concerning the financial analyst increase or decrease on the basis of a percentage deviation from their preceding status, compound growth is a matter of importance to the financial community.

There are two fundamental distinctions that must be thoroughly understood in the theory of compound interest. These are:

1. Future Value versus Present Value
2. Lump Sum versus Annuity

Future value is the value at some point in the future of a quantity subject to compound growth. An example would be the value 10 years from now of $1,000 invested at 5% compound interest. Present value, on the other hand, is the current or beginning value of a quantity subject to compound growth. An example of present value is the value which must be invested now at 5% compound interest in order to have $1,000 accumulated in 10 years. The relationship between future and present value can be shown graphically by the use of a time line.

If the present value is known:

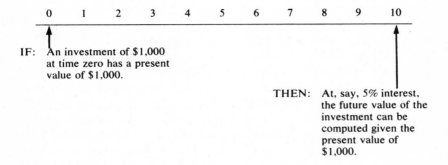

IF: An investment of $1,000
     at time zero has a present
     value of $1,000.

THEN: At, say, 5% interest,
       the future value of the
       investment can be
       computed given the
       present value of
       $1,000.

Alternatively, if the future value is known:

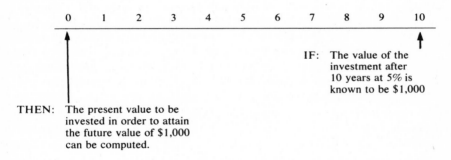

IF: The value of the
     investment after
     10 years at 5% is
     known to be $1,000

THEN: The present value to be
       invested in order to attain
       the future value of $1,000
       can be computed.

From the time lines, it can be seen that future values can be converted into present values and vice versa. Notice that money can have different values at different times because it is subject to the law of compound growth.

Lump sum quantities are easily explained because they are the quantities with which the analyst is most familiar. The examples in the preceding paragraph were lump sums — the future value of a lump sum of $1,000 or the present value of a lump sum of $1,000 received 10 years from now. A lump sum is merely a single payment which is either given or received on a specified date. Annuities are only slightly more complicated, being a fixed amount such as $1,000 which is paid or received once each time period for a stated number of time periods. An example of an annuity received might be an arrangement to receive $1,000 annually for 20 years. An example of an annuity paid might be the investment of $1,000 annually for 10 years. In terms of time lines, the annuity can be shown as:

The periodic payment of, say, $1,000
is made each year.

0	1	2	3	4	5	6	7	8	9	10

The value of the annuity at this point
is its present value. For example,
the amount of money that would have
to be invested at 5% now in order to
receive $1,000 annually for 10 years.

The value of the annuity at this
point is its future value. For
example, the amount of money
that would be accumulated in 10
years if $1,000 were invested
annually at 5%.

From the time line of the annuity, it can be seen that this type of investment has both a present value and a future value. In this sense, annuities are similar to lump sum payments. In order to solve problems involving the compounding process, then, it is necessary to know whether
the problem involves a lump sum or an annuity and then to decide whether
it is necessary to begin with a known present value and calculate an unknown future value or to begin with a known future value and calculate an
unknown present value. Once the type of problem has been recognized, it
is possible to use financial tables simply to look up the solution. There are
four basic tables commonly available for this purpose. See Appendix B.

1. Amount of 1 at Compound Interest. Table B–1 is used in lump sum
problems with a known present worth to compute an unknown future
worth.

2. Present Value of 1 at Compound Interest. Table B–2 is used in
lump sum problems with a known future worth to compute an unknown
present worth.

3. Amount of Annuity of 1 Per Period. Table B–3 is used in annuity
problems when the annual payment is known and the future worth is
needed.

4. Present Value of Annuity of 1 Per Period. Table B–4 is used in
annuity problems when the annual payment is known and the present
worth is needed.

ILLUSTRATIVE PROBLEMS

The use of these tables can be explained most easily in the context of
practical examples, and a few applications are presented for this purpose.
The types of problems selected do not in any way exhaust the possibilities of this type of an approach in investment analysis.

Example 1

As a portfolio manager, you are discussing retirement plans with a
55-year-old man. He does not wish to touch his current capital upon

retirement, and he wishes to receive $10,000 annually from the additional capital which he is willing to place in your care at the beginning of his retirement. He will retire at 65 and you both are willing to assume that he will die at 75. In addition, you agree that a 10% return is possible. How much should he present to you on his 65th birthday?

This problem can be attacked by using the approach outlined above. Is it a lump sum or an annuity problem? Since he wishes $10,000 *annually,* it is an annuity, and it is to run for 10 years. Is it necessary to convert the annuity into a present worth or into a future worth? Since he will be presenting the lump sum at the *beginning* of the term of the annuity, the present worth at age 65 is needed. Note that this is present worth in terms of the life span of the annuity, not in terms of the particular year that the portfolio manager considers the problem. Since the problem is to convert an annuity to a present worth, Table B–4 is used. The entry in this table for 10 periods at 10% interest is 6.145 (or $6.145). This is the lump sum needed in order to receive $1.00 per year. Since he needs $10,000, we multiply 6.145 × $10,000 = $61,450, which must be invested at age 65 to receive $10,000 annually for 10 years. If he were expected to live 15 years, the table entry would be 7.606, implying that $76,000 would be needed to produce the annuity from age 65 to age 80. If he were expected to live precisely 10 years, but a return of only 5% was available, the table for 10 periods at 5% shows 7.722, implying that $77,220 would be needed in this case. This compares to $61,450 for the same annuity at 10%, a substantial increase in the investment needed. If a 20% return were possible, only $41,930 would be needed.

Example 2

Assuming the original problem stated in Example 1, assume further that the man states that he now has $500,000 capital that he wants safely invested and that he intends to leave to his children. Since he is willing to assume very little risk, a 5% interest rate is assumed. He further states that he is able to save $5,000 per year (at the level of risk associated with a 10% return) toward the annuity which he wishes to begin receiving when he retires. He then asks several questions, assuming that the 10% return and 5% low-risk return can be attained. Will he have accumulated enough personal funds to have financed his retirement without drawing upon the money which he has set aside for his children? What will be the value of the fund for his children when he retires? When he dies? If he has more than ample funds for retirement and invests these funds at 10% for his children, how much additional money will they have when he dies? This is now a set of problems in compounding theory, and they can be solved by simply breaking them into a series of individual problems.

First, it is already known from Example 1 that $61,450 will be needed at age 65 to finance the annuity. The problem, then, is discovering the value of the $5,000 saved each year for 10 years at 10%. This is an annuity problem because more money will be paid each year. It is the future worth which is needed because the problem is to find the value at the *end* of the term of the annuity (this annuity builds funds from age 55 to age 65). From the description of the tables, this conversion of annuity to future worth can be seen to require the use of Table B–3. The entry in this table for 10 periods at 10% interest is 15.937. This is the future value of a $1.00 annuity, and since $5,000 will be paid annually, we multiply 15.937 × $5,000 = $79,685. This is the value of the money accumulated by the annual $5,000 payments as of age 65. Since only $61,450 will be needed for retirement, $18,235 will be available to be invested at 10% for the children. The children will receive this money after it has been invested for 10 years (from age 65 to age 75).

What will be the total value of the money at that time? This is the next problem, and we begin as usual by asking whether it is an annuity or a lump sum. It is a lump sum because all of the money to be invested is available at one time. Is the present worth or the future worth needed? The number desired is the value of the fund at the end of the ten-year period that it will be invested. It is therefore a future worth. Referring to the description of the tables, converting lump sum present worth into future worth is solved by using Table B–1. The entry in this table for 10 years at 10% is 2.594. This is the value of $1.00 after 10 years at 10%, and since we are investing $18,235, we multiply 2.594 × $18,235 = $47,301.59 as the value to be received by the children when the investor reaches age 75.

This solves all of the problems except the value of $500,000 at 5% when the man reaches age 65 and age 75. This is a lump sum, future value problem using Table B–1. The entry at 5% for 10 years is 1.629 and for 20 years is 2.653. The $500,000 will therefore be worth 1.629 × $500,000 = $814,500 at age 65 and 2.653 × $500,000 = $1,326,500 at age 75. The total value of the funds available for the children at age 75 is therefore $47,301 + $1,326,500 = $1,373,801.

Example 3

An investor wishes to have $500,000 in 14 years and expects to be able to achieve an 8% return during this period. How much money does he need to have now in order to achieve his goal? This is a lump sum problem because it asks for the single payment necessary now in order to have $500,000 in 14 years (assuming that it is invested at 8%). The present worth is the desired value. Referring to the description of the tables, converting lump sum future worth into present worth is the function of Table B–2. The table entry for 14 periods at 8% is 0.340. This is the amount which must be invested now in order to have $1.00 in 14 years at 8%. Since we must have $500,000, we must multiply 0.340 × $500,000 = $170,000.

Example 4

The investor in Example 3 is in the unfortunate position of having only $100,000 available for investment. How far short of his goal will he fall at 8%? What rate of return must he have to achieve his goal? The value of $100,000 in 14 years at 8% can be found using Table B–1 to convert present worth to future worth. The table entry is 2.937, which when multiplied by $100,000 equals $293,700, or $206,300 below the goal. The solution to the second question is found by dividing $500,000 by $100,000, getting 5.0. The rate of return which in 14 years will provide a future value of $5.00 for every $1.00 in the present is the minimum return which will achieve the goal. Looking in Table B–1 (which converts present worth into future worth) under 14 periods, we find that 12% return would produce $4.387 and 14% would produce $6.261. The required return is therefore about 13%.

Example 5

A company had earnings per share 10 years ago of $2.00 and the current EPS is $3.26. If only one growth rate can be used to characterize the increase, what would that growth rate be? This is obviously not an annuity problem, and the problem is to find the return which would convert the present worth of $2.00 into the future worth of $3.26. This is the conversion performed by Table B–1. By dividing $3.26 by $2.00, we get $1.63 as the future value per $1.00 of earnings. Looking at Table B–1 under 10 years for some rate of return which would produce 1.63, we find an entry of 1.629 under 5%. The EPS can therefore be characterized as having grown at approximately a 5% rate over the last 10 years.

Example 6

As a portfolio manager, you receive a set of estimates from the research department concerning the future price action of two different stocks which will pay no dividends in the foreseeable future. The first stock is expected to sell at 65 in three years, with a current price of 50. The second stock is currently selling at 30 and, although results from year to year are unpredictable, it can be estimated to be selling at 45 in four years. Assuming that you have no additional information, you can buy only one of the stocks, and the estimated rise in the S&P 500 in the intermediate future is 8% per year, which stock do you purchase? One possible solution to this problem is based upon using the 8% per year return on an "average" investment in a "cost of capital" sense. Since this return could be earned on the capital by simply investing in the averages, it seems clear that an investment in either stock recommended by the research department has an expected opportunity cost of 8%. Using Table B–2 (which converts future values into present value) it seems reasonable to find the present value of the capital appreciation per dollar of investment which would be produced by each stock and then select the issue having the largest present value. If the estimates are correct (and we have no other information upon which to base a decision, making the assumption of accuracy necessary), this approach will maximize the capital appreciation of the account relative to the appreciation of the S&P 500. Incidentally, if either stock has a present value less than the assumed $1 initial investment, its purchase would provide less appreciation than the purchase of the "averages." This is the same thing as saying that the stock will provide less benefit than its opportunity cost, which in turn is equivalent to maintaining that the stock should not be purchased.

Actually performing the indicated calculations, we find that:

Stock	Current Price	Price in		Indexed Appreciation	
		3 years	4 years	3 years	4 years
A	50	65	—	1.30	—
B	30	—	45	—	1.50

These values can be reduced to present values by using Table B–2 at the 8% level with each time period corresponding to the year in which the gain is estimated to be received:

Stock	Time Period	Appreciation	"Discount" Factor	Present Value
A	0 yr.–3d yr.	1.30	.794	1.0322
B	0 yr.–4th yr.	1.50	.735	1.1025

This table indicates that although both investments would provide a more attractive return than the market average, stock B is expected to be substantially more beneficial to the portfolio than stock A. It is interesting to note, however, that if the return on stock B were not obtained until the fifth year, the discount factor would be .681 and the present value would be 1.0215. This would be less attractive than stock A's 1.0322.

This approach in the selection of securities is more flexible than simply dividing the expected appreciation by the number of years required to achieve the benefit. This flexibility stems from the ability to deal with multiple time periods when using the present value method. For example, if the market were expected to rise 20% in the fourth year, the present value of an investment in stock A would be unaffected but the present value of an investment in stock B would decline very dramatically.

When the portfolio manager has expectations concerning varying returns over varying time periods, for both the averages and the set of stocks being analyzed, the present value technique will still permit him to select the set of stocks which is most consistent with his set of expectations. Using the average annual rate of return for the different stocks, on the other hand, can never provide the proper weighting of the value of each issue over each time period relative to the behavior of the market during that period. Present value technique reduces the large number of expectations over a complex set of time intervals to a single number which indicates the value of each security as an investment vehicle.

FINANCIAL FORMULAS

The financial tables are calculated from four basic formulas which can be used directly when tables are not available. The formula for the compound amount of one which converts present worth into future worth is:

$$S = (1 + i)^n$$

where:
  i = the interest rate per period
  n = the number of time periods

This equation can easily be solved by the use of logarithms. Find the log of $1 + i$ and then multiply the log by n. Take the result (which is a logarithm) and find its antilog. This antilog is the solution, that is, it is the value of S.

The formula which provides the discount factor used to find present worth given future worth is:

$$\text{Discount Factor} = (1 + i)^{-n}$$

This formula can also be solved using logarithms. The technique is exactly the same as the first formula, except that the log is divided by n rather than multiplied.

The formula for the future value of an annuity is:

$$\frac{(1 + i)^n - 1}{i}$$

The formula which provides the present value of an annuity is:

$$\frac{1 - (1 + i)^{-n}}{i}$$

COMPUTING AN UNKNOWN ANNUITY

The techniques presented up to this point will permit the analyst to move easily from present worth to future worth and back again. In addition, it is already possible to move from an annuity having a known annual payment to either the present worth or the future worth of the annuity. Unfortunately, it is not yet possible to compute an unknown annual payment when the present or future worth is known. The following examples show how to overcome this problem and why computing annual payments is important.

Example 7

Assume that you are a portfolio manager and a client wishes to have $100,000 available when he retires in eight years. You agree that a 7% return is possible on investment and use the future worth to present worth conversion table at eight years and 7% to find a discount factor of .582. Multiplying this by $100,000 you get $58,200 as the amount which should be invested now in order to have the desired amount upon retirement. The client, however, indicates that he prefers to make annual payments into the portfolio in order to obtain the $100,000 instead of providing the $58,200 lump sum. He asks for the size of payment needed. Since this problem deals with the conversion of future worth into the size of the annual payment, it is the reverse of Table B–3 (the Amount of Annuity of 1 per period table, which converts the payment into the future worth). Looking in this table under eight years and 7%, you find 10.260. Since the problem is "reversed," you divide 10.260 into 1.0 in order to find the annual payment, getting .0975 as the annual payment needed to have $1.00 upon retirement. Since $100,000 is needed, you multiply .0975 times $100,000 to find the payment needed. This produces a solution of $9,746.

Example 8

As a portfolio manager, you are approached by a client for advice concerning an investment opportunity which he has encountered. He has a chance to invest $10,000 in a local business which will provide a constant annual return for 12 years, at the end of which the assets will be worthless. What is the minimum annual payment that will make the investment worthwhile if the client has the alternative of obtaining a 9% return by investing in bonds? In this problem, the 9% opportunity cost can be taken in the cost of capital sense, and the investment can be regarded as attractive if the present worth of the stream of income that is generated has a positive value using a 9% discount rate. In other words, the capital which the investor would have after 12 years of bond investment would be greater than the capital which would be produced by this investment *unless* the investment produced a return greater than or equal to 9% per year. Any annual payment from the investment that would be less than 9% would dissipate the capital which could have been produced by the purchase of bonds. The present worth is known to be $10,000, and the unknown quantity is the amount of the annual payment which would provide a 9% return. To move from the present worth to the annual payment, we "reverse" the process of moving from payment to present worth which is covered in Table B–4. This table at 12 years and 9% has an entry of 7.161. In order to "reverse" this entry, you divide this value into 1.00, getting .1396 as the amount for the annual payment which would give a present value of $1.00. Multiplying this by $10,000, you get $1,396 as the minimum annual return which would make the investment profitable (i.e., make it provide a 9% annual return).

SUMMARY

Four very simple tables can provide the financial analyst with the solutions to a very substantial set of problems. They can be used to calculate the values for any process which changes according to the compounding principle, and the model of compound growth is useful in an extremely high percentage of the items considered by the investment community. Probably the most important applications stem from the fact that money (and also the products which can be purchased with money) has a time value. A dollar today is worth more than a dollar to be received ten years from now, even if the purchasing power of money is held constant. The analyst deals with many variables, and these variables have values at different points in time. By using the techniques shown in this chapter, he will be able to simplify the diversity of his data by expressing many of the quantities at their present worth. In this way, he will be able to consider a high percentage of his problems without regard to the variations caused by the time dimension and the time value of money.

The specific techniques discussed enable the analyst to convert present worth to an unknown future value, convert future worth to present value, convert annual payments to the future total value of an annuity, or convert annual payment to an unknown present worth of an annuity. In addition, if both values are known (both present and future worth or both annual payment and future worth, for example), then the implied table entry can be computed and compared to the actual table values to find the implied interest rate. Example 5 showed how this can have practical application. Finally, problems requiring the conversion of either the future or present worth of an annuity into the required annual payment were found to be solved by simply dividing the appropriate table entry into 1.00.

Chapter
5   Averages and How to Use Them

In statistical analysis, it is often necessary to select one number, or an "average" to represent a large collection of numbers. The "average" most often used is the arithmetic mean, but at times other "averages" are more appropriate. The harmonic mean and the geometric mean are explained, as are the median and the mode. In addition, an average is more meaningful if the dispersion of the data around the average is known. The range, the variance, and the standard deviation are illustrated, together with the coefficient of variation, which is used to compare dispersion among several series of data.

INTRODUCTION

Elementary statistics is the study of how data can be effectively summarized. It attempts to describe the important aspects of large sets of data without inundating the reader in a mass of detailed numbers. By using the simple models of descriptive statistics, important characteristics of the information being studied can be made more evident because the general tendencies of the data are presented clearly and without the distraction of the individual peculiarity of each observed datum. The dangers in the use of the tool of descriptive statistics can be deduced from the purpose of this approach. First, it is possible to fail to locate a significant feature of the data. Second, it is possible to misuse the tools and indicate a characteristic which is not actually present. The two most important features of a data set are its tendency to cluster around some central value, and its tendency to deviate from that central value. These two features are the topics of the two following sections of this chapter.

MEASURES OF CENTRAL TENDENCY

Arithmetic Mean

Whenever an analyst wishes to simplify a large group of numbers by characterizing the group by a single number, he quite naturally gives serious consideration to using an *average*. The arithmetic mean, commonly called the "average," is probably one of the two most frequently used mathematical models in the investment community (the compound annual growth rate being the other). This section is not an attempt to establish the uses of the average but instead is designed to show the limitations of the model and to show several other "averages" which in certain cases are more appropriate than the arithmetic mean.

The basic, underlying concept implied in the use of an average is that all of the data being used are observations from one population which has a common property. It would, for example, be absurd to average the *P/E* of Standard Oil of New Jersey, the earnings per share of U.S. Steel, and the current ratio of Xerox. This point is obvious, but it indicates two very important points in the use of the mean. First, the arithmetic of the average is simply $\frac{\Sigma x_i}{N}$ (read: the total of all x's, divided by the number of x's). It will work on any group of numbers indiscriminately, producing absurd results if not used with some care. Second, the characteristic of the population which is being measured can easily be misrepresented unless some care is taken. The average is a number "pulled" out of the set of data by the model and which is supposed to *represent* or "stand for" the particular characteristic of the data set which is needed. If the model is not appropriate for the data at hand, or if the data do not refer to the particular item for which a measurement is desired, the results can be fallacious.

One of the most misleading uses of an average is to characterize a highly diverse group with an "average" which is not representative of any member at all. Table 5–1 below is an illustration of this situation. Although a number of misleading conclusions can be drawn from this

TABLE 5–1
"Speculative" Industry

Company	Five-Year Price Appreciation (%)
A	− 40
B	− 60
C	− 80
D	− 20
E	+550
Average	70%

"average," the arithmetic procedure used is correct. It is the model that is wrong, in the only sense that a model can be wrong: it is not helpful in analyzing the data.

Another example occurs in the averaging of P/E ratios. If the earnings of one company are almost zero, its P/E will be enormous and any average which includes this company will be unrealistic. This suggests that great care is necessary when averaging ratios of any sort.

Harmonic Mean

In some cases, the *harmonic mean* should be used instead of the more generally known arithmetic mean. This average is employed in certain cases where rates or where prices are being characterized by an average. Mathematically, the average is:

$$H = \frac{N}{\sum \left(\frac{1}{x_i}\right)}$$

It is used when the x_i are such things as miles per hour, dollar earnings per dollar market value, and so forth. Whenever the analyst averages numbers which are expressed as an "x per something," the harmonic mean should be considered. This mean is more appropriate than the average if the variations in the data are in the "per something" instead of in "x" (as is normally the case). For example, when averaging miles per hour, we might find that "miles" are constant and that "per hour" varies. Consider the following observations:

60 miles	taking	2 hours
60 miles	taking	1½ hours
60 miles	taking	3 hours
60 miles	taking	1 hour
60 miles	taking	2½ hours
60 average	÷	2 average = 30 mph average

We would find that because it is the hours, not the miles, that varied, the mean of the mph would produce the incorrect answer:

Arithmetic Mean

30 mph
40 mph
20 mph
60 mph
24 mph
174 mph ÷ 5 = 34.8 mph

But by taking the harmonic mean, we find that:

Harmonic Mean

$$H = \frac{N}{\sum \frac{1}{x_i}} = \frac{5}{\left(\frac{1}{30} + \frac{1}{40} + \frac{1}{20} + \frac{1}{60} + \frac{1}{24}\right)} = \frac{5}{\frac{40}{240}}$$

$$= \frac{(5)(240)}{40} = \frac{1200}{40} = 30 \text{ mph}$$

giving the average which was already
shown to be correct.

Another example stems from the financial measure "dollar earnings per dollar market value." If we are comparing the "expensiveness" of four stocks, it is the "per dollar market value" of the issues which varies, and this calls for the harmonic mean. The following example shows both calculations:

Comparison of Means Using $ Earnings per $ of Market

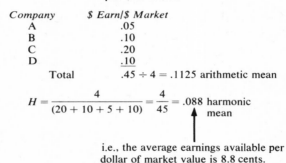

Company	$ Earn/$ Market
A	.05
B	.10
C	.20
D	.10
Total	.45 ÷ 4 = .1125 arithmetic mean

$$H = \frac{4}{(20 + 10 + 5 + 10)} = \frac{4}{45} = .088 \text{ harmonic mean}$$

i.e., the average earnings available per
dollar of market value is 8.8 cents.

If we then check the result by using another measure of "price," the price-earnings ratio, the following shows what happens:

Mean Using P/E Ratio

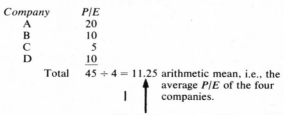

Company	P/E
A	20
B	10
C	5
D	10
Total	45 ÷ 4 = 11.25 arithmetic mean, i.e., the average P/E of the four companies.

This P/E is equal to .088 $ earnings per $ market, as given by the *harmonic mean*. It is *not* equal to .1125 $ earnings per $ market value as indicated by the *arithmetic* mean of the $ earnings per $ market.

The following should clarify the situation:

Calculation of the Average When Earnings Vary

Company	Price	Earnings	P/E
A	$100	$ 5.00	20
B	100	10.00	10
C	100	20.00	5
D	100	10.00	20
	$100 ave.	$11.25 ave.	11.25 ave.

$100 ave. ÷ $11.25 ave. = an 8.88 ave. P/E, which is not equal to a direct average of the P/E's.

Calculation of the Average When Prices Vary

Company	Price	Earnings	P/E
A	$40	$2.00	20
B	20	2.00	10
C	10	2.00	5
D	20	2.00	10
	$22.5 ave.	$2.00 ave.	11.25 ave.
	$22.5 ave. ÷	$2.00 ave. =	11.25 ave. P/E

These results show that the harmonic mean *does* measure what it is designed to measure. It gives the average when the "per something" aspect of the data is the part which is fluctuating (earnings, in this case). The arithmetic mean is correct, however, when prices fluctuate and earnings are constant. Each model serves its own particular purpose, depending on what part of the ratio the analyst regards as "basic." If studying the average earnings available for a given size of investment, the harmonic mean is valuable; if studying the relative price which must be paid for earnings, the arithmetic mean is appropriate.

Geometric Mean

The geometric mean is frequently used in averaging quantities such as the base data for indices, the observations of a time series which has a compound growth rate, ratios, and ratios of change over time. It is mathematically defined as:

$$G = \sqrt[n]{x_1 \, x_2 \, x_3 \ldots x_n} \quad \text{or} \quad G = \sqrt[n]{\Pi(x_i)}$$

Recall that Π indicates that the product of all x's is to be found, producing a single number.

The simplest way to calculate the geometric mean is to find the logs of x_i, then add these logs, divide by N, and finally take the antilog of the result. Mathematically,

$$\log (\text{Geometric Mean}) = \frac{\Sigma(\log x_i)}{N}$$

Then, Geometric Mean = antilog [log (Geometric Mean)]

A major computational limitation of the technique is that G cannot be found if any x_i is zero or negative.

The main use of the geometric mean in financial analysis is in averaging changes over time. For example, if the rate of return on a portfolio which has received no dividends is needed, calculating the ratio of the current year's value to the preceding year produces the following:

Year	Market Value	Market Value Relative to Previous Year
1963	$100.00	—
1964	110.00	1.10
1965	88.00	.80
1966	101.20	1.15
1967	121.44	1.20
	Total	4.25
	Arithmetic Mean	1.08

To compute the geometric mean, add the logs of the x_i:

$$\log 1.10 = .4139$$
$$\log\ \ .80 = .90309 - 1 = -.09691$$
$$\log 1.15 = .06070$$
$$\log 1.20 = \underline{.07918}$$
$$\text{Total } .08436$$

We then find the average of the logs:

$$.08436 \div 4 = .02109$$

And then to find the value of the answer, we take the antilog of the average:

$$\text{Antilog } .02109 = 1.05 = \text{Geometric Mean}$$

As a result of these calculations, the arithmetic mean of 1.08 and the geometric mean of 1.05 were found as alternative numbers which might possibly be used to characterize the same set of data. In order to determine which method is more valuable, it is logical to start with the beginning portfolio value and apply the "average" change each year in order to see how accurately the final value of the portfolio is approximated by the use of the averages. For the arithmetic mean:

**Beginning Portfolio Value Increased
at Arithmetic Average Rate**

$100   × 1.08 = 108.0 in 1964
108   × 1.08 = 116.6 in 1965
116.6 × 1.08 = 125.9 in 1966
125.9 × 1.08 = 136.0 in 1967

Since the arithmetic mean yields a 1967 value of 136.0 instead of the actual 121.44, it has an optimistic bias. For the geometric mean:

**Beginning Portfolio Value Increased
at Geometric Average Rate**

100   × 1.05 = 105   in 1964
105   × 1.05 = 110.2 in 1965
110.2 × 1.05 = 115.7 in 1966
115.7 × 1.05 = 121.5 in 1967

which is accurate within
rounding error.

Other Averages

If an analyst divided his stocks into ten equal groups based on their *P/E* ratio, he might display the results in a later presentation as shown in Figure 5–1.

FIGURE 5–1

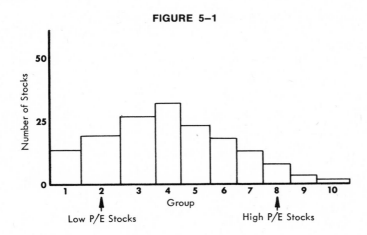

This graphic presentation is called a histogram and clearly shows the frequency with which events occur and the distribution of these frequencies within a population. The only point to be made by the histogram at this stage, however, is that it is not "balanced"; it has a concentration on the left-hand side, in the area of the low P/E ratios. The average which is to be used to represent the population, then, must represent a "skewed" population.

This creates a rather severe problem, because the relatively few observations in the high-priced range are given, obviously, a high P/E and hence a high weight when the arithmetic mean is computed. The arithmetic mean, in other words, automatically weights the frequencies by their numerical values, and this produces distorted results if the distribution is radically skewed. If the weights (the P/E ratios) are ignored, it is possible to emphasize the companies themselves by asking which company has exactly half of the companies below it in "expensiveness" and the other half above it. In this way, the "middle" company would be found, and in a very real sense this company is very representative of the group as a whole. This type of average is called the *median*. It would be the analyst's "best bet" if he wished to guess what P/E a particular company possessed, worrying about the *number of companies* that would fall between his estimate and the actual value.

The arithmetic mean, on the other hand, would be the "best bet" when guessing the P/E of a company while worrying about the number of P/E's that would fall between the estimate and the actual value. In other words, the median represents the *companies* while the mean represents the $P/E's$. The mean is more sensitive to extreme values. Therefore, while the two will be equal in balanced distributions, the mean will tend to be "pulled" off center in skewed populations. Since the median is simply the "middle" number, no mathematical technique is available to calculate it. The median can be found only by examining the set of numbers and selecting the middle value. For example, in the following set:

$$5 \qquad 8 \qquad 10 \qquad 14 \qquad 23$$

The number "10" can be seen to be the median. On larger problems, however, locating the median can be a tedious task. Because of this (and also because it has no mathematical formula which might make it useful in more advanced mathematical use) the median is seldom used in statistical analysis.

The *mode* is defined as the most frequent value in the population. It represents the single P/E which the largest number of stocks in our example possess. In balanced distributions, it equals the mean and median, but in skewed distributions it is less sensitive to extreme values than either of the other two measures. If each value in the following set of numbers represents the number of years that a stock has been held in a portfolio,

1   2   3   2   3   4   3   5   4   3   2   1

the mode is 3 years, as can be found by counting the frequency with which each value occurs. This procedure is the only means by which the mode can be discovered, and as a result the mode is seldom used.

MEASURES OF DISPERSION

Unfortunately, the use of one of the various types of averages cannot completely describe the basic data. One very important characteristic which the average completely neglects is the "closeness" of the various observations to the average. The need to supplement the average with another measure which characterizes this "spread" has been recognized by analysts for many years, so that, for example, the mean price of a stock frequently is supplemented by the range for the year.

Range

The range as a measure of the amount of dispersion that is present in a data set has the advantage of conceptual simplicity and ease in calculation. Its disadvantage is that one extreme value will greatly affect the range but is not really typical for the population as a whole. For example, if a stock at the close of each month sells for:

32   34   30   35   33   37   34   38   49   37   35   37

the range can easily be found by inspection to be 30–49. The number 49 was a most unusual value, so that the range presents a picture of greater market volatility than is justified by the data. One possible solution would be simply to throw out extreme observations before finding the range, but since it is impossible to define "extreme" with precision, this technique is too subjective.

Variance and Standard Deviation

If the analyst decided to reject the use of the range and instead used deviation from the mean as a measure of "spread," he would be using the lines in the diagram shown in Figure 5–2.

FIGURE 5–2

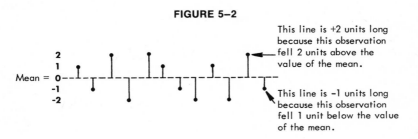

If the total of the length of these vertical lines is large, the population has a broad dispersion; if small, a small dispersion. But on closer examination, we find that the lines for observations *below* the average are negative. By the definition of the mean (it must fall in the middle of the observations), the total of the negative lines *must* equal the total of the positive, yielding an answer of zero in every case. In the graph, we find that:

$$+ 1 - 1 + 2 - 2 + 2 + 1 - 1 - 2 + 1 - 2 + 2 - 1 = 0$$

In order to measure these lines *as lines* without regard to the sign of the numbers that they touch, it is necessary to avoid negative signs. The simplest way to do this is to square all of the lines, that is, to square every deviation from the mean. This works because $(+2)^2 = +4$ and $(-2)^2 = +4$, making equal length lines have equal positive length without regard to the original sign. By summing the squared deviations and then dividing by the number of observations, it is possible to find the "average squared deviation." This is called the *variance* in statistical theory. If the variance is then "unsquared," the root mean square is found. This is called the standard deviation. The following formulas are helpful:

Variance	*Standard Deviation*
$\sigma^2 = \dfrac{\Sigma(x - \bar{x})_i^2}{N}$	$\sigma = \sqrt{\dfrac{\Sigma(x - \bar{x})_i^2}{N}}$

where:

σ = the greek letter "sigma," traditionally used in statistics to indicate standard deviation.

x_i = the observation value.

$\bar{x}$ = the mean of the observations.

N = the number of observations.

Assume, for example, that the quarterly P/E ratio of a stock being analyzed has the set of values:

10	12	14	10	9	11	12	13

These numbers have a mean of 11.375. The mean value is useful in providing a single number which can be used to characterize the entire set of eight numbers, but it does not give any indication of the "diversity" of the set. The eight values might as easily have been:

0	0	0	0	22.750	22.750	22.750	22.750

or:

11.25	11.25	11.25	11.25	11.5	11.5	11.5	11.5

The mean of any of these sets is still 11.375, but the accuracy with which the mean characterizes the data is quite different in each case. The variance indicates the adequacy of the mean as representing the numbers and at the same time is in itself a valuable measure of the variability of the data, which in this case shows the volatility of the market's valuation of the company's earning power. The standard deviation is simply the square root of the variance. Each measure has selected uses in more advanced statistical techniques.

In the first set of numbers shown above, the variance is computed by: (1) subtracting the mean from each number, (2) squaring the result, (3) adding all of these squared values together, (4) dividing this sum by 8. Step one produces the following set of numbers:

-1.375 .625   2.625 -1.375 -2.375 $-.375$ .625   1.625

Step two squares these numbers, producing:

1.89   .39   6.89   1.89   5.64   .14   .39   2.64

Step three simply adds these numbers together, getting 17.625. Step four divides by 8, getting 2.203 as the value for the variance. The standard deviation is merely the square root of 2.203, or 1.484.

The advantage to the use of the variance or the standard deviation is that it takes every value in the population into account when measuring the dispersion in the group being studied. In a normally distributed set of numbers, approximately 68% of the numbers will fall within one standard deviation of the average. For example, if the average is 48 and the standard deviation is 2, an analyst would expect about 68% of the numbers to be between 46 and 50. He would expect about 95% to lie within 2 σ of the mean (44 to 52), and about 99% to lie within 3 σ (42 to 54). The standard deviation is always measured in the same units as the average. An average P/E of 20 would have a σ of, say, 3 P/E multiples (from 17 to 23); an average sales of $40 million might have a σ of, say, $8 million (from $32 million to $48 million); and so forth.

Coefficient of Variation

The advantage of having the measure of dispersion expressed in the same units as the mean disappears, however, when an analyst wishes to compare the volatility of two different sets of data. For example, it may be necessary to compare the variation from average profit margin in the grocery chain industry to the retail trade industry. If the net margin in grocery chains is 1.5% with $\sigma = 0.45\%$ and retail trade has a mean margin of 5.0% with a σ of $=0.75\%$, it is difficult to see which industry has more "scatter." Certainly, the 0.75% of retail trade is greater, but its mean is also higher and so a larger σ is to be expected. The solution is to calculate the standard deviation as a percentage of the mean. This produces the *coefficient of variation*, a "percentage dispersion" figure. In the example, the coefficient of variation (symbolized by V) for grocery chains equals $0.45\% \div 1.5\% = 30\%$. For retail trade, $V = 0.75\% \div 5.0\% = 15\%$. From the data, it is now clear that grocery chains have about twice the dispersion found in the retail trade industry. It is the data that provide the basis for the conclusion, but the information within the data was made visible to the analyst through the coefficient of variation. For reference, the formula is:

$$V = \frac{\sigma}{x} \times 100$$

Mean Absolute Deviation

An alternative to the standard deviation as a measure of dispersion is the mean absolute deviation. In this technique, the absolute values of all deviations from the average are totaled and the resulting sum is then divided by the number of observations. The formula for this procedure is:

$$\text{Mean Absolute Deviation} = \frac{\Sigma|x_i - \bar{x}|}{N}$$

In the chart of deviations presented in the section on variance, the deviations were:

$$+ 1 - 1 + 2 - 2 + 2 + 1 - 1 - 2 + 1 - 2 + 2 - 1 = 0$$

The absolute values can be found and totaled, producing:

$$+ 1 + 1 + 2 + 2 + 2 + 1 + 1 + 2 + 1 + 2 + 2 + 1 = 18$$

Since there are 12 observations, the mean absolute deviation equals $18 \div 12 = 1.5$.

The advantage of the mean absolute deviation is that it is less sensitive to extreme deviations than the variance. The disadvantage is that it is not used extensively in more advanced mathematical techniques, while the variance is found in many applications.

Chapter

6 Linear Regression or How to Express the Relationship between Two Variables

A common task of the financial analyst is to simplify a mass of data into a simple statement and then to see whether a relationship exists between two variables. Linear regression is a technique for determining whether and by how much a change in one variable will result in a change in another variable. A crude method to visualize the relationship is to plot the data on a graph, but a mathematical equation can express the relationship more precisely. The standard error of estimate will show by how much the equation misses expressing the relationship, and the coefficient of correlation will show the extent to which the two variables are related. Finally, the coefficient of determination will indicate the percent of variance in one variable that is explained by the second variable.

BASIC CONCEPTS

The logical manipulations in the chapter on algebra have some direct practical value, but the problem for a financial analyst is not fundamentally the execution of operations on mathematical terms. The really basic problem in quantitative applications is the reduction of a fantastic mass of data into a manageable set of simple statements. Simplification is the first job of a research analyst or portfolio manager, and this task is the subject matter of elementary statistics. But basic statistics and algebra combine to provide the foundation for the study of the *relation-*

ship between variables. Algebra permits the manipulation of functions such as:

$$Y = a + bx$$

but does not provide the analyst with the technique by which he can discover whether two variables have such a relationship. Even given the function, the analyst is unable to decide upon the values to use for *a* or *b* and so cannot use the equation for practical applications. Statistics, however, permit the researcher to reduce data on two variables to the equation by using the tool called simple regression.

Returning to the rather time-worn example of *P/E* and *G* (growth in earnings), assume that a research analyst suspects that these two aspects of individual stocks are closely related. As a result, he naturally believes that high *P/E*'s are associated with high *G*'s, and low with low. Being aware of the use of graphs, he decides to "picture" a set of 23 stocks in which he is interested. He therefore plots 23 pairs of (*G, P/E*) values on a graph, and each pair, naturally, is represented by a point, as shown in Figure 6–1. All of the pairs fall in the upper right-hand quarter of the graph (quadrant I) because all of the issues in which he has an interest

FIGURE 6–1

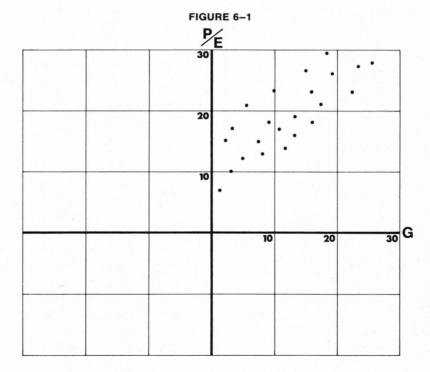

have a positive growth rate and a positive level of current earnings. This is not necessary for either the graph or the regression technique.

The most conspicuous thing about this graph is that the "swarm" of points appears to have a pattern. They tend to form a "channel" running diagonally across the paper. The easiest way for the analyst to simplify this "swarm" is to draw a straight line through the "middle" of the points, as shown in Figure 6–2.

FIGURE 6–2

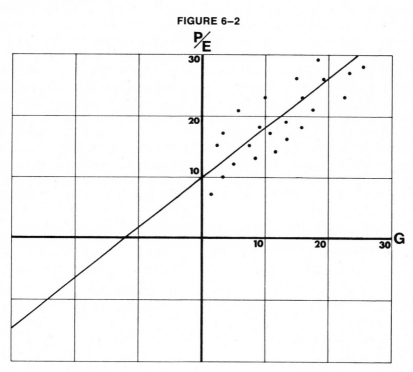

The line describes the pattern of the observations (points) without the "clutter" which was in the original system. By using this graph he is able to take a stock which he is analyzing, estimate its growth rate, and then go over on the *G* axis to this growth rate, up to the line, and read the *P/E* from the vertical axis. This *P/E* is the expected "general" area around which he would anticipate the market's valuation of the stock to fluctuate. The technique is workable and can be used by any analyst.

Assume now that an analyst using this graphic technique showed the "scatter diagram" to a statistician. The first thing that he would hear, of course, would be that the equation for a straight line is:

$$y = a + bx$$

or in this case:

$$P/E = a + bG$$

Since the analyst already had his line, the statistician may well argue, "Why not use its equation to derive the P/E for the stocks instead of this over on G, up to the line approach?"

Actually, the analyst had already found a and b when he drew the line on the graph. The value of a is the "intercept" — the value of the P/E when $G = 0$ algebraically; the point at which the line crosses the P/E axis geometrically. The analyst could find "a" by simply looking at his graph. Now b is the amount of additional P/E gained when G goes up one. It can be found from the graph by going over one on the G axis and observing how much P/E goes up. An example might be: G up one, P/E up 0.8. The value of b is therefore 0.8. Algebraically, it is the rate of change in $P/E;$ geometrically, it is the slope of the line drawn by the analyst.

Performing these simple examinations, the researcher finds that:

$$P/E = 10 + 0.8G$$

and this equation can predict P/E just as well and certainly much faster than the cruder graphic method. He has moved from a graphic to an analytic approach, trading one model in for a superior one.

INCREASING PRECISION

There are still some problems involved in the way the analyst is attacking the problem. First, he is still wasting a great deal of time because he must draw the scatter diagram so that he can "fit" his line and observe the values of a and b. Second, when he fits his line, he is using freehand methods and will be slightly inaccurate as a result. Since he has already taken the first step in the analytic approach, he could very easily use algebraic techniques to avoid these difficulties by applying the method of least squares.

To find a and b by least squares, all that is needed is to plug values into the following two equations:

$$\Sigma Y = Na + b\Sigma X$$
$$\Sigma XY = a\Sigma X + b\Sigma X^2$$

where:

Y is the dependent variable (P/E in this case).
X is the independent variable (G in this case).
N is the number of observations (number of points in the scatter diagram).

Since all of the symbols in the two equations can be converted into numbers except *a* and *b*, the analyst has a system of two equations in two unknowns, which he can then solve algebraically.

In order to use this analytic approach, the analyst only needs to calculate for each observation:

$$Y = \text{the } P/E$$
$$X = \text{the growth rate}$$
$$XY = (P/E)(G)$$
$$X^2 = G^2$$

and then add all of the observations together, giving:

$$\Sigma Y$$
$$\Sigma Y$$
$$\Sigma XY$$
$$\Sigma X^2$$

and then "plug" these into the "normal equations" along with N (the number of observations). Solving the equations then gives *a* and *b*.

This approach will give the *precise* equation which will minimize the amount by which the line "misses" the points in the diagram as shown in Figure 6–3.

FIGURE 6–3

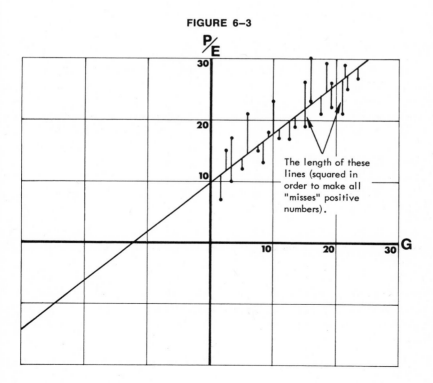

This technique, then, permits the investment man to use the "best" equation, or function, which describes the relationship underlying his data on two variables and minimizes the error that might occur in a line drawn freehand. It reduces literally dozens of numbers to a simple formula. In addition, it reduces the "essence" of the scatter diagram to a simple mathematical expression. But least squares is a *model* of the diagram. It does not reproduce every aspect of the graph. And some of these aspects are very important to the analyst. For example, it was the presence of the "pattern" which first verified to the analyst that a relationship existed. Second, the "width" of the channel made by the points indicated the accuracy of the line in describing the relationship. If analysis is to replace graphs, measures of these factors are necessary.

STANDARD ERROR OF ESTIMATE

Even if a relationship exists, an analyst is not especially interested in it unless it produces practical results. If a regression line can tell the analyst the *P/E* of a stock given the growth rate, give or take a little because of the limitations of the data, then the analyst is interested in just *how much* this "give or take" figure is. For example, Figures 6–4 and 6–5 show a relationship.

FIGURE 6–4   FIGURE 6–5

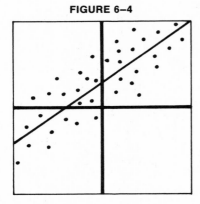
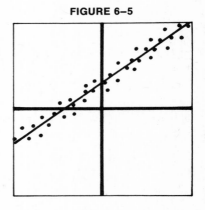

The first graph, however, has a very wide channel, while the second graph closely approximates the regression line. The value of the regression is obviously greater in the second graph, because the line will more closely characterize the data. The model will not have lost as much information in this case—it will have captured the "essence" of the base data. What the analyst needs is an analytic measure of the size of this channel.

The standard error of estimate $(s_{y,x})$ provides this information. This figure is the standard deviation of the points around the regression line. As a result, if there is a great deal of "scatter," the $s_{y,x}$ will be very large, indicating a high standard deviation of the points from the line. If the line fits the data well, $s_{y,x}$ will be small. The importance of $s_{y,x}$ in measuring the "channel" can easily be seen in Figures 6–6 and 6–7.

FIGURE 6–6

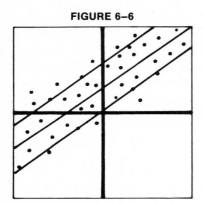

FIGURE 6–7

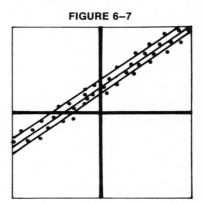

The wider scatter in the first graph caused a "broader" channel (a higher $s_{y,x}$). Notice that not all of the points are included in the channel, just as not all observations in a sample fall within one standard deviation of the mean. In general, about 68% of the points would be expected to fall within the lines. If we doubled the width of the channel, about 95% of the points would be included. It is interesting to note that the line of regression can be regarded as a sort of "mean" around which there is a standard deviation, which in this case is called the standard error. This idea corresponds to the intuitive idea of the line on the diagram being the most likely P/E "give or take a little" and the idea of the regression line being a "best estimate."

The standard error is measured as the distance from the regression line to one of the "bracketing" lines of the channel. This distance in any one study, of course, is always the same regardless of where it is measured because the two lines are parallel to the regression line. See Figure 6–8. The length of this line can be read from the vertical axis (P/E axis in the example). Because of this, an $s_{y,x} = 1.2$ in the example would mean 1.2 P/E multiples, that is, about $2/3$ of the time the actual P/E would fall within 1.2 P/E multiples of the P/E calculated from the growth rate. The unit of measurement (P/E in this case) for $s_{y,x}$ is always the same as for the variable being predicted because both are read from the vertical axis.

FIGURE 6–8

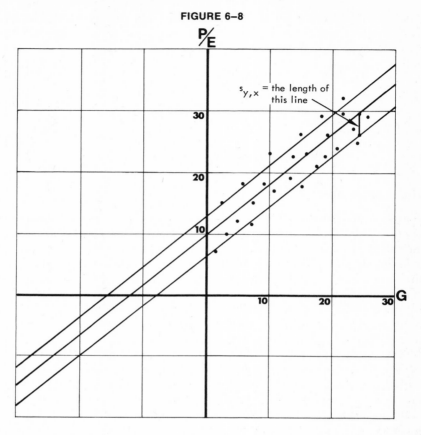

In order to calculate $s_{y.x}$ without resort to a scatter diagram, the following formula is used:

$$s_{y.x} = \sqrt{\frac{\Sigma(y - \hat{y})_i^2}{N - 2}}$$

where for each observation:

> $y =$ the item being predicted (P/E, for example).
> $\hat{y} =$ the predicted value for the y, found by using the regression equation and the observation's value of x (growth in the example). $\hat{y}$ is sometimes referred to as y_c.
> $(y - \hat{y})_i =$ the amount by which the equation "missed" the actual value of the observation.

and for the study as a whole:

> $\Sigma(y - \hat{y})_i^2 =$ the total of the squared deviations of the observed y from

the value $\hat{y}$, predicted by the equation for each observation. All of the $\hat{y}$ values will fall on the regression line.

N = the number of observations being totaled.

$\dfrac{\Sigma(y - \hat{y})_i^2}{N - 2}$ = the average squared deviation from the regression line. (The "variance" from the line). The denominator is $N - 2$ instead of N because of rather complicated concepts involved in the theory of statistical inference. $N - 2$ can most easily be thought of as the number of observations adjusted to eliminate bias.

THE COEFFICIENT OF CORRELATION

All of the work related to the regression model up to this point has assumed that the two variables being considered actually do have a relationship. In the example, this means that P/E has been assumed to be a function of G. Obviously, in many cases, the data may indicate that the fundamental relationship indicated by theory has not been substantiated by real events. In the scatter diagram, this would be shown by the absence of any pattern in the points. Analytically, a measure of how well the variables are related is provided either by the coefficient of correlation or the coefficient of determination.

The coefficient of correlation r (sometimes referred to as rho) is simply an index number which can be used to gauge the extent to which two variables are related (it has more advanced statistical features discussed in a later chapter). If $r = 0$, there is no tendency for one variable to vary with the other, i.e., there is no linear function tying the two variables together. If $r = +1.0$, the value of y can be perfectly predicted from a knowledge of the value of x. In addition, this shows that when x rises, y rises also. In this situation, two variables are said to have a perfect direct relationship. If $r = -1.0$, the value of y can still be completely predicted from a knowledge of the value of x, but when x rises, y falls. In this case, the two variables are said to have a perfect inverse relationship.

This behavior of r permits the analyst to use the absolute value of r, or $|r|$, as a measure of relationships. A high $|r|$ indicates a high degree of association between the variables, while an $|r|$ close to zero indicates that whatever relationship is present in the data may very well have been caused by chance. The real value of r, however, is in more advanced statistical applications. When an analyst is simply attempting to gain an intuitive feel for relationships, the coefficient of determination has a much more obvious interpretation and is therefore more frequently used.

The coefficient of determination, R^2, is the percentage of the variance in y which is "explained" by x. The reason why this is a helpful intuitive statistic may be made clearer by the following illustration.

Assume that you have been required to guess the value of some y (the P/E of an unknown stock at the end of next year, for example). In addition, assume that you are not permitted to use any other variable in guessing. About all that you could do would be to look at the past P/E's of stocks and guess the mean of these numbers as the actual value which will occur next year. You will probably be wrong, but you haven't been permitted to use very much information, either. How wrong will you be? The variance of the P/E's of a large group of stocks around their mean P/E is a good measure of how many P/E's you may be misguessing. If these stocks have a variance of 6 P/E's, your estimate will be fairly accurate; if they have a variance of 15, you could have a problem.

Now assume that you are permitted to know the growth rate of the earnings of the company and that you are familiar with regression theory. Instead of simply guessing the mean P/E, you can now guess the value of the P/E which is associated with the company's earnings growth. Now how wrong will you be? The width of the channel in the scatter diagram measures the amount of error which would be likely, and analytically this is $s_{y,x}$.

If the error in this new problem, which can be measured by $s_{y,x}$ or by $s_{y,x}^2$ is less than the error in the original problem as measured by the variance of P/E around the mean, then you will have reduced the extent of your error. But this is the same as saying that a knowledge of growth rates is helpful in predicting P/E's. And this could only be the case if the two variables are related. How can you measure how much error has been eliminated? The remaining error after the regression has been performed divided by the original error (the original variance) is the *percentage* of error which was wiped out by the use of the regression model. Mathematically, this is:

$$R^2 = \frac{\Sigma(\hat{y} - \bar{y})^2}{\Sigma(y - \bar{y})^2} \longleftarrow \text{the variance of the predicted values of } y.$$
$$\longleftarrow \text{the variance of the actual value of } y.$$

The mathematical relationship between R^2 and r is easily pointed out by showing the formula for r:

$$r = \sqrt{\frac{\Sigma(\hat{y} - \bar{y})^2}{\Sigma(y - \bar{y})^2}}$$

r therefore equals the square root of R^2.

AN ADDITIONAL APPLICATION

Simple regression has been used frequently in investment studies to examine the relationship between stocks and a stock market average such as the Standard & Poor's 500. If it is true that the price movement of a given stock is sensitive to the movement of the "average," then a regression using the percentage change in the average as x and the percentage change in the stock as y would quantify the relationship. Studies of this type show the extent to which a stock is related to the movement of stocks in general, because R^2 shows the percentage of the stock's behavior which can be explained by the behavior of the average.

If this type of study shows a significant relationship (a high R^2), the regression line $y = a + bx$ can be used to describe the movement of the stock. The value of b shows the "sensitivity" of the stock to the average. If b equals 1, the stock will show the same percentage gain as the average. If b equals 2, any change in the market will precipitate a change in the stock that is twice as great, indicating a highly sensitive stock. If b equals one-half, the stock will change only half as much as the average, showing that the security is stable. In investment literature, b is frequently called the "beta coefficient" of the stock.

This approach can be extended to portfolio analysis, since a portfolio is simply a group of securities. The value of "b" in this case indicates the sensitivity of the portfolio to fluctuations in the average, and the value of "a" is the return on the portfolio which does not stem from movements in the average.

Chapter

7 The Calculus or How to Deal with Rates of Change between Variables

Calculus deals with dynamic rather than static situations and thus concentrates on rates of change, or how one variable changes as another changes. If the changes are constant, the relationship is simple and is said to be linear; if the changes vary, the problem is curvilinear and more complex. Calculus permits the determination of an instantaneous rate of change and also of the change in the rate of change, involving acceleration or deceleration. Finding the instantaneous rate of change, called the derivative, is called differentiation. The inverse process, using the derivative to find the function, is called integration. The uses of calculus are so vast that it is impossible to describe even a small number of the potential uses in investment analysis. This chapter rather stresses the concepts as a basis for a broader understanding of later work.

RATES OF CHANGE

The study of rates of change is the realm of the calculus, the fundamental tool of the physical sciences. In a dynamic and changing world, the static concepts of algebra prove to be insufficient and so an extension of the basic mathematical tools must be made. The world of business is certainly in a state of flux at least equal in complexity to the changes in the physical world, and the valuable applications for calculus in this area are numerous even though not highly publicized.

Calculus studies functions, but from a new standpoint. Algebra deals with equations as a means of tying two variables together and "screening out" inadmissible pairs of values. Calculus, on the other hand, asks how the value of y varies as the value of x varies. Returning to the example of the simplest of graphs, see Figure 7–1.

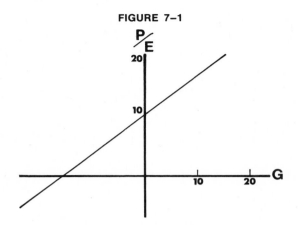

FIGURE 7–1

Algebra treats this line, or function, as the set of points satisfying a linear equation. In other words, it is the static set of permissible pairs of (x,y). Calculus takes the line and asks how y changes as x changes. For example, as x increases, how does y change?

The two significant questions which deal with this change are the direction of change and the *rate* at which the change is occurring. The direction of change is simply the direction of the line — positive if the line is rising, negative if the line is downsloping. The rate of change is a more difficult concept and deserves further discussion.

Every analyst is familiar with graphs of a time series. The typical economic time series shown in Figure 7–2 can serve as an illustration of the rate of change. The solid line is the history of the series; the dotted line is an extrapolation of its current trend. As can clearly be seen, the series is changing as time passes and in general appears to be rising. Given the most recent results of the series, the projection appears to be a reasonable continuation of the trend. At what rate is the series increasing? This can be found by seeing how much the projection of series y rises when one year passes. If it goes up $20 billion per year, that is the rate of change. If it rises $1 million, that is the rate. Mathematically, the rate is *defined* as the change in y as x changes. Since the projection is a straight line, this rate is always the same ($20 billion ÷ 1 year; $40 billion ÷ 2 years; etc.).

Let's examine the same series five years later, as shown in Figure 7–3. The projection was far from accurate, but that is beside the point in this

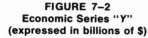

FIGURE 7–2
Economic Series "Y"
(expressed in billions of $)

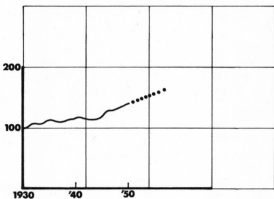

example. The important thing is that the rate of change is now different; the rate of change in y is changing. The projection indicated the rate at one point in time but did not "fit" the function five years later. The rate of change of the *projection,* however, is the same as the rate of change of the function *at the time* of the projection. In addition, the projection has only one rate of change because it is a straight line, and it is (as can be seen from the graph) tangent to the curve at the time that it was made. From this fact, mathematicians have *defined* the rate of change of a curve as being *the rate of change of the tangent to the curve at the point being*

FIGURE 7–3
Economic Series "Y"
(expressed in billions of $)

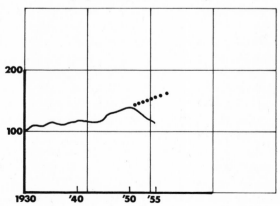

considered. Finding the rate of change of the tangent is a simple matter because the tangent is a straight line.

Once again, the rate of change on a straight line is the amount by which *y* changes when one more unit of *x* is added. If one more *x* produces one more *y*, the rate of change is 1. If one additional *x* yields one half an additional *y*, the rate of change is 1/2. If one more *x* results in a decline in *y* of 2, the rate is −2, and so on. The rate of change of the function at the point where the tangent is drawn is exactly the same as the slope of the tangent on the graph. As a result, it is possible to deal with the fundamental questions of the calculus either as rates or as the slopes of lines. This equivalence has generated some confusion among students in this subject when too little attention is paid to the viewpoint of regarding graphs, slopes, tangents, and so forth as being simply models which visually portray the concepts of change being considered. If these *models* at times seem irrelevant to problems in the real world, the student can at least remain confident that the characteristics *of change* which they represent are valuable in practical descriptions of reality.

INSTANTANEOUS RATES OF CHANGE

The calculus treats all "simple" functions, not just straight lines. This means that before beginning the subject, it is necessary to extend the idea of "rate," because the idea of rate used in the linear function is only approximately correct for curvilinear functions, as could be seen from the examination of series *y* in the previous charts. In the case of a straight line, it is possible to ask how much *y* increases when *x* increases by two units and then divide this answer by 2 in order to get the rate of change. This is because the rate of change is constant for a linear function. If the rate of change is *not* constant, using *two* units as the increase in *x* instead of *one* unit is too "broad" an increase to use and the results will only be approximate. In fact, *one* unit is too broad an increase, and so is *one half* a unit. In order to find the *exact* rate of change, we have to locate the *instantaneous* rate of change—the rate which is being more and more closely approximated when we change from using two units of *x* to using one unit, then one half a unit, and so on. The instantaneous rate is the *limit* being reached by these successively more accurate calculations of average rates. The "mathematical" justification for using the tangent is that it is the limit which is being approached as the "average" rates are slowly refined by considering smaller and smaller intervals.

Graphically, the calculation of the "average" rate of change in *y* when two units of change in *x* is permitted can be portrayed as in Figure 7–4. The line is straight because an "average" rate is only one number, and when this number is evaluated over a fixed interval such as "two units,"

FIGURE 7–4

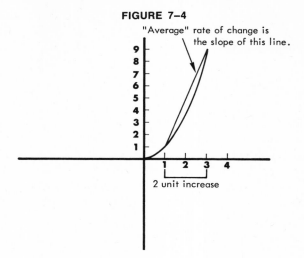

it is a constant. The line starts at $x = 1$, but this is an arbitrary choice implying that the rate of change when x is 1 is desired. The rate could as easily be found for another value of x. If we now portray the same graph but also show the average rate when using a "one unit of x" approach as *another* straight line, Figure 7–5 results.

FIGURE 7–5

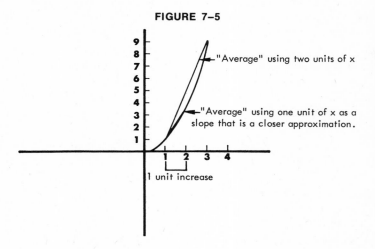

Now these approximations, as we take smaller and smaller increases in x, approach the instantaneous rate of change, which is seen on the graph (as may have been suspected) as the tangent to the function. Loosely speaking, when the chord is moved down the function so that its endpoint drops from three to two, it becomes a better approximation of the rate of change. When its endpoint reaches one, it becomes a tangent instead of a chord and is no longer an approximation but rather the rate of change itself, as shown in Figure 7–6.

FIGURE 7–6

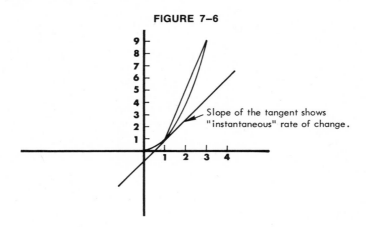

Slope of the tangent shows "instantaneous" rate of change.

This is intuitively clear if we regard the function as being the graph of an economic time series similar to the Series *y* example earlier in the chapter. At the last point plotted on the graph as shown in Figure 7–7, we would extrapolate the trend by projecting a continuation of the most recent rate of change—by drawing the instantaneous rate of change.

FIGURE 7–7

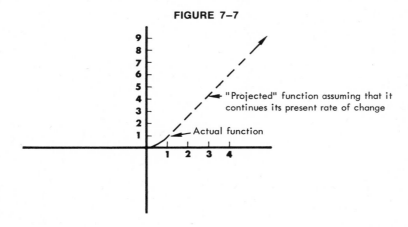

"Projected" function assuming that it continues its present rate of change

Actual function

This line is geometrically tangent to the curve if we then draw the remainder of the function, just as the projection of series *y* was tangent to series y when the remainder of the years were included in the graph. See Figure 7–8.

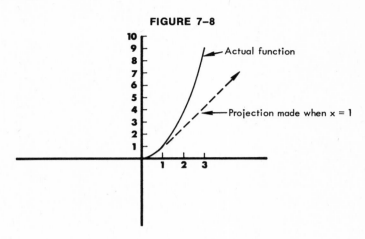

FIGURE 7–8

THE FIRST DERIVATIVE

At this point, it is possible to state (very nonrigorously) that change has been examined from two standpoints — the amount by which y increases when x increases by a small amount, and also as tangents to graphed functions. Intuitively, every analyst is familiar with the concept, for when he drives away from a stop sign, he goes from 0 mph to, say, 30 mph. Each of the values of the speedometer between 0 and 30 represents a rate of change, and when the speedometer was at 20 the car was traveling at 20 mph if only for an "instant." Calculus calls the rate of change the "derivative" and uses the mathematical symbol $\frac{dy}{dx}$ to stand for the rate of change in y with respect to x. Another symbol frequently used is y' for change with respect to x and $\dot{x}$ for change with respect to time where x is a function of time.

Now it is possible to examine a few examples of derivatives.

$$\frac{dy}{dx}(bx) = b$$

This simply means that the rate of change of a linear function is constant and is equal to the slope of the line when the function is graphed, a fact which has already been discussed in this chapter. Another fantastically illuminating result is:

$$\frac{dy}{dx}(c) = 0$$

The rate of change of a constant is zero; a constant doesn't change. The rate of change of more difficult functions can also be found using calculus. For example:

$$\frac{dy}{dx}(x^2) = 2x$$

or more generally:

$$\frac{dy}{dx}(cx^n) = ncx^{n-1}$$

THE SECOND DERIVATIVE

The above analysis indicates that the rate of change in, say, x^2 is $2x$. Since $2x$ is a variable, this is an example of the fact that in many cases the rate of change in the function changes, depending upon the value of x. Graphically, it appears as Figure 7–9.

FIGURE 7–9

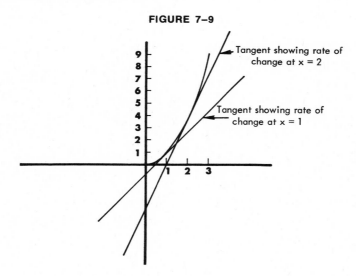

As x becomes larger, the rate of change becomes greater, as can be seen from the upward "curve" of the line. This, of course, means that the derivative (the rate) changes as x changes. In fact, if the rate of change could not assume different values for different values of x, all functions would necessarily be straight lines.

The occurrence of a changing rate of change is certainly no unusual phenomenon to an investment analyst. Changes in the rate could be seen quite clearly in series y and are evident in virtually all of the relationships considered in investment work. But since the rate of change is the subject matter of the calculus and the first derivative is changing, it is logical to expect calculus to include the study of how this rate of change changes. As it happens, the change in the rate of change can be expressed as a derivative (called the second derivative and symbolized $\frac{d^2y}{dx^2}$ or y'' or $\ddot{x}$).

The rate at which a rate of change is changing may be a tongue-twisting phrase, but the concept is actually very familiar to analysts. Examine Figure 7–10.

FIGURE 7–10

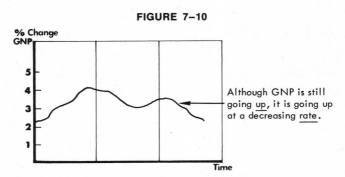

In this chart, the rate of change in GNP is plotted instead of GNP itself. The graph actually shows, then, the movement of the first derivative of GNP. It plots the rate of change, and changes in the value of this curve are changes in the change of GNP. When an analyst is interested in the *direction* of the line on this graph, he is dealing with the rate at which the curve is changing, and since the curve is the first derivative of GNP, he is considering the derivative of the first derivative. This is obviously the second derivative, and equally obvious is the fact that investment men have been using the concept for quite some time.

The second derivative tells us the direction and the "speed" of change in the rate of change of the function being studied. It has a direct physical interpretation in the concept of *acceleration*. If an analyst is describing the motion of a car leaving a stop sign, he needs to indicate the rate of change in position, say 20 mph, but also that this rate of change is rapidly increasing—the car is accelerating. If he is interested in the trend of earnings, he is not only interested in whether earnings are rising, he wishes to know whether they are rising at an increasing or at a decreasing rate.

The first derivative, then, is the rate of change in a function; and the second derivative is the rate of change in the rate of change. The second derivative, the acceleration, is used in such statements as "increasing at an increasing rate, increasing at a decreasing rate, the rate of decline is slowing." Even higher derivatives can be found but are seldom needed in practical business analysis. The section of calculus known as *differential* calculus, then, has provided the investment analyst with the two new tools $\dfrac{dy}{dx}$ and $\dfrac{d^2y}{dx^2}$. The usefulness of these devices is much broader than might at first be suspected.

1. Obviously, derivatives can be used to describe rates of change.
2. Since the rate of change must be positive when the function is increasing and negative when it is decreasing, it must be zero when the function is at a maximum. Derivatives are therefore valuable in finding maximum (and also minimum) values.
3. Since calculus describes the relative impact of changes in x on the value of y, it can be used to explore the "nature" of functions, providing information that may be valuable in determining which function is most appropriate for use in a particular problem.

HOW RATES OF CHANGE ARE FOUND

At this point, the intuitive and geometric aspects of differential calculus have been examined and a few simple results have been presented. The question which naturally follows is how those results were obtained analytically. This problem can be presented graphically in the following diagram as the visual process of moving the point A down toward the point B (making the line $\overline{AB}$ more and more closely approximate the tangent line C). How can this process be stated mathematically? See Figure 7–11.

FIGURE 7–11

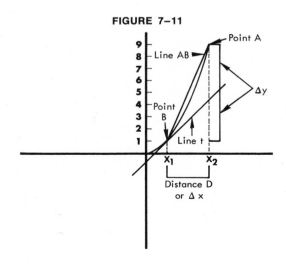

Notice that as A moves down the curve (forcing x_2 to move to the left), the distance D between x_1 and x_2 becomes smaller. Calling this distance Δx (pronounced "delta x"), we can say that as we visually move A toward B, Δx approaches zero. Since the endpoint of the line $\overline{AB}$ is "stuck" on the curved line, we can say that *adding* a Δx to the value of x will force the endpoint *higher* on the curve, and this makes the value of y larger. Calling the increase in y by the name Δy, we can see that adding Δx to one side of the equation for the line will add Δy to the other side of the equation. But more important than this is the fact that as *we move Δx toward zero* (make line $\overline{AB}$ smaller and smaller) we find that Δy *moves toward zero* as well. Expressing these ideas in an equation, we can use the function x^2 as an example:

$$y = x^2$$

Increasing y and x by Δy and Δx, respectively, produces:

$$(y + \Delta y) = (x + \Delta x)^2$$

But this equation can be simplified by algebra, so:

$$(y + \Delta y) = x^2 + (2x)(\Delta x) + (\Delta x)^2$$

It is possible to make the equation simpler by merely subtracting the first equation from this last result, so:

$$y + \Delta y = x^2 + (2x)(\Delta x) + (\Delta x)^2$$

minus:

$$y = x^2$$

gives:

$$\Delta y = (2x)(\Delta x) + (\Delta x)^2$$

All of this manipulation has been strictly according to ordinary algebra and has been done in order to produce the equation:

$$\Delta y = (2x)(\Delta x) + (\Delta x)^2$$

But before the manipulation began, it was decided that the analyst was interested in the value of the tangent at the point where Δx is zero. This is where algebra stops and the calculus begins, for now it is possible to examine the equation by asking what happens as Δx approaches zero. Dividing the equation through by Δx, we find that:

$$\frac{\Delta y}{\Delta x} = 2x + \Delta x$$

As Δx approaches zero, $2x + \Delta x$ approaches $2x$. If we pass to the limit, the value *is* $2x$, and $\frac{\Delta y}{\Delta x}$ (expressed at the limit as $\frac{dy}{dx}$) is seen to equal $2x$. As a result, we have the expression:

$$\frac{dy}{dx}(x^2) = 2x$$

A similar approach can be used to find the derivative of virtually all of the elementary functions (such as sin x, log x, etc.), but the results have already been calculated and tabulated by mathematicians and can easily be found in any calculus textbook. An example of one way in which the derivative can be used is included in the addendum to this chapter.

INTEGRATION

The second major application of calculus is finding the function when only the rate of change is known. This can be seen to be merely the inverse of the process of differentiation. It is the attempt to use the derivative of the function to find the function instead of the other way around. The function, when derived from a rate, is called the integral, and the process of finding the integral is called integration.

The problem of integrating a function is mathematically touchier than differentiating, but it is possible to provide some idea of the problem here. Assume that some country's *GNP* is known to be increasing at a constant annual rate of $6 million. At the end of one year, this will still be the rate of gain, and the same is true for two and three years. Graphically, this can be shown as in Figure 7–12.

FIGURE 7–12
Rate of Increase in GNP
(millions $)

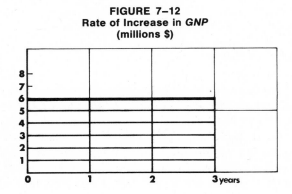

Since the economy is growing at a constant rate, and the graph plots the rate, the graph naturally shows a "constant." Suppose now that an analyst wished to calculate the total increase in the economy after three years. He would multiply $(6)(3) = \$18$ million. This can be seen on the graph as the *area* under the function between zero and three on the x

axis. Counting the number of "blocks" in this area, we find that there are 18 blocks (where each block represents $1 million on the graph), or $18 million for the total increase in *GNP* for the three years. This is an example of the problem of moving from a rate to the value of a function and therefore is an integration. The example shows that integrating is equivalent to finding the area under a curve and also that the solution (the integral) can be found by multiplication when the rate being integrated is constant. At this point, it is obvious that integration is simply a generalization of multiplication to allow for the many cases where the rate of change is not constant.

Moving one step further, consider a graph having a changing rate as in Figure 7–13.

FIGURE 7–13
Rate of Increase in *GNP*
(millions $)

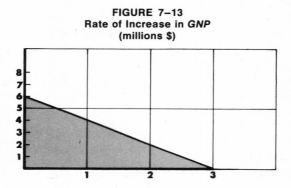

In this case, the rate is constantly declining. More precisely, the rate of change in *GNP* is decreasing at a constant rate. In order to calculate the value of the function (in our example, the total increase in *GNP* for all three years), the analyst would integrate the rate from zero to three. This is the shaded area on the graph. The total area is the integral, or the *amount* of increase given a knowledge of the *rate* of increase. Unfortunately, however, multiplication applies only for a *constant* rate. Integration, on the other hand, applies to virtually any rate of change that can be expressed mathematically, and when the rate is not constant, the integral must be found by techniques more complicated than multiplication.

Notice that the solution will only provide the amount of change that resulted from the *GNP*'s fluctuations. It does not give *total GNP* but only the *total change* in *GNP* over the three years being considered. To get the total value of *GNP,* it would be necessary to add the starting value (the value before any years had passed) of *GNP* to the value of the integral. This "starting value" is obviously a constant and is called, understandably, the constant of integration. Since only one variable is being integrated in this case, there is one "starting value." If two variables were involved, there would be two such constants, and so on.

The use of integrals certainly goes well beyond this very basic application, but the intuitive ideas involved remain similar to the above example. No single technique for finding the integrals of all functions has ever been developed, but a large number of integrals have been found by mathematicians using various means, and the resulting tables showing the various formulas can be used in most practical applications.

The practical application of the calculus is more subtle than the application of the simple statistical techniques that have been covered in previous chapters. The reason for this is that the calculus provides the research worker with assistance in the *formulation* of a problem instead of in the development of specific solutions once a line of attack has already been formulated. This means that the calculus is more powerful in *developing* models than it is in providing one specific model for the solution of one specific type of difficulty.

Suppose, for example, that a research analyst knows that the time series which he is studying increases at a rate which is a constant percentage of its actual value as time passes. Before any mathematical models can be used to work with the time series, the mathematical equation which describes it must be found, and this can only be found by converting the known characteristics of the rate of increase into the correct equation. This, of course, is a typical problem of integration, and the use of the integral calculus is advantageous in defining the "law" affecting the time series. Once this law is found, statistical models can be applied to gain further insight into the problem.

Calculus provides the analyst with the ability to convert his knowledge about how quantities vary in relation to each other into the implied function which mathematically defines their relationship. Once the characteristics of the change in a variable have been specified, the calculus can be used to find the precise mathematical statement which would produce this pattern of change. This certainly enhances the quantitative approach, for it provides the means by which complex relationships between variables can be discovered through an examination of their behavior pattern in the real world. The characteristics of change defined by the analyst are not restricted to how *GNP* changes over time. The technique applies just as well in cases where changes in the variables are related to changes in *other* variables. If an analyst has a theory concerning the way that the savings rate changes as income changes, he can use the calculus to move from the function relating the changes to the function which relates the two quantities.

MULTIDIMENSIONAL CALCULUS

The techniques of differentiation and integration are not restricted to the consideration of y as a function of x. In the real world, y is almost always a function of more than one variable, and $y = f(x_1, x_2, \ldots x_n)$ is therefore a far more realistic approach than the simplified material presented up to this point. Unfortunately, the treatment of many variables through the use of the calculus is a very complex subject, and only two of the techniques will be briefly described in this chapter.

The partial derivative of a function is an extension of the concept of the derivative in the simple (x,y) case. It describes a rate of change, as did its simpler counterpart. But the presence of several independent variables (many x_i) complicates the matter and forces a broader interpretation. The partial derivative with respect to, say, x_1 indicates the rate of change in y as x_i changes and all of the other x_i are held constant. In the simple case of one x, $\dfrac{dy}{dx}$ indicated the rate of change in y as x changed.

In the multivariate case, $\dfrac{\partial y}{\partial x_1}$ shows the rate of change in y as x_1 changes and does not consider the other x_i.

The extension of the idea of a derivative complicates matters because for any given set of values for the x_i, y will have a certain rate of change if only x_1 is increased, another rate of change if only x_2 is increased and so on through x_n. This means that for any set of values for the x_i, y will have a partial derivative with respect to x_1, $\dfrac{\partial y}{\partial x_1}$; a different partial derivative with respect to x_2, $\dfrac{\partial y}{\partial x_2}$; and so on through x_n, $\dfrac{\partial y}{\partial x_n}$. The values of each of these partial derivatives will in most cases not be equal to each other because y will be more sensitive to changes in some of the x_i than others.

Assuming that the function is not too complicated, y will have a partial derivative with respect to all of the x_i for every possible set of values which the x_i might be given. It is important to note, however, that the values of the "partials" will usually change when different values for the x_i are substituted for the original ones. This is simply a way of saying that the rate of change of y with respect to the x_i changes with the values of the x_i and is a condition which the reader might have expected as a result of having just studied changing rates of change for simple functions. As it happens, these changes in the partial derivatives can be studied by taking the second-order partial derivatives. However, the important point here is that the $\dfrac{\partial y}{\partial x_i}$ change for different values of x_i.

Multiple integration is the extension of integration to the multidimensional case. The integral of y with respect to x has been shown to be the area under the curve of y. Multiple integration gives the volume of the region which is "under" y. The simple example of multiplication providing the area of a rectangle underneath the rate of change of GNP has a counterpart in multiple integration as the multiplication of y, x_1, and x_2 which gives the volume of the "box" which lies underneath y. Multiple integration allows the analyst to find the total amount of change when only the rates of change of all of the variables are known.

ADDITIONAL READINGS IN CALCULUS

ALLEN, R. G. D. *Mathematical Analysis for Economists*. London: Macmillan & Company, 1938.

This book covers the calculus from a practical standpoint, showing applications in economic theory (542 pages). The work is substantially more readable and more practical than other books in the field. Unfortunately, when the field is calculus, this is not saying a great deal. While the value of calculus in improving the reader's mathematical sophistication is indisputable, its value in immediate business applications is small. If an analyst wishes to learn the subject in order eventually to be able to attack truly advanced quantitative problems, this book is by a wide margin his best choice. As a side benefit, his understanding of economic theory should improve rather dramatically as the relationship between calculus and economic functions is explored in the applications sections.

ALLEN, R. G. D. *Mathematical Economics*. 2d ed. London: Macmillan & Company, 1959.

This work assumes that the reader has covered the material in the above work and continues by presenting a number of the more important quantitative economic models (803 pages). The development is mainly in terms of the economic concepts, but chapters covering mathematical topics are included whenever the next economic theory presupposes some new quantitative technique. The material is difficult, but if an analyst has succeeded in mastering Allen's first work, the additional insight into economics gained by attacking the theories described in this book is well worth the extra effort. Put another way, the marginal profit from the second work is sufficient to cover the overhead cost of grinding through the first. This is the nature of calculus and its related techniques: amazingly high rewards are gained, but only after an extended initiation process.

COURANT, R. *Differential and Integral Calculus*, Vols. I & II. 2d ed. New York: John Wiley & Sons, Inc., 1937.

This book is an outstanding work in advanced calculus. It is included here only for those analysts who may have become infatuated with the subject. Strangely enough, if an analyst wishes to consider only the purely mathematical aspects of the calculus, this classic work is actually more readable than most of the standard texts.

ADDENDUM TO CHAPTER 7

The Nature of Applications

The applications of calculus usually appear in the "background" of business applications, that is, the calculus is used to develop a model which is then useful in business applications, but the developed model does not itself require a knowledge of calculus in its application. This places the calculus in an unusual status when attempts are made to evaluate its usefulness. It has little direct use in quantitative analysis, but the models which *are* used were almost invariably developed by means of the calculus.

It could be said that the application of the calculus is "to develop applications," or to develop models which are useful. The value of calculus is therefore enormous, for it has been instrumental in the development of many very valuable applications. The value of a detailed knowledge of the calculus by a businessman not interested in developing new models but rather in applying existing ones is less clearly seen. On the one hand, such knowledge instills precision of thought and an appreciation of the underlying characteristics of other models. On the other hand, the investment in time required for a working knowledge of calculus is substantial. That such an investment, once made, is highly rewarding, is an opinion universally held by researchers in the exact sciences.

The presentation of elementary concepts in this chapter, however, could hardly be regarded as an investment in the sense described above. As a result, elegant applications of the calculus cannot be presented. Even useful examples are almost impossible to locate without first introducing far more mathematics than discussed in this chapter. The chapter serves only to develop an intuitive "feel" for the manner by which calculus attacks a problem. Two treatments of problems using the calculus are included in this addendum in order to provide additional insight into this "line of attack." The problems are certainly not of monumental business significance, but the approach used in the solutions is interesting. The treatments are not included in order to provide solution techniques to be memorized, but rather to indicate in the broadest possible terms the general approach of the calculus in handling problems.

Reconsidering the Mean

The mean and variance have been explained in an earlier chapter, but it is possible at this point to use calculus to point out an interesting characteristic of the mean. To begin the example, recall that the variance is defined as $\Sigma(x_i - \bar{x})^2$ where the x_i are the observations and $\bar{x}$ stands for the mean of the set of observations. In the following equations, it is more convenient to refer to the x_i as a_i because they are constants which are presented at the beginning of the problem.

Suppose that instead of using the mean in the formula for the variance, an analyst instead decided to use a number (which will be called x). In the new notation, this means that the analyst's formula for the "variance" using *his* number instead of the mean would be $\Sigma(a_i - x)^2$. Obviously, if he chose various different values for x, his "variance" would have a different value for each x chosen. His "variance" is a function of the value chosen for x and since the value of the function changes as x changes, the problem appears to fall into the realm of the calculus. Since the problem is a study in change, in other words, it is natural to ask for a precise description of the *rate* of change.

The rate of change in $\Sigma(a_i - x)^2$ is defined to be the derivative of the function. Writing the variance out in full instead of using the Σ notation produces:

$$(a_1 - x)^2 + (a_2 - x)^2 + , \ldots , + (a_n - x)^2$$

By simply squaring the appropriate values, it is possible to produce:

$$(a_1^2 - 2a_1x + x^2) + (a_2^2 - 2a_2x + x^2) + , \ldots , + (a_n^2 - 2a_nx + x^2)$$

The derivative of this function can be found by differentiating each term on a one-at-a-time basis. The fact that the derivative of a constant is zero and the derivative of x^2 is $2x$ has been discussed earlier in the chapter, and using this information produces:

$$(-2a_1 + 2x) + (-2a_2 + 2x) + , \ldots , + (-2a_n + 2x)$$

as the value for the derivative of the analyst's "variance."

One use of the calculus that has already been mentioned is the fact that the derivative is zero when the value of the function is at a maximum or a minimum. Rearranging terms and setting the derivative equal to zero produces:

$$\sum_{i=1}^{n} \left(-2a_i\right) + 2nx = 0$$

as a necessarily true equality whenever the analyst's "variance" is at its largest or smallest value (smallest, in this case). Examining this equation should therefore provide information about the nature of x when the analyst's "variance" is as small as possible:

$$\sum_{i=1}^{n} \left(-2a_i\right) + 2nx = 0$$

can be written as:

$$2\left(\sum_{i=1}^{n} \left(-a_i\right) + nx\right) = 0$$

This can equal zero only if:

$$\sum_{i=1}^{n} \left(-a_i\right) + nx = 0$$

transposing:

$$nx = \sum_{i=1}^{n} \left(a_i\right)$$

isolating x:

$$x = \frac{\Sigma(a_i)}{n}$$

which is the definiton of the mean.

This result shows that of all of the numbers which the analyst might choose to compute his "variance," the smallest "variance" would be produced only if he chose the mean. This explains why the mean is used in the formula which defines variance in statistical analysis.

Calculus and Probabilities

Calculus provides the foundation for almost all of the statistical techniques. Its use in this area is a complex topic, but it is possible to consider a simple example which indicates some of the flavor of mathematical statistics.

Consider one of the simplest cases of a random variable, where any value between two numbers may occur, and the likelihood that any particular number within this range will occur is equal for all such numbers. This is called a rectangular distribution and can be graphed as Figure 7–14, showing that any number between one and three is equally probable and that no other number may occur.

FIGURE 7–14

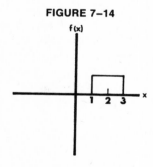

Probabilities are defined to be *desired* events divided by all *possible* events. In cases where the number of possible events could be counted, this definition is simple enough. But when the possible events include *all* numbers between one and three, a simple enumeration of events becomes impossible because there are an infinite number of such events. It therefore becomes necessary to partition the set of events into the desired versus the undesirable outcomes while weighting each of the events by their likelihood of occurrence. The distribution (rectangular, in this case) performs this weighting. Partitioning the weighted events is accomplished by finding the area under the distribution which falls in desired regions of x and then dividing the result by all possible events, which in this case is the entire area under the distribution.

Assume for a moment that the top of the rectangular "box" is one unit high (its vertical coordinate is "one"). How can the probability that the random variable will assume a value greater than zero be calculated? It obviously does not need to be calculated because if all possible values must fall between one and three the probability of a value greater than zero must be 1.00 (must be 100% probable). Nevertheless, it is useful in mathematics to start with the very simple and then generalize to the realistic problem. How could the probability that x will be greater than zero be found *analytically?*

The rules for probability when the number of events cannot be counted indicate that the area under the curve in desired regions of x must be found and then divided by the total area under the curve. The desired region for x in this case is $x > 0$. The area of the rectangle in this region is two units of length times one unit of height, or two. The total area under the distribution is two. Dividing the former by the latter produces $2 \div 2 = 1.00$ as the probability that x will be greater than zero.

Generalizing to a more realistic case, what is the probability that x will be greater than 2.5? The area under the distribution in the desired region is 0.5 times 1.0, or 0.5. The total area is 2.0. The probability is therefore $0.5 \div 2.0 = .25$. It is interesting to note that the height of the distribution does not affect the probabilities. If, for example, the rectangle were two units high, the desired area would become 0.5 times $2.0 = 1.0$ and the total area would become 2.0 times $2.0 = 4.0$. The probability would therefore be $1.0 \div 4.0 = .25$, as was just calculated using a height of one.

It is obvious at this point that the probabilities relating to the rectangular distribution can be found through the use of simple multiplication. Why should the framework of the calculus, with its areas under curves and its integrals, be dragged into so simple a problem? The answer to this question stems from the unfortunate fact that not all random variables have a distribution of outcomes where each possible result is equally likely. In fact, even very simple processes involve distributions having wide variation in the probabilities of various results. When the "top" of the distribution is not a constant value, the use of multiplication breaks down, but the use of integration is still valid. Calculating probabilities as areas under curves is therefore far more general (and hence more practical) than using multiplication. Multiplication once again proves to be the special case of integration which occurs when only constants are involved.

Chapter
8 Probability Theory or
How to Treat Uncertain Events

The field of investments constantly deals with uncertainty. Probability theory can be used effectively to make the treatment of uncertainty more realistic and less dependent upon intuition or hunch. Understanding the probability of a single event is relatively simple, but problems become more complex (and the rewards of understanding the theory become greater) when events are combined into joint probabilities, union of probabilities, and conditional probabilities. The concept of maximizing expected values is discussed because it is so useful in considering the benefits and costs of alternative investments and investment strategies. Moreover, consideration is given to measuring the loss in return as a result of the presence of uncertainty, therefore indicating the amount that can be paid for information that will improve choices.

BASIC CONCEPTS

Anyone who has ever played a game of chance has an intuitive feel for the meaning of probability. And since life itself is one of the most uncertain of projects, the gambling that is forced on man by virtue of his merely being alive makes probabilities one of the most fascinating of subjects. The mathematical theory of probability deals with the "chance" of something occurring which is not certain to occur, but it treats the subject with a precision and objectivity not found in the subjective, experiential approach. Since probabilities provide information concerning uncertain events, they are ideally suited for management and investment functions, which could be *defined* as *decision making in the face of uncertainty.*

Probabilities are expressed on an arbitrary scale, or index. If an event must necessarily occur, it is absolutely probable and has a probability of 100%—expressed as 1.00. If it cannot possibly occur, it has a probability of 0. Naturally, most real-world problems fall somewhere between these extreme values. A probability of .5 means that it is equally likely that an event will occur or not occur. A figure of .25 means one chance in four, .10 means one chance in ten, etc.

The simplest examples stem from the simple games of chance. If a coin is flipped, the probability of heads is .50; if a die is rolled, the probability of a "three" is one in six, or .167. Any analyst can determine these results intuitively. Intuition, however, breaks down in more complicated problems, requiring the use of math. Mathematically, the solution was found by dividing the event being analyzed by the number of events (all events being equally likely). In flipping the coin, the probability of heads was therefore:

$$\frac{H}{N}$$

where:

$$H = 1$$
$$N = 2$$

It is simple to expand the problem a bit by asking about the behavior of N. If the coin were tossed three times, N would equal $2 \cdot 2 \cdot 2$, or 8. The probability of throwing three successive heads is therefore one in eight, or .125. The formula holds for more complicated problems, like the probability of ten successive heads ($N = 2^{10}$), where the answer is one chance in 1,024 or a probability of .00098.

CALCULATING PROBABILITIES

These results are not sufficient to make probabilities useful, but the theory can easily be extended by *combining* probabilities. If an analyst estimates that XYZ Corp. has a probability (p_i) equal to .10 of dropping 15% in price and Widgits Inc. has a p_2 equal to .20 of dropping 15%, what is the probability of *both* of these events occurring? If the price movements of the two stocks are completely unrelated, the answer is:

$$(p_1)(p_2) = (.10)(.20) = .02$$

The probability of *at least one* of the events occurring is slightly more complicated. At first glance, this would appear to be the sum of p_1 and p_2. This would produce a probability of .30. This result, however, has the probability of both events occurring simultaneously added into the total twice. Figure 8–1 shows how this happens.

FIGURE 8–1

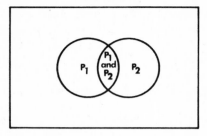

When p_1 is added to p_2, the area "p_1 and p_2" is included both in the probability of p_1 *and* in the probability of p_2. The addition therefore adds the "p_1 and p_2" area into the result twice. The solution to this problem is to subtract one of the "p_1 and p_2" values out of the original addition, producing the answer:

$$p_1 + p_2 - p_1 p_2 = .10 + .20 - .02 = .28$$

If the price movements of the two stocks are related (that is, if a decline in one stock would lead the analyst to expect a decline in the other), then it would be necessary to know the probability of a decline in the second stock given that a decline in the first stock occurred before any calculations could be performed.

The notation for the probability concepts developed so far is shown in Table 8–1.

The use of tree diagrams to show the structure of problems in conditional probability has become quite common. For example, assume that a

TABLE 8–1

Mathematical Symbol	Mathematical Term	English Equivalent
$P(A)$	Marginal Probability	The probability of the occurrence of A.
$P(A$ and $B)$	Joint Probability	The probability of both A and B occurring.
$P(A$ or $B)$	Addition of Probabilities	The probability of either A or B occurring.
$P(A|B)$ or $P(A$ given $B)$	Conditional Probability	The probability of A given that B has occurred.

potential investor is giving consideration to the purchase of the common stock of a company. He is, however, faced with possibilities of a good, neutral, or bad market during the coming year. In addition, his particular stock may perform well, neutrally, or poorly relative to the market in any of the three markets. If the hypothetical investor is familiar with probability theory, he would attempt to determine the probabilities of each of the three market conditions and also the probabilities for the particular stock's relative performance in each of the market conditions. Assume that he subjectively provides these probabilities, which are then used to construct the tree diagram, Figure 8–2.

FIGURE 8–2
Example of a Simple Decision Tree

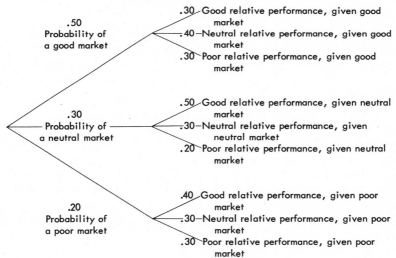

This information is interesting in itself, but it can be manipulated to provide even more interesting results. For example, what is the probability of both a good market and a poor relative performance in the stock? What is the probability of the stock's performing relatively well even though a poor market occurs? In order to answer these questions, Table 8–2 can be constructed.

The column dealing with marginal probability is dealing with the unconditional probability which is shown in the tree diagram at the leftmost set of branches, the branches which do not depend on any prior event. In this particular example, this is the probability of a given market condition. The conditional probability column gives the probability of each of the branches on the tree diagram which depend on a prior event. In this

TABLE 8–2

Marginal Probability		×	Conditional Probability		=	Joint Probability
Good market	.50		.30	Good performance		.15
			.40	Neutral performance		.20
			.30	Poor performance		.15
			1.00			
Neutral market	.30		.50	Good performance		.15
			.30	Neutral performance		.09
			.20	Poor performance		.06
			1.00			
Poor market	.20		.40	Good performance		.08
			.30	Neutral performance		.06
			.30	Poor performance		.06
	1.00		1.00			1.00

particular case, of course, these probabilities are related to the performance of the stock relative to the market *given* some specific market condition. The joint probabilities column is the solution column in this particular table and refers to the probability that *both* a given market condition and a given performance for the common stock are in fact realized after one year. It is obtained by multiplying the market probability by the stock probability. From this table, it is possible, for example, to discover that there is a .15 probability of both a good market and a bad relative performance of the common stock occurring. In addition, there is a .08 probability of both a poor market and a good relative performance in the stock. By adding together all of the joint probabilities dealing with good relative performance, the investor can determine the total probability of his investment proving to be more successful than the alternative investment of a very broadly diversified portfolio which would behave exactly like the market. In this case, his calculation would be:

$$.15 + .15 + .08 = .38$$

The total probability for a neutral performance would be:

$$.20 + .09 + .06 = .35$$

The probability of poor results can be calculated as:

$$.15 + .06 + .06 = .27$$

Naturally, the total for the three possible results of good, neutral, or bad is 1.00:

$$.35 + .27 + .38 = 1.00$$

This is simply because there is a 1.00 probability that the stock will perform *either* well, neutrally, or poorly. By using this form of analysis, the investor has discovered that he can expect his common stock to do somewhat better than average. If his assessments of the probabilities are correct, he would perform fairly well in the long run if enough common stocks having this probability pattern were purchased, because the probability of outperforming the market (.38) exceeds the probability of performing less well than the market (.27).

EXPECTED VALUE

One of the most useful results of the theory of probability is the concept of expected value. In a game of chance, there is some price at which a rational gambler would be indifferent to the game because he would expect to neither lose nor win. If a man offers to flip a coin with you paying $1.00 if it is heads and gaining $1.00 otherwise, you would expect to break even—the expected value of the game would be zero. On the other hand, if you received an offer to flip a coin and receive $2.00 if tails are thrown but nothing for heads, what would you be willing to pay? The game must be worth something, because you have an opportunity to receive money but cannot possibly lose anything other than the amount paid for the privilege of playing the game. The problem is to determine the precise amount that the game is worth. Over the long run, tails will occur about half the time, and so you will receive $2.00 about half the time. The rest of the time, you receive nothing. It seems reasonable to assume that $2.00 half the time is the same as $1.00, and this is the expected value of the game. Over the long run, the game would be profitable for you if you paid anything less than this $1.00 expected result. Actually, of course, you can pay $1.05 for the privilege of enjoying the game, but over the long run this decision would result in the loss of money.

If this discussion appears to have more value in after-five problems than in business situations, the approach can easily be extended to virtually every situation involving uncertainty. For example, the expected value of a particular stock at the end of the year could be calculated by the use of probabilities. Assume that the analyst estimates the prices and probabilities shown in Table 8–3.

TABLE 8–3
Expected Value of a Typical Stock

Probability	Price
.10	70
.20	75
.30	80
.20	85
.20	90

The expected value of the stock would be the "average" of its estimated values at the end of the year. But since the probabilities vary, a "weighted total" of the various possible prices is needed in order to find the "average":

$$(.1)(70) + (.2)(75) + (.3)(80) + (.2)(85) + (.2)(90) = 7 + 15 + 24 + 17 + 18$$
$$= 81 \text{ expected value}$$

The expected value of any investment project which is to be undertaken, experiment which may be performed, or the like, can be calculated in a similar fashion. In investments, the advantage of expected values is that they facilitate a comparison between potential investments, and so provide a way by which probabilistically weighted relative values can be used in decision making. This is possible because the maximization of expected value can be regarded as a rational business strategy.

The approach could be broadened somewhat by saying that the maximization of utility can be regarded as a rational business strategy. This modification allows the decision maker to allow for risk. For example, if you received the coin-flipping offer described at the beginning of this chapter, but the wager was for $100,000 if tails occurred, would you be willing to pay, say, $40,000 for the opportunity to play? The expected value of the game is $50,000, but most individuals would prefer to avoid the wager due to the risk involved. Utilities are numerically measured dollar values reduced by the individual's personal feelings concerning his distaste for risk. Techniques for the measurement of utility and also for its maximization exist; however, because of the complexities that are involved, only maximization of dollar values will be considered in this chapter.

The use of expected values can be expanded by building tables which show the probability of given events and what would happen to various investments if the events actually occurred. As an example, assume that the economist for the investment department has projected three different business assumptions for the next year. Because no additional information is available concerning possible alternatives for the economy, the investment department head chooses to assume that these three events completely exhaust the possibilities for the environment in which the various companies which he analyzes will operate in the near future. Quite naturally, he feels that the price appreciation of most of the various companies which are covered by the department will greatly depend upon which particular economy actually happens to occur. In addition, he knows that his staff would be much more capable of correctly predicting price appreciation if they were certain of the economic conditions in which the companies were operating.

The preceding analysis implies that the department head can obtain reasonably accurate estimates of price appreciation given the economy (the conditional price appreciation) and also that these estimated returns will vary substantially from one potential "economy" to some alternative potential "economy." As a result of these considerations, he decides to ask each analyst to submit the expected value of each company's price appreciation for each possible economy. After the estimates are returned, the following table (Table 8–4) is presented to him.

TABLE 8–4
Estimated Conditional Capital Appreciation

		Company			
	A	B	C	D	E
Economy I.............	11%	14%	8%	16%	6%
Economy II...........	10	12	7	12	6
Economy III..........	9	6	7	4	5

Because the staff is in this particular case familiar with the theory of probability, each of these numbers is the probabilistically weighted "spread" of possible returns in the company *given* one particular level of economic activity, that is, the 11% entry for Company A in Economy I was derived in the same way that the $81 expected value was derived in Table 8–3. For example, an analyst may have felt that stock A in Economy I has a .25 probability of rising 14%, a .50 probability of 12%, and a .25 probability of 6%.

$$(.25)(14\%) + (.50)(12\%) + (.25)(6\%) = 11\%$$

Given the data in Table 8–3, the department manager then decides to "merge" the three economies together to form a single expected value for each of the stocks being considered. In order to do this, he assigns a probability to each of the economies and then weights the returns for each of the stocks by these probabilities, as in Table 8–5.

TABLE 8–5
Calculation of Expected Values from Conditional Values

	Prob-ability	A	B	C	D	E
Economy I.............	.3	11	14	8	16	6
Economy II...........	.5	10	12	7	12	6
Economy III	.2	9	6	7	4	5
Expected value		10.1	11.4	7.3	11.6	5.8

At this point, a single expected value has been obtained for each of the stocks. The 10.1% expected return in Company A is obtained by weighting the three possible returns for the company by the three probabilities for the economies. The particular calculations in this case would be:

$$(.3)(11) + (.5)(10) + (.2)(9) = 10.1\%$$

Using Table 8–5, commonly called a payoff table, the manager would direct the purchase of Company D, and he might possibly use Company B as an alternative purchase if circumstances required it. This action is called for because Company D has the highest expected value at 11.6% while Company B is a close second at 11.4%. It is important to point out several facts about this table. First, the probability weights which were given to the economies obviously had an impact on the expected value of the securities. Second, the sum of the probabilities assigned to the economies was 1.00 because it was absolutely certain that one of the three economies would occur (given the assumption of the department head). Third, each of the rates of return estimated by the analysts was derived by the use of a probability weighting of the various possible performances of each of the issues, given the particular economy in the estimate.

Suppose that the department head decided that the economy next year was somewhat less promising than his initial probability weightings indicated. He could still use the three potential economies developed by the department's economist, but he would want to change the probabilities assigned to these three conditions. As a result, he may profitably set up another payoff table, such as Table 8–6, of the same stocks using different probabilities.

TABLE 8–6
Revision of Expected Values

	Prob-ability	A	B	C	D	E
Economy I	.1	11	14	8	16	6
Economy II	.6	10	12	7	12	6
Economy III	.3	9	6	7	4	5
Expected value		9.8	10.4	7.1	10.0	5.7

Now Company B is the most attractive, due to its more defensive price characteristics. This is simply due to the change in weightings, for the conditional returns of the various stocks (the returns *given* a specific economy), have not changed. What has happened is that the less promising economy has received a larger weight, and because of this the returns of the stocks in an adverse environment have become more important in determining the final expected value of the stock. Since Company B is more attractive than Company D in an adverse environment and this type of an economy has become more important in determining the stock's expected return, Company B quite naturally has become more attractive. If the economic climate continued to worsen and the department head decided to assign the probabilities 0.0, 0.6, and 0.4, Table 8–7 would determine the relative attractiveness of the companies.

TABLE 8–7
Revision of Expected Values

	Prob-ability	A	B	C	D	E
Economy I	.0	11	14	8	16	6
Economy II	.6	10	12	7	12	6
Economy III	.4	9	6	7	4	5
Expected value		9.6	9.6	7.0	8.8	5.6

Companies A and B now tie with an expected return of 9.6% per year. Company D has now dropped to an estimated 8.8%. As can be seen, the application of expected value and payoff tables can portray the impact of changing expectations on the relative attractiveness of alternative investments.

STRATEGIES

The use of expected monetary value as a criterion for business decision is only one of a number of possible strategies. A potential investor may, for example, decide to use an alternative strategy which causes him to invest in that stock which provides the largest possible gain under some possible condition. For example, in Table 8–5 the payoff table shows that stock D given Economy I has an expected profit of 16%. Since this possible profit is the largest which can be obtained from any investment being considered, this strategy (called "maximax") would purchase stock D. The problem with this approach is that it does not consider the probability of the various economic developments. It purchases the largest *possibility* without regard to its *probability*. If the probabilities of various economic developments changed, as shown in Table 8–6, the maximaxer or "crapshooter" would still purchase stock D because of its possible 16% return even though Economy I (and hence the 16% return) is highly improbable.

If the alternative approach of using the expected monetary value of an investment in each of the stocks is applied, this cavalier approach to investment is avoided because the behavior of the stocks under all expected conditions is given the proper consideration (the proper weight). On the other hand, the maximax strategy, if carried to its extreme, will cause the investor to opt for the largest possible value under conditions where the probability of that value occurring is so minute as to be virtually zero, as found in Table 8–7. In this case, the "crapshooter" would still purchase stock D even though the 16% figure is for all practical purposes irrelevant to any investment decision. In fact, he would still purchase stock D (given some minute probability of Economy I) even if the expected returns under Economies II and III for this stock were zero instead of the actual 12% and 4%.

A more reasonable approach toward investment is the "minimax" style. This investor minimizes his maximum loss, (or in a bull market maximizes his minimum gain). This means that the minimaxer will choose that particular stock which will perform best given the worst possible development that could occur. Examining Table 8–5, it can be seen that the worst returns that could be produced by each of the stocks are 9%, 6%, 7%, 4%, and 5%, respectively. The minimaxer would choose stock A in order to insure a 9% return regardless of what economy was encountered. This strategy has some intuitive appeal, for it is the most conservative stance that can be taken.

In order to understand the problem in the minimax strategy, it is necessary to examine the minimaxer's choice when the probabilities are changed, as in Table 8–6. In this payoff table, the minimaxer will still choose the stock having the maximum performance under the most adverse conditions. He will, in other words, continue to purchase stock A. This will always be the case regardless of the probabilities because, (*given* the economies) the conditional value for the stock does not change when the probabilities of the various economies change. This means that the minimaxer completely disregards the probabilities for the various economies. As a result, he would make his selection on the basis of the performance of companies in the most adverse economy regardless of the probability of that economy actually occurring. This appears to be carrying safety to an extreme, for it disregards a great deal of the information which is available for making business decisions. It disregards the probabilities of the various economies despite the fact that information concerning their relative importance is available.

EXPECTED OPPORTUNITY LOSS

Another strategy which will always produce the same results as the expected monetary value but which is more subtle and provides more value in the more complicated problems of decision theory is the minimization of the expected opportunity loss. In order to understand this concept, Table 8–6 appears below, as Table 8–8, with one minor modification. The value of the stock which produces the best conditional return in each economy is circled. This is the stock which would be purchased if the economy presented in the row were known with absolute certainty to be the correct operating environment for the companies during the coming year. In this particular case, the "best" purchase in each of the three economies in Table 8–8 is different.

TABLE 8–8
Revision of Expected Values

	Prob-ability	A	B	C	D	E
Economy I	.1	11	14	8	16	6
Economy II...........	.6	10	12	7	12	6
Economy III	.3	9	6	7	4	5
Expected value		9.8	10.4	7.1	10.0	5.7

These are the stocks which would be purchased if uncertainty were not present, that is, if one or the other of the economies were known with certainty to be correct. Naturally, it was the presence of uncertainty in the first place that required the use of probabilities and the calculation of expected value. It is possible using the above table, however, to move one step further in the analysis of the influence of uncertainty by showing the *loss in return* which the investor would suffer by choosing the incorrect company *given the occurrence* of the economy. For example, if Economy I does in fact occur and Company A were chosen for investment, the investor will receive only 11% instead of the 16% return which could have been obtained by selecting the best stock given Economy I. This means that the choice of Company A would have resulted in a 5% opportunity loss, that is, a 5% lower rate of return than would have been possible if the economy had been known with certainty. If Company B had been chosen and Economy I actually occurred, a 14% rate of return would have been achieved instead of the optimum 16% for Company D. This implies that a 2% opportunity loss would have been suffered because it was not known with certainty that Economy I would occur. Examining Economy II, the purchase of Company A would produce a 10% return, 2% below the 12% optimum return achieved by Companies B and D. Naturally, if Company B had actually been chosen, there would be a zero opportunity loss. In Economy III, the purchase of Company D would have produced a 4% return, 5% less than the optimum 9% return achieved by Company A. This means that the fact that the occurrence of Economy III was not known with certainty produced an opportunity loss of 5% given the purchase of Company D. The opportunity losses from each of the investments in these five companies can be placed in a table such as Table 8–9.

TABLE 8–9
Conditional Opportunity Loss

	A	B	C	D	E
Economy I............	5%	2%	8%	0%	10%
Economy II...........	2	0	5	0	6
Economy III	0	3	2	5	4

As can be seen, this is a table of *conditional* opportunity losses, for the entries are the losses which will be incurred *given* the actual occurrence of one or the other of the various economies. Further analysis is unfortunately impossible unless these conditional opportunity losses are "merged" into a single opportunity loss figure for each of the companies. After all, the objective is to select that company which has a minimum opportunity loss, and this would be impossible unless each company were represented by only one number.

Up to this point, the analysis has not considered the problem of uncertainty at all. Each entry in the table is the correct entry for the company given that the economy actually occurs. But it is known that each of the economies will occur only with some given degree of probability. As a result, the *actual* opportunity loss resulting from an investment in any of these stocks cannot be discovered. Only the *expected* opportunity loss (EOL) can be computed. In order to do this, each of the conditional opportunity losses is weighted by its probability and the results are then totaled. This calculation then gives the investment analyst the "best bet" concerning the opportunity loss which is involved in the purchase of any of the companies. These calculations (using the probabilities which were used in Table 8–5) are shown in Table 8–10.

TABLE 8–10
Expected Opportunity Loss

	Prob-ability	A	B	C	D	E
Economy I............	.3	5%	2%	8%	0%	10%
Economy II	.5	2	0	5	0	6
Economy III	.2	0	3	2	5	4
EOL		2.5	1.2	5.3	1.0	6.8

The company having the lowest expected opportunity loss is Company D, showing that the use of EOL produces the same decision as the use of expected monetary value in Table 8–5.

Table 8–11 calculates EOL using the probabilities in Table 8–6.

TABLE 8–11
Revised Expected Opportunity Loss

	Prob-ability	A	B	C	D	E
Economy I............	.1	5%	2%	8%	0%	10%
Economy II	.6	2	0	5	0	6
Economy III	.3	0	3	2	5	4
EOL		1.7	1.1	4.4	1.5	5.8

The minimum EOL is now Company B, corresponding to the selection of Company B which was made by the use of expected monetary value with the same probabilities.

As can be seen from the last two tables, the expected opportunity loss (EOL) is not the *actual* opportunity loss which will be incurred from the investment but rather the analyst's *expectation* of the amount of opportunity loss which he will suffer. The EOL, then, is the "best bet" in an uncertain world of the amount of opportunity loss that will be suffered. But since opportunity loss is by definition the amount by which the actual selection will be inferior to the *optimum* investment due to the presence of uncertainty, opportunity loss is a calculation of the *cost of uncertainty*. This, in turn, means that the *expected* opportunity loss is the "best bet" that can be made concerning what this cost of uncertainty will actually be. It is, in other words, the optimum *estimate* of the cost of uncertainty.

As has been shown, the investment which minimizes the estimate of the cost of uncertainty is also the investment which maximizes the expected monetary value of the investment. As has also been shown, the EOL is sensitive to changes in the probabilities of the various economies. This completely identical performance of EOL and EMV at first glance makes the use of opportunity losses appear to be redundant. This is not the case, however, because the EOL not only provides the optimum investment decision, but also provides the "price" which the investor is paying as a result of the presence of uncertainty. In other words, if the analyst could eliminate the uncertainty concerning the economies, he could reasonably expect to gain a larger return on his investment, and the amount which he would expect to gain is precisely the amount of the expected opportunity loss.

Even though the analyst has already minimized the effect of uncertainty by choosing the lowest expected opportunity loss, some cost of uncertainty nevertheless remains and is precisely measured by the EOL. If this uncertainty could be eliminated, the expected value of the investment would increase by a known amount (by the EOL). Certainly, the investment manager would be willing to pay anything up to this amount in order to receive perfect information concerning the economies because he would be reimbursed by his additional return on investment. This means that the minimum expected opportunity loss (the expected opportunity loss of the "best" security) is equal to the expected value of perfect information (EVPI). In the example, this means that perfect information concerning the correct economy for the coming year would have a value to the investor equal to 1.0% of his investment if he assumed the (.3 .5 .2) probabilities shown in Table 8–10 because the EOL of the best investment in this situation is 1.0%.

Unfortunately, it is not often possible to find sources of perfect information, but the manager could reasonably spend a portion of the money available for *perfect* information in order to buy *imperfect* information, i.e., information which is helpful but is not a complete solution to the decision problem. Naturally, he would be willing to spend less money for imperfect advice than for perfect information, and the precise amount which he would spend would depend upon the degree of imperfection as well as the amount of money which was available from the expected opportunity loss. A large proportion of the more advanced uses of decision theory is devoted to the problem of determining the precise amount of money which should be used to purchase various imperfect pieces of information. Although this subject is beyond the scope of this book, the applicability of the problem to the field of investments is obvious, for a number of sources of imperfect information are available. The particular application discussed here does, however, show that the value of information stems from both economic and analytic considerations.

ADDITIONAL READINGS IN PROBABILITY THEORY

FELLER, WILLIAM. *An Introduction to Probability Theory and Its Applications, Vol. I.* New York: John Wiley & Sons, Inc., 1957.

This book is a solid mathematical treatment of the elementary aspects of probability (436 pages). The material has less immediate practical value than the following text and requires a mathematical orientation on the part of the reader. It is valuable to the reader already familiar with probability theory, however, because it clarifies the mathematical aspects of the theory. Volume II treats the mathematical problems of continuous probability distributions and requires a much higher level of mathematical expertise than is required in actual business applications.

SCHLAIFER, ROBERT. *Probability and Statistics for Business Decisions.* New York: McGraw-Hill Book Co., 1959.

This book is the classic text in the field of statistical decision theory (669 pages). It is readable and practical, but the level of presentation will hardly insult the reader's intelligence. Numerous examples are used and are directly related to business situations. The introduction and part one treat the nature of subjective probabilities. Part two covers the various simple probabilities. Part three uses Bayesian theory to analyze the results of samples. Part four covers the value of additional information, and part five deals with the classical approach to statistics.

Chapter
9 Hypothesis Testing or How
Certain Are Patterns in the Real World?

Although financial analysis involves processing vast amounts of data, questions often arise whether samples of data taken from a universe or population are representative of the population itself. Statistical techniques have been devised for this purpose that involve testing the null hypothesis, that is, determining with what level of confidence the opposite of what you are trying to prove can be rejected. Parametric tests deal with data drawn from a population with known characteristics, which usually means that they are normally distributed. Nonparametric tests deal with data not normally distributed. Two parametric tests are the t test, which measures whether the difference between the arithmetic means of two samples is significant and whether they are representative of the population, and the F test, which answers questions concerning the equality of variances. The principal nonparametric test is the Chi Square test, which tests data to see if it matches an already established idea of what it should look like. Illustrations are given for applications of these tests in financial analysis.

SCIENTIFIC METHOD AND STATISTICAL TESTING

The *method* of statistics is quite often overlooked or at least underemphasized when quantitative techniques are first applied to a new field. This is probably no less true of the quantitative applications in investments than of any other field. In the tentative, testing phase of quantitative applications, the use of tools without a systematic technique quite often leads to a piecemeal approach to problems and to results of only limited value. In quantitative analysis, just as surely as in investment or economic analysis, methodology tends to predetermine the answer. This is simply because the line of attack chosen by the analyst can reasonably be expected to provide the most significant step toward the development of the particular answer which will be obtained.

The body of knowledge now referred to as classical statistics originally developed as a device by which scientific theories or tentative hypotheses about the nature of reality could be subjected to empirical testing. The basic pattern of the scientific method is procedural in nature, going from basic observation of data to the formation of an hypothesis and then checking that hypothesis against additional observations in the world of experience. The strength of the technique lies in the impossibility of theorizing in contradiction to available facts or about unobservable matters, i.e., matters not subject to empirical verification. Agreement with observed reality is the fundamental criterion of science, and the perpetual modification of tentative theories therefore lies at the heart of the scientific method. The value of the results achieved, however, depends upon two factors:

1. The power of the new creative hypothesis.
2. The ability of the analyst to obtain data to be used for verification.

Both the power and the limitation of statistics lie in this latter area, for the methods of statistical theory are highly useful tools for the *verification* of hypotheses but can never jump beyond this application into the *formation* of theory.

With the techniques provided by the efforts of previous thinkers, the analyst is able to determine the validity of an analysis of the great masses of available data. But, strictly speaking, he is not able to analyze the data directly because he must have some plan or concept in mind in order to direct his efforts. Without the formation of a coherent, useful and original theory or hypothesis, statistics could not provide any information other than the "boiled-down" results of numerous observations. This "summary presentation" is not statistics at all, but rather arithmetic on a massive scale.

Classical statistics *begins* with a scientific hypothesis and then attempts either to verify or to refute it. Unfortunately, however, it is impossible in a scientific sense ever to prove anything to be absolutely correct. As a result, statistical technique is forced into the position of making probability statements about the possibility of being correct. Actually, the probability statements of classical hypothesis testing take the opposite of the hypothesis or theory and attempt to show that it is very likely to be wrong. If, for example, a theory says that the P/E ratio of a stock is higher than average if the growth in the stock's earnings is above average, statistics would reverse this theory and deal with the following statement: "It is not true that a stock's P/E is higher if its earnings growth is higher." An attempt is then made to reject this statement. This "reverse methodology" is called the attempt to reject the *null hypothesis* (H_o) and can never be totally successful simply because it is impossible to observe every instance pertaining to a universal "law." It is considered satisfactory if the null hypothesis (H_o) can be rejected with some confidence that the rejection will not later be proven to have been in error. The "level of confidence" as a result has become a dominant statistical theme and quite naturally has been expressed in terms of probabilities. The hypothesis is tested by actually observing a number of examples of the population and then using statistical inference to move from statements about the examples to statements about the population in general.

Classical statistics, then, is a methodology which formally states a currently accepted theory concerning the nature of the world and then attempts to prove that the scientific evidence makes it highly improbable that the theory is true. This approach is really much less mysterious than first appearances would indicate. After all, if an analyst were to argue that the commonly accepted notion that "high multiple stocks outperform low multiple stocks" was an incorrect theory, he would probably state the theory and then show facts tending to refute it. This approach would certainly be more direct than the alternative of stating some opposing view and then trying to establish the new theory without refuting the currently established thinking on the subject. Classical statistics simply states the current hypothesis and attempts to refute it. It is by nature only a "bubble burster," a destroyer of illusions. The theory which is to be tested (and possibly rejected) is the null hypothesis, and the level of confidence is the desired level of accuracy in rejecting the null hypothesis. For example, if a 95% level of confidence is chosen, 5% of the null hypotheses which are rejected will, in fact, be true. This possibility of error cannot be eliminated because there is always a possibility that the particular data selected were misleading. The advantage to statistics is that such errors can be controlled and kept within acceptable limits. Frequently used levels are 95% and 99%, although some scientific applications require substantially higher certainty.

Once a student moves beyond the most basic aspects of statistical analysis, he discovers that the value of the use of statistics is not determined by the models evaluating the data, but rather by the usefulness of the hypotheses put forward by the analyst. Formal statistics is not a decisive technique when used simply to summarize data or "pulverize" information in a wild search for some hidden meaning. Hypothesis testing when properly used clearly specifies the theory to be tested and the test procedure, providing a clear and decisive acceptance or rejection. And the value of an acceptance or rejection of a theory is completely dependent upon the value of the theory being tested. Statistics cannot provide theories for testing (only a valuable insight by an analyst can do

that), but statistics can be of great value in relieving the burden of verification from the analyst and so allowing more time for the formation of
concepts which may prove useful in investment operations.

The subject of hypothesis testing is divided into two broad areas of
application — parametric tests and nonparametric tests. The parametric
tests assume that the data being tested are drawn from some population
having known characteristics, usually that the population is normally
distributed. The nonparametric tests do not assume normality and as a
result can be applied to a broader number of practical situations. In fact,
a number of these tests can be applied when the data are only ranked and
have no numerical value at all.

The advantage of the nonparametric tests is that they require fewer
favorable characteristics in the problem being analyzed. Unfortunately,
actual problems (especially in the investment field) have a pronounced
tendency to defy formulation in classical terms. Data frequently are not
normally distributed, often are only a ranking of preferences, and sometimes consist only of the classifications "good" and "bad," or "buy"
and "sell." In such cases, the assumptions of the parametric tests obviously are not met, and this means that these models cannot be used
because they are not relevant to the problem at hand. The only recourse
at that point is a nonparametric test. It is important to point out, however, that if the data *do* fit a parametric model, then *this* approach should
be used. This is because the parametric tests (when their assumptions are
met) produce less chance of an error in classifying the null hypothesis as
true or false. In this chapter, only two of the parametric tests will be
discussed: the *t* test (also called "student's *t*") and the *F* test.

THE *t* TEST

The *t* test is applied in a number of problems, the most important of
which deals with finding a probability concerning the means of statistical
populations. For example, one possible *t* test could be applied to the following problem. A portfolio manager receives an account from a new
client and is interested in testing to see if the ability of the former manager
in handling equity investment is significantly superior to a random selection of stocks. Since this particular account is invested 100% in equities, it
presents a unique opportunity to "sample" the other manager's performance. He finds the project to be worthwhile and proceeds by building a "control" account which can be used to show the results of completely random performance. This can be done by taking a random
sample (say, by throwing darts or using random number tables until the
desired number of issues has been selected) of stocks of investment
quality, because this is the population from which the previous manager
was making his decisions. All of the stocks in the actual account which

is being analyzed have about the same total market value, and so the manager has two samples:

x_1 The account (a sample of the previous manager's performance)
x_2 The random sample

The portfolio manager at this point has two different sets of data at hand. The random sample of stocks provides information concerning the performance of investments which were not under any investment management. The account provides information concerning the performance of investments under a previous manager's control. If it can be shown that these two groups of data are essentially identical, then it follows that the control of the previous manager was equivalent (in terms of performance) to having no investment management at all.

Two problems immediately present themselves in this study. First, since the data in the samples are unwieldy, it would be useful to find a representative number typical of each set of stocks. The average, or arithmetic mean can be used for this purpose. The manager is therefore interested in whether the average results of the account's stocks equal the average results of the random sample.

If we agree to call the average performance of the prior manager μ_1 (mu) and the average for all stocks μ_2, we can state mathematically that he is interested in whether $\mu_1 = \mu_2$. Note that μ_1 and μ_2 are not the sample averages. This is a subtle but important point: μ_1 is not the average performance of the stocks in the account, but refers to the average performance of the first manager of the account. The account merely provides one sample of this manager's performance, and its average may be different from the true average performance capability of the manager. μ_1 is the *true population average* which the sample average $\bar{x}_1$ is estimating. μ_2 is the true population average estimated by $\bar{x}_2$, where $\bar{x}_2$ is the average of the random sample of stocks.

Another problem is that, since the data are only samples, it is impossible ever to prove *absolutely* either equal or unequal performance. It is only possible to prove results in terms of some level of confidence which always leaves some small probability of an incorrect decision. In this particular problem, the null hypothesis is $\mu_1 = \mu_2$ and the portfolio manager decides that a 95% confidence level is sufficient. This means that if the other manager performs better than the random sample and also if he can reject the null hypothesis at the .95 confidence level (indicating that the difference in performance is a *significant* difference), then he will consider the other manager to have established a performance better than random. He will, however, still have a 5% chance of this being the wrong conclusion due to the possibility that the data may not represent the true performance picture. The next problem is that of finding a method by which $\mu_1 = \mu_2$ can be subjected to a precise testing procedure even though the subject matter is probabilistic in nature.

In this problem, the equality of the means of two samples is being tested, and this is an ideal use for the t test. Since the portfolio man is assuming in his null hypothesis that the two samples are being drawn from the same population, he assumes that the variances of the two samples are approximately equal. In addition, it can be shown that the means of reasonably large samples drawn from any population are normally distributed. The assumptions of the t test are therefore at least closely approximated, and the next problem is the actual calculation of the t statistic.

Let:

n_1 = the number of items in sample one; the account
n_2 = the number of items in sample two; the random sample
$\bar{x}_1$ = the mean of the values in sample one
$\bar{x}_2$ = the mean of the values in sample two
s_1^2 = the variance of the values in sample one
s_2^2 = the variance of the values in sample two

Then the t statistic can be found by the following formula:

$$t = \frac{\bar{x}_1 - \bar{x}_2}{\hat{\sigma}_{\Delta\bar{x}}}$$

←————— The numerator is simply the difference between the means of the two samples.

The denominator is an estimate of the amount by which the two means might be expected to differ. It is the standard error of the numerator. For our purposes, it is possible simply to regard it as a number which can be calculated by the following formula:

$$\hat{\sigma}_{\Delta\bar{x}} = \hat{\sigma}\sqrt{\frac{n_1 + n_2}{n_1 n_2}}$$

Where $\hat{\sigma}$ is an estimate of the variation in the performance of stocks and is determined by the formula:

$$\hat{\sigma} = \sqrt{\frac{n_1 s_1^2 + n_2 s_2^2}{n_1 + n_2 - 2}}$$

In actual calculation of the value of t, the analyst would first compute $\hat{\sigma}$. This would provide an estimate of the variability of the performance of stocks — the standard deviation of the "stock universe" from which the data on performance were selected. Next, the value of $\hat{\sigma}_{\Delta\bar{x}}$ could be found. This is a measure of how great a difference between the two means could be expected simply on the basis of chance variation. It is the standard deviation of the possible values of $\bar{x}_1 - \bar{x}_2$. In other words, the manager would not expect $\bar{x}_1$ to equal $\bar{x}_2$ exactly because the data simply are not that perfect an indicator of performance. He would, however, expect $\bar{x}_1 - \bar{x}_2$ to be reasonably close if there is no real difference in the performance of the other manager and the performance of a random sample. The statistic $\hat{\sigma}_{\Delta\bar{x}}$ is a precise measure of how great a difference between $\bar{x}_1$ and $\bar{x}_2$ might be expected. The difference $\bar{x}_1 - \bar{x}_2$ would be expected to be zero give or take $\hat{\sigma}_{\Delta\bar{x}}$ about two-thirds of the time if the assumption of equal performance is correct. The manager can then compute t as $(\bar{x}_1 - \bar{x}_2)/\hat{\sigma}_{\Delta\bar{x}}$. This is the amount by which the two samples actually differ divided by the amount by which they would be expected to differ if there is no essential difference in performance characteristics. The value of t is the difference in means divided by the "range" of difference that we would expect to result from our having taken random samples. If t equalled ".5," then the difference would only be one-half of what might be expected simply on the basis of chance variations in the data. The difference in this case would hardly be significant. If t equalled "4," however, the difference in performance was four times the amount which might reasonably be attributed to chance, and t might very well be significant.

As an example of the calculation of t, working through the example that has been used may be helpful. Assume the following results from the samples:

Other Manager		Random Sample Management	
n_1	12 stocks	n_2	15 stocks
$\bar{x}_1$	15%	$\bar{x}_2$	10%
s_1	3%	s_2	2%

Note that n_1 is the number of observations, $\bar{x}_1$ is the average performance, and s_1 is the standard deviation of the performance of the stocks under control of the other manager. The same letters with the subscript "2" refer to the comparable data for the "random" manager. Also, note that the standard deviations s_1 and s_2 are much lower than an experienced analyst would expert from any set of stocks; they are set at an unrealistically low level for purposes of this example. It is important to note that larger standard deviations make it much more difficult to establish a significant difference in performances.

Using these initial data, it is possible to calculate $\hat{\sigma}$, the estimated standard deviation in the performance of stocks in general:

$$\hat{\sigma} = \sqrt{\frac{n_1 s_1^2 + n_2 s_2^2}{n_1 + n_2 - 2}} = \sqrt{\frac{12 \cdot 3^2 + 15 \cdot 2^2}{12 + 15 - 2}} = 2.59$$

Next, $\hat{\sigma}_{\Delta\bar{x}}$ can be computed,

$$\hat{\sigma}_{\Delta\bar{x}} = \hat{\sigma} \sqrt{\frac{n_1 + n_2}{n_1 n_2}} = 2.59 \sqrt{\frac{12 + 15}{12 \cdot 15}} = 1.00$$

The value of t can now be found as the difference between the two means divided by the expected difference stemming from the random nature of the data:

$$t = \frac{\bar{x}_1 - \bar{x}_2}{\hat{\sigma}_{\Delta\bar{x}}} = \frac{15 - 10}{1.00} = 5.00$$

The result of this rather complex set of calculations is a single number — the value of t in this particular test. At this point the value of t is still of no use to the portfolio manager whatsoever. He was attempting to find the actual probability of being in error if he rejected the null hypothesis. But the probabilities of error have already been worked out and stored in tables for any particular value of t. As a result, once t has been found, the problem of deciding whether or not the null hypothesis can safely be rejected is solved by simply locating a number in a table. A portion of a t table is reproduced below in Table 9–1.

TABLE 9–1

Degrees of Freedom	Risk		
	.10	.05	.01
1	6.314	12.706	63.657
5	2.015	2.571	4.032
10	1.812	2.228	3.169
20	1.725	2.086	2.845
25	1.708	2.060	2.787

A number of important points can be drawn from this table. First, all of the entries in the table are values of t, and if the t which the manager calculated is *larger* (disregarding the sign) than the value in the table, the H_o can be rejected. But which table value should be used? This depends upon two things: (1) the level of risk which the analyst is willing to accept (.05 in the example, i.e., he wished to be 95% certain); (2) the degrees of freedom involved in the particular test being made.

"Degrees of freedom" is a rather complicated topic, but it essentially refers to the number of observations involved in the data used in the test. If more observations are used in the sample, the "value" of the results is better, and the confidence in the results can naturally be increased. The phrase "degrees of freedom" is used instead of "number of observations" because it frequently happens that the mathematicians will destroy the value of one or more observations when they set up the formulas being used in the statistical test. The phrase "degrees of freedom" refers to the number of observations minus the number of the observations which were lost by using any particular formula. In the case of our example, the d.f. equals $n_1 + n_2 - 2$, showing that two observations were rendered useless because the formula for the two-sample t test was used in order to find the value of t, leaving the balance of the observations in the samples available for service as degrees of freedom.

This information concerning the use of the t table is sufficient to permit the final solution to the problem of the portfolio manager. In this example, the confidence level was set at .95, implying a .05 risk level. The number of stocks in each sample were 12 and 15, respectively. This means that the degrees of freedom $n_1 + n_2 - 2$ equal $12 + 15 - 2$ equal 25. The probability of t can therefore be found in the table in the .05 column and the 25 d.f. row. Referring to the table, this value for t is 2.060. This means that in this particular study, the value of t would be less than 2.060 95% of the time if in fact the performances were equal. But the manager found a value for t of 5.00. The logical conclusion is that such a large value for t would not have occurred if performances were equal, and so the null hypothesis (of equal performance) is rejected. This, of course, is the same as accepting the alternative hypothesis that they are unequal. Because the computed t is greater than the table value of t, the manager can therefore reject the null hypothesis with .95 confidence.

Several additional points concerning the nature of t are useful. For example, since the analyst wishes to reject the H_o and this is done if the absolute value of t is greater than the value entered in the table, the presence of small entries in the table is advantageous to him. The fact that the t table entries become smaller as more degrees of freedom are involved indicates that larger samples have more power than small ones. More observations increase the chance of success of rejecting the H_o when it should in fact be rejected. In addition, the size of the t table entry decreases as the level of risk increases, indicating that it is easier, for example, to reject the null hypothesis if a risk of .10 is acceptable than if a risk of .05 is the maximum permitted. This stands to reason, because it is more difficult to prove the validity of a 95% confidence than it is to prove a 90% confidence.

The behavior of the *table* values of t therefore shows that larger samples will produce fewer errors than smaller samples and also that it is easier to reject an hypothesis if a greater risk of error is allowed. But the ability to reject a null hypothesis (to "prove" something) depends not only upon the table value of t but also upon the calculated value. In other words, for any given degrees of freedom and confidence level, larger values of the *computed* t would make rejection easier. This leads to the interesting question of how the variables used in the calculation affect the value of t. As the difference between means becomes greater, t becomes larger. This is reasonable, because it is more likely that performances differ if our sample means show a greater difference, other things being equal. Also interesting is the fact that as the standard deviations of the performance of the stocks in the "portfolio" (s_1 and s_2) become smaller, t becomes larger. This means that the same difference between average results ($\bar{x}_1 - \bar{x}_2$) is more significant if there is less chance variation in the populations being sampled. In the example, it would have been more difficult to prove a difference in performance had s_1 and s_2 been, say, 10%. This is simply because the 5% difference in means ($\bar{x}_1 - \bar{x}_2$) would have a greater possibility of having been caused by the (now much larger) random fluctuations in the data.

Regardless of the particular application which may have caused an analyst to compute a particular t statistic, the same t table is used. The t table is therefore valuable in any application involving a t test of any kind, and our example covered only one particular application. All of the commonly used t tests deal with population means, but a number of variations are possible. For example, a population mean can be tested to see if it equals a specific value, two populations can be tested for equal means with an alternative hypothesis that one specified population has a higher average value, one population can be tested to see if it is greater than some specified value, etc. Despite the diversity in applications, however, the t test can always be reduced to the calculation of a simple formula which can be found in any elementary statistics text. In addition, all t tests always use the same t table and are always formulated in terms of a null hypothesis which may be rejected at some stated level of confidence.

THE F TEST

The F test, like the t test, is parametric, for it assumes that the populations being tested are normally distributed. And just as the t test has many applications, so does the F. But while t tends to deal with the means of the groups being studied, the F tends to be concerned with problems dealing with the variances. As a matter of fact, the most powerful use of F is the statistical technique known as "analysis of variance," which is covered in a separate chapter. The only application of the F test that will be considered here is concerned with the equality of variances.

In the example of the t test, the portfolio manager assumed that the variance of the portfolio was a good estimate of the variance in the previous account manager's buy selections *and* that this variance was equal to the variance in stock performance in general. This assumption was necessary for the *t* test to be applicable. Unfortunately, this assumption may prove to be invalid, so that the manager would be well advised to test whether the variances of the two populations may be assumed to be equal ($\sigma_1^2 = \sigma_2^2$) before applying the *t* test. If it is established that $\sigma_1^2 \neq \sigma_2^2$ with 90% confidence, then there would only be 10 chances out of 100 that the *t* test would be valid. In this case, of course, the *t* test would have to be abandoned. Discretion being the better part of valor, the manager decides to determine the probability of $\sigma_1^2 = \sigma_2^2$. No direct method of discovering this probability is available, so he calculates:

$$F = \frac{\text{The variance of the group of stocks having the larger variance}}{\text{The variance of the group of stocks having the smaller variance}}$$

This value will be a single number and, of course, will be a value equal to or greater than one. But *F*, like *t*, has no direct value to the portfolio man; he wants the probability. The probabilities associated with *F* have been computed and are available in tables, a section of which is reproduced in Table 9–2.

TABLE 9–2

Degrees of Freedom 2 (.05 risk)	Degrees of Freedom 1 (.05 risk)		
	1	*2*	*3*
1	161	200	216
2	18.51	19.00	19.16
3	10.13	9.55	9.28

The value of the computed *F* is compared to the appropriate value in the table; if it is greater than the table entry, the H_o is rejected (which means that $\sigma_1^2 \neq \sigma_2^2$). The problem is now reduced to locating the proper value in the table. Since the manager is working at the 90% confidence level, 10% risk is acceptable. However, since he has two alternative hypotheses ($\sigma_1^2 > \sigma_2^2$ and $\sigma_1^2 < \sigma_2^2$), he has a 5.0% level of risk *per alternative* and so the .05 table is used. But which number in the table is to be chosen? This depends, once again, upon the concept of degrees of freedom. In this particular test, one degree of freedom is lost from each of the two groups being tested. The d.f. for each group is therefore the number of observations in that group minus one. The $d.f._1$ locates the proper column, and the $d.f._2$ locates the proper row, and this isolates the single number in the table which is to be used for the test.

In the example of the portfolio manager's problem, $n_1 = 12$; $n_2 = 15$; $s_1 = 3$; $s_2 = 2$. Since variance is equal to the standard deviation squared, the variance of the other manager's account was $3^2 = 9$ with degrees of freedom of $12 - 1$, or 11. The variance of the "random" control sample was $2^2 = 4$ with degrees of freedom equal to $15 - 1$, or 14. Since the other manager's account had the greater variance, it is used as the numerator in the F ratio and we have:

$$F = \frac{\text{greater variance}}{\text{lesser variance}} = \frac{9}{4} \qquad \begin{array}{l} \text{numerator has 11 d.f.} \\ \text{denominator has 14 d.f.} \end{array}$$

The value of F_{14}^{11} at the 5% level is 2.56. Since the computed value for F of $\frac{9}{4} = 2.25$ is not greater than the table value of 2.56, the null hypothesis cannot be rejected and the assumption that the variances are equal is not statistically invalidated. Once again, under the assumption of equal variances, the t test is valid.

CHI SQUARE

The chi square (χ^2) distribution is the leading example of the non-parametric tests. It can be used in a number of applications, only one of which will be considered here. The applications do, however, all have a common concept which is characteristic of χ^2 – they test the data to see if they match an already established idea of the way the data *should* appear. If the test shows significant deviation from the *expected* results, then the theory which caused the analyst to expect a certain behavior in the data must be discarded. This ability of χ^2 to check theories to see if they are an adequate model of the real world makes the χ^2 test very valuable in the investment profession, where untested theories are found in abundance. This power of χ^2 as a "bubble-burster," coupled with the fact that it does not assume normality in a world unfortunately abnormal probably makes the tests using χ^2 the most underrated simple statistical application in the world of finance.

Assume that an analyst has discovered a stock having excellent prospects and a *P/E* of 13. He wishes to recommend the stock in the Investment Committee meeting but knows that several members favor high-multiple stocks on the grounds that low-multiple issues offer lower prospects for strong capital appreciation. This theory, of course, does not necessarily eliminate the purchase of this one stock; it merely covers the overall approach toward stocks in general, leaving room for exceptions. Nevertheless, the analyst feels that the approach would be applied in this particular case and that the only hope for a purchase lies in discrediting the theory at least to the extent that it will allow minor exceptions (e.g. this stock). The theory would lead the committee to *expect* a certain performance from high and low multiple issues, and it is logical to see if the *actual* performances matched these expectations. The analyst knows that a $P/E < 15$ is considered low, and a $P/E > 25$ is considered high by the committee. He also knows that a compound annual rate of return $< 5\%$ is poor while $> 15\%$ is good. Examining the stocks normally analyzed by the staff, he locates the cheap and expensive issues in the past and checks their performance, placing each stock as in Table 9–3.

TABLE 9–3

	Good Performance	Poor Performance	Total
Low *P/E*	8	14	22
High *P/E*	12	13	25
Total	20	27	47

Thus far, the results aren't too convincing to anyone. The analyst was hoping for the results in Table 9–4.

TABLE 9–4

	Good Performance	Poor Performance	Total
Low *P/E*	25	0	25
High *P/E*	0	22	22
Total	25	22	47

The committee would expect a tendency toward the results in Table 9–5.

TABLE 9–5

	Good Performance	Poor Performance	Total
Low *P/E*	0	25	25
High *P/E*	22	0	22
Total	22	25	47

The fact that the pattern desired by the committee did not occur is hardly evidence that the theory is false, and the analyst is to be congratulated for not presenting this argument to the committee. Instead, he decides to test the hypothesis that there was no relationship between *P/E* and the performance *at all* — to see if the two ideas were completely independent. Since he has already filled out a contingency table, he decides to use a test for independence. If the "expected" results were *independent,* it is possible to place the expectations in parentheses in Table 9–6.

TABLE 9–6

	Good Performance	Poor Performance	Total
Low *P/E*	8 (9.35)	14 (12.65)	22
High *P/E*	12 (10.65)	13 (14.35)	25
Total	20	27	47

These figures were easily derived. The 9.35 was found by first locating the "percentage" (more accurately, the proportion) of *all* of the stocks which performed well. This was $20 \div 47 = .425$. In other words, .425 of all stocks analyzed could be expected to perform well, without regard to their *P/E* ratios. If *P/E* is assumed to be unrelated to performance, it would therefore be natural to expect .425 of all low *P/E* (or high *P/E*) stocks to perform well. Since there are 22 low *P/E* stocks, .425 of these 22 stocks would be expected to show a good performance. The arithmetic is $.425 \times 22 = 9.35$. Once this number is found, the remaining values are very easy to compute because 9.35 plus one of the unknown numbers must be equal to one of the row or column totals. For example, 9.35 plus the expected number of high *P/E* good performance stocks must equal 20. Only 10.65 will satisfy this requirement. The 10.65 is merely $20 - 9.35$ because the total of 9.35 and this number is already known from the table to be 20. The other two values are found by subtracting the expected value from the appropriate row total. The expected number of low *P/E*, poor performance stocks when added to the expected number of high *P/E*, good performance stocks must obviously equal the total number of low *P/E* stocks considered in the study (22). The indicated arithmetic is $22 - 9.35 = 12.65$. The expected value of the high *P/E*, poor performance stock is found through the same line of reasoning, with the resulting arithmetic of $25 - 10.65 = 14.35$.

Once the expected values are known, the amount by which the data deviate from the expectation can easily be found. The problem is whether the deviation is *significantly* large. No one would expect a *perfect* match even if the assumption of independence is true, but at what point do the data deviate to such an extent that they disprove the hypothesis? To answer this, χ^2 must be computed.

Let:

x_{ij} = the actual value in row i and column j.

$\bar{x}_{ij}$ = the expected value in row i and column j.

Then:

$$\chi^2 = \sum_i \sum_j \left[\frac{(x_{ij} - \bar{x}_{ij})^2}{\bar{x}_{ij}} \right]$$

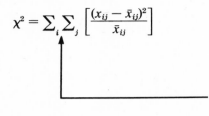

Recall that Σ_j means "sum all of the j observations" (columns). $\Sigma_i\Sigma_j$ means "first total all of the columns and then add all of these totals together."

This is a single number which is the χ^2 value in the particular test. It can then be compared to a χ^2 table to determine the validity of the hypothesis, as in Table 9–7.

TABLE 9–7

Actual	Expected	$x_{ij} - \bar{x}_{ij}$	$(x_{ij} - \bar{x}_{ij})^2$	$\dfrac{(x_{ij} - \bar{x}_{ij})^2}{\bar{x}_{ij}}$
8	9.35	−1.35	1.82	.195
12	10.65	1.35	1.82	.171
14	12.65	1.35	1.82	.144
13	14.35	−1.35	1.82	.123
				Total .633

This value of χ^2 can be compared to the χ^2 table, a portion of which is shown as Table 9–8.

TABLE 9–8

Degrees of Freedom	Risk		
	.10	.05	.01
1	2.71	3.84	6.63
2	4.61	5.99	9.21
3	6.25	7.81	11.34

If the value of the computed χ^2 is greater than the table value, then the actual deviation of the data is significantly greater than the amount of deviation which could be expected under the assumption that P/E and performance are not related. The hypothesis that P/E and performance are independent would therefore be rejected.

The appropriate column of the table is found by selecting the level of risk which is considered to be acceptable. In the example, the analyst chooses a 10% level of risk in order to make it relatively easy to reject the assumption of independence. This is because he is asserting the truth of the independence hypothesis and wishes to make the test as capable of working against him as possible. At the 90% level, independence will be rejected much more easily than would be the case at, say, the 99% level of confidence. The appropriate row in the table is found by selecting the correct number of degrees of freedom. The d.f. is (the number of rows in the contingency table less one) times (the number of columns in the contingency table less one). In this particular case, d.f. $= (2 - 1)(2 - 1)$ $= 1$ d.f. Looking at the χ^2 table, the appropriate value is 2.71. Since .633 is certainly not larger than 2.71, the null hypothesis is not rejected and the data do not provide any evidence that would justify the conclusion that P/E is related to performance. The χ^2 technique used in this example can be applied to a very broad variety of problems, including contingency tables of any size. χ^2 also has other applications not related to contingency tables, but all applications relate to the problem of evaluating the significance of the deviation of observed data from expected results.

METHODOLOGY AND ETHICS

The previous example showed, among other things, a particular case of how business ethics enters into statistics. The choice of the confidence level in the example was made in such a way that the analyst's position was not shown favoritism. This example, plus the fact that this is the close of the chapter dealing with statistical method and the discovery and verification of scientific truth, make a few comments on the relationship between statistics and business ethics appropriate.

Statistics has been assailed for years for being a device by which lies might be "proven" to be the truth. Graphs are shown in advertisements without a scale to show the appropriate numbers. Graphs occur in annual reports with the bottom two-thirds chopped off so that a rise in sales from $65 million to $100 million goes from the bottom of the chart to the top. "Independent laboratories" prove anything superior to everything. The government has at times been accused of misusing numerical data. All of this is occurring at the same time that statistical technique is providing invaluable assistance in the natural and social sciences and is becoming indispensable in such diverse fields as quality control, auditing, and market research.

Unfortunately, almost anything *can* be "proven" by statistics, but only if statistical technique is deliberately and systematically misused in order to serve nonscientific motives. It might be possible to say that although statistical *data* can be manipulated by statistical *technique* to "prove" anything, the use of the statistical *method* will produce scientific truth, and very possibly may be the *only* means by which scientific truth can be developed.

The point to this section, and perhaps to this entire chapter, is that statistics as a discipline does not permit the introduction of self-interest in its method. It sets up an hypothesis and then attempts to reject that hypothesis, with the burden of proof always on the new, unestablished theory (the analyst's theory). When statistical manipulations are reduced to tools to be used to "back up" an untenable position, the misrepresentation is not only unethical from the standpoint of the financial analyst, it is an act of dishonor in man's attempt to develop a scientific view of the world.

ADDITIONAL READINGS IN HYPOTHESIS TESTING

CHOU, YA-LUN. *Statistical Analysis.* New York: Holt, Rinehart & Winston, Inc., 1969.

This book treats the problems of point estimation, interval estimation, and tests of hypotheses in Chapters 9 and 10 (78 pages). These pages clearly define the procedure necessary to execute each particular technique, and each type of problem is specifically identified as a separate section in the table of contents. This clear organization, coupled with an unusually usable set of tables, makes the text a valuable reference handbook when computational or definitional problems are encountered. The description of the procedure of testing (pages 304–13) is entirely verbal and is a statement of method which can be very profitably read by any analyst in about one hour.

JEDAMUS, PAUL AND FRAME, ROBERT. *Business Decision Theory.* New York: McGraw-Hill Book Company, 1969.

This book deals with hypothesis testing and estimation from the standpoint of minimizing the dollar cost of error to the firm (239 pages). This work considers the possibility of replacing the classical statistical idea of an arbitrary level of confidence (such as 95%) with a level of confidence which will minimize the sum of the cost of uncertainty and the cost of obtaining information. This approach points out that uncertainty has a true dollar cost to management because it produces some chance for erroneous decisions and errors therefore *must* eventually occur. It is reasonable to assume that management should be willing to attain only that level of confidence which will bring costs to their lowest point, for a desire for additional confidence would produce exorbitant expenses in gathering information. No quantitative background beyond the probability and hypothesis testing chapters of this book is needed. The entire text can be covered in two weekends and will restructure the reader's thinking concerning the nature of risk and business information.

SIEGEL, SIDNEY. *Nonparametric Statistics.* New York: McGraw-Hill Book Company, 1956.

This book is a presentation of the nature of the nonparametric techniques and a description of 27 specific nonparametric tests (239 pages). A verbal description of their characteristics, an example of their application, and a step-by-step statement of their calculation is included. The calculations are extremely simple, the emphasis is on practical application, and numerous examples are drawn which are simple enough to be understood by the nonexpert. The entire book is excellent and shows how quantitative precision can be achieved in the analysis of problems which at first appear to be completely qualitative.

Chapter

10 Analysis of Variance or Are the Differences between Averages Significant?

This chapter provides a more extended discussion of the material in the previous chapter on hypothesis testing, considering more elaborate uses of the F test in analyzing the difference between the average value of groups. One-way analysis of variance measures the difference when only one variable between two groups is considered; two-way analysis of variance permits the measurement of the effects of two variables. Finally, another test permits measurement of the interaction between the two variables.

AN EXPANSION ON HYPOTHESIS TESTING

The analysis of variance is a major statistical technique which has been used extensively in problems relating to the natural and social sciences. It is an hypothesis testing procedure, constituting the most significant application of the F statistic, and it is the basis for the scientific design of experiments. The technique is parametric, that is, it assumes that all of the random variables involved in the study are normally distributed. Studies have indicated that the results are very sensitive to deviations from normality in the data being tested. Although the subject goes well beyond this elementary presentation, only one-way and two-way analysis of variance will be considered at any length.

As an example of an application of this technique, assume that the head of the portfolio management division wishes to determine whether there is a significant difference in the performance of the various portfolio managers. In order to make this decision, he assumes that the results of the managers during the past year can serve as good estimates of the managers' abilities in any year. He then has his statistical worker select at random 15 accounts managed by each of the four portfolio men and calculate the dollar increase or decrease per dollar of market value during the most recent complete calendar year (in these accounts, there were no contributions or disbursements). Several days later, he receives the following data shown in Table 10–1.

TABLE 10–1
Performance Analysis
($ increase per $ market value, multiplied by 100 for convenience)

Man 1	Man 2	Man 3	Man 4
12	15	13	16
10	12	10	8
14	8	7	6
13	9	4	11
20	18	11	12
9	10	16	14
8	11	8	9
14	7	14	7
10	14	12	15
13	20	13	4
9	14	11	8
11	12	8	9
10	10	9	11
8	13	11	13
12	7	14	12
11.5 average	12.0 average	10.7 average	10.3 average

With these data, the manager is able to say with certainty that the second portfolio man had a better average performance on the particular 15 accounts chosen for this analysis during the year being studied. Unfortunately, however, he is *not* able to jump from this absolute statement to a conclusion that portfolio analyst two is definitely a better analyst than the others. After all, only one year was included in the study, and only 15 accounts were selected. Another sample of a different set of 15 accounts, through the normal workings of chance, would probably show different results. And even if all of the accounts supervised by any of the portfolio managers were considered, the accounts are only being used as examples of the man's performance, and he might have performed better with more accounts had they been available. This means that all of the portfolios handled by a manager are still only a sample of the man's performance capabilities and so are subject to random error.

The problem at hand is not whether manager number two is better; it is whether or not he is *significantly* better than the other managers. The sample of 15 accounts shows that the second portfolio manager outperformed his colleagues, but the immediate question which would have to be asked by any rational man is whether that performance was due to his own capabilities or to the mere workings of chance embodied in the investment process being studied. It is obvious that one of the managers would have to appear more capable than the others if the sample data were not tested for significance, because the average results of each of the four men would almost certainly be different. But to move automatically from this virtual certainty of performance measurement to a conclusion that the particular portfolio manager having the highest average is in fact a superior manager is an error which may cause the head of the department to give promotions on the basis of the chance technique by which the file clerk located the 15 accounts used in the study.

THE NULL HYPOTHESIS

The head of this particular department decides that the simple arithmetic results may be misleading and so applies the scientific method. The problem is clearly an example of hypothesis testing because the *significance* of the data is desired. Converting the problem into mathematical terms, the manager sets up an hypothesis which he can then attempt to reject. This null hypothesis (H_o) is that the means of the four managers' accounts are equal. Calling the mean of manager i's accounts a_i,

$$H_o : a_1 = a_2 = a_3 = a_4$$

If the department manager can use a statistical technique to reject this H_o, he will have scientifically established that there is a significant difference between the performance of his various portfolio men. Naturally, the alternative hypothesis (H_a) is that the means are not equal.

Moving somewhat more deeply into the mathematical aspects of this problem, it is possible to rephrase the preceding analysis slightly by introducing the new concept of the grand mean, which is the overall average of all of the data being considered. In this particular example, the grand mean is the average performance of all 60 accounts being managed by the various portfolio men in the department, which works out to be 11.1. The null hypothesis states that each portfolio manager's average performance will be equal to the performance of every other manager. This may quite easily be rephrased by saying that the average performance of each particular portfolio manager will be the same as the grand mean. This is the same as stating that the null hypothesis asserts that the performance of any one particular manager will be about the same as the average performance for the department as a whole. If this can be rejected, then it would be possible to say that at least one manager significantly outper-formed the department. The problem is that one or more men may out-perform the grand mean (or department results) simply because of the workings of chance. It is quite possible that one or two of the portfolio men happened to have a good performance simply because they were lucky.

In effect, this analysis maintains that there are three possible reasons why an account would have a given change in market value. First, any account is affected by the grand mean. This is the general performance characteristic of any account which is managed by the department. Second, each account is controlled by a specific portfolio manager, and if there is a significant difference between the abilities of the various managers, then this will have an important effect upon the performance characteristics of the account. Third, each account has investments and a diversification unique to itself, and, to some extent at least, these characteristics will subject the account to random variation. This varia-tion could not have been foreseen and cannot be attributed to either the general behavior of accounts or the capability of the particular manager in charge of the portfolio.

Putting the above analysis into mathematical notation, it is possible to call the performance of each account x_{ij}. The performance of each ac-count can be attributed to (is equal to) three causes. The first is the grand mean (μ for the actual mean, $\bar{x}$ for the estimate of the mean as calculated from the sample data), the second is the ability of the portfolio manager i (α_i for their actual performance ability, $\bar{x}_j$ for their estimated means as calculated from the sample), and the third is chance variation (e_{ij}). The resulting equation is:

$$x_{ij} = \mu + \alpha_i + e_{ij}$$

In this equation, α_i stands for the effect on the accounts' performance which stems from the ability of the ith portfolio manager. Using this nota-tion, it is possible to restate the null hypothesis that the managers have equal ability by simply stating that the effect of the particular portfolio manager handling the account is zero — that it makes no difference which manager handles the account. Mathematically, this is:

$$H_o : \alpha_1 = \alpha_2 = \alpha_3 = \alpha_4 = 0$$

ONE-WAY ANALYSIS

The problem now is to break apart the three factors which influence the performance of the portfolios so that some numerical measure of the value of α_i can be tested for statistical significance. In other words, be-fore the effects of the ability of the managers can be tested to see if they deviate significantly from zero, some technique must be used to determine the size of the effect. The analysis of variance is a statistical model which permits the department head to "decompose" the sample data which he has collected for each manager into the three underlying components of overall mean, effect of the managers, and chance variation.

The technique by which the various effects are separated from the mass of data at hand is quite subtle. First, the overall variation in the data set is calculated. This "total variation" is defined as the variance of all of the data from the grand mean. This is found by the formula:

$$\Sigma\Sigma(x_{ij} - \bar{x})^2$$

This quantity is called the total sum of the squares, or *SST* for short. In effect, the variation of each account from the grand mean is computed and squared, and then these deviations are totaled.

The grand mean $\bar{x}$ naturally provides an estimate for the performance characteristics of accounts in general, but an additional measure is necessary if the effect of the portfolio managers is to be found. For this purpose, the total variation in each manager's accounts is calculated separately for each manager. The variation within the managers' accounts is found by calculating the amount by which each of manager 1's accounts deviated from his average performance, then calculating the amount by which manager 2's accounts deviated from *his* average performance, etc. The deviations within each manager's accounts are squared and totaled, producing a variance for each of the managers as a statistical measure of the variability of the performance of each manager's accounts. These four variances are then added together, and the total is called the sum of the squares error (*SSE* for short).

Next, it is important to have a measure of the extent to which the performance of the various managers differed from each other. Since the average performance of each manager will be at least slightly different from the results of the other managers, it is natural that the model would require some quantitative measure of the extent to which the managers' performance diverged from the performance of the department as a whole. This is measured by the deviation of each manager's average performance from the grand mean. These deviations are then squared and added together, producing a single variance which is called the between samples sum of squares (*SSB* for short).

SSB, then, is a statistical measure of the amount by which the average results of the various portfolio managers deviated from the overall results of investment accounts in general. Now, if the performance of the portfolios did depend on the portfolio manager, then one or two of the managers would do substantially better than the grand mean while the others would do substantially worse. This naturally means that the variance of the managers (the *SSB*) would be large whenever there was a difference in performance between the managers. On the other hand, if the choice of manager did not matter, each manager's average performance would not differ substantially from the grand mean. All of the managers would do about equally well because each would have equal ability and there would be no reason for their performance to deviate from the department's result. In this case, the SSB (the variance of their performance from the grand mean) would be small.

The net result of this analysis is that the department head is interested in whether 11.5, 12.0, 10.7, and 10.3 vary *significantly* from the grand mean of 11.1 — he wants to know whether SSB is significantly large. The problem is that it is important to determine how much of the variation measured by SSB might normally be expected on the basis of chance. But the analysis of variance technique has already provided a measure of chance variance in the calculation of SSE. After all, this is simply the total of the variances of the accounts handled by each portfolio manager.

Using SSE as a measure of the completely random variation in the performance of the accounts, the significance of the portfolio managers (measured by SSB) can easily be calculated. This is done by relating SSB to SSE, which is in effect the relationship between the impact of the managers and the random "impact" which might be expected on the basis of chance alone. SSB and SSE are total values, however, and because of this fact, they cannot be directly compared. The SSB is a total for all four managers, while the SSE is a total for all observations. It is reasonable to put each measure on an "average" basis, dividing SSB by the number of managers and SSE by the number of observations. Due to rather complicated matters related to the degrees-of-freedom problem that was discussed in the chapter on hypothesis testing, however, SSB is divided by $k - 1$ (the number of managers minus one) and SSE is divided by the number of observations minus the number of managers.

As a result of this "averaging," SSB is converted into MSB (the mean square between samples). The SSE is converted into the MSE (mean square error). Since the data after this conversion are on a comparable basis, it is possible to relate the manager's impact to chance results. This is done by simply dividing MSB by MSE, and the result is an F statistic.

In other words, if the department head wishes to determine whether the difference in the performance of the managers is significant, he must express the actual difference in their results as a ratio or "percentage" of the amount by which he would expect the portfolio managers' results to vary simply on the basis of chance. This ratio of actual difference to expected difference is the F statistic. A value for F of "1.0" would mean that the difference in the results of the managers was exactly what he might have expected from chance variations in the data. A value for F of "5.0" would mean that the difference between the managers was five times what would be expected from chance, indicating that the difference may well be real. The analysis of variance is useful because it allows the total variation (SST) in the data to be broken into the effect stemming from the managers (SSB) and the results of chance (SSE). Mathematically,

$$SST = SSB + SSE$$

Verbally,

| The total difference in the performance of the accounts in the department | = | The difference in the ability of the managers | + | The difference in the impact of chance upon the accounts |

In addition to providing this valuable breakdown, the model provides the F statistic so that the significance of the managers (of the MSB) can be tested. In order to use the F statistic which is provided, it must be compared to the F table. If the computed F is greater than the table F, then the difference in the performance of the managers is real. In other words, the null hypothesis that $\alpha_1 = \alpha_2 = \alpha_3 = \alpha_4 = 0$ is rejected. In order to find the proper table value for F, the degrees of freedom in the numerator equals $k - 1$ (the number of managers -1). In the denominator the d.f. equal $n - k$, where k equal the number of managers $= 4$, and $n =$ the total number of observations in the data $= 60$.

CALCULATION OF ONE-WAY ANALYSIS

In order to provide some practice in the technique, it is a simple matter to use the theory developed to this point to work through the example which has been considered.

The actual calculation of SST, SSB, and SSE in any particular problem can be most easily accomplished through the use of the following three formulas:

$$SST = \Sigma\Sigma x_{ij}^2 - N\bar{\bar{x}}^2$$
$$SSB = \Sigma n_j \bar{x}_j^2 - N\bar{x}^2$$
$$SSE = \Sigma\Sigma x_{ij}^2 - \Sigma n_j x_j^2$$

where:

$x_{ij}^2 =$ the square of the ith observation in the jth column. In the example, the ith account of manager j.
$\bar{\bar{x}}^2 =$ the square of the grand mean.
$n_j =$ the number of observations in the jth column.
$\bar{x}_j^2 =$ the square of the average of the observations in column j. In the example, the average performance of the jth manager.
$N =$ the total number of observations in the study.

By simply computing the desired quantities and inserting their numerical value into the equations, the SST, SSB, and SSE can easily be found.

Actually, only three quantities are necessary for the solution: $\Sigma\Sigma x_{ij}^2$, $N\bar{\bar{x}}^2$ and $\Sigma n_j\bar{x}_j^2$.

Actually performing the calculations for the example, we execute the following steps:

1. Calculate the grand mean $\bar{\bar{x}}$.
   Result: 11.1.
2. Calculate $N\bar{\bar{x}}^2$.
   Result: $60 \cdot 11.1 \cdot 11.1 = 7{,}392.60$.
3. Square all of the observations and then total them. $(\Sigma\Sigma x_{ij}^2)$
   Result: 8,125.
4. Multiply each column average squared by the number of observations in the column. $(\Sigma n_j x_j^2)$
   Result:
   $$15 \cdot 11.5^2 = 1{,}983.75$$
   $$15 \cdot 20.0^2 = 2{,}160.00$$
   $$15 \cdot 10.7^2 = 1{,}717.35$$
   $$15 \cdot 10.3^2 = \underline{1{,}591.35}$$
   $$\text{Total} = 7{,}452.45$$
5. Insert the values into the formulas.
   Result:
   $$SST = \Sigma\Sigma x_{ij}^2 - N\bar{\bar{x}}^2$$
   $$= 8{,}125 - 7{,}392.60 = 732.40$$
   $$SSB = \Sigma n_j\bar{x}_j - N\bar{\bar{x}}^2$$
   $$= 7{,}452.45 - 7{,}392.60 = 59.85$$
   $$SSE = \Sigma\Sigma x_{ij}^2 - \Sigma n_j\bar{x}_j^2$$
   $$= 8{,}125 - 7{,}452.45 = 672.55$$
6. At this point, it is possible to check the calculations by using the fact that $SST = SSB + SSE$. This will be true of the computed numbers if no calculation error has been made.
   Result:
   $$SST = SSB + SSE$$
   $$732.40 = 59.85 + 672.55$$
   $$732.40 = 732.40$$

It is now possible to see in concrete terms that the total variation in the data (the SST) has been broken into two distinct components. The first of these, $SSB = 59.85$, is the variation in account performance which can be attributed to the managers. The second, $SSE = 672.55$, is the variation due to particular characteristics of the accounts chosen, in other words, random variation. Using these values, MSB and MSE can be calculated as:

$$MSB = 59.85 \div 3 = 19.95$$
$$MSE = 672.55 \div (60 - 4) = 12.01$$

The next step is to compute F according to the following formula:

$$F = \frac{MSB}{MSE}$$

which in this case is:

$$F = \frac{19.95}{12.01} = 1.6611$$

Once again, the F ratio can be given intuitive meaning by considering the denominator (12.01) to be an estimate of the variation between the performance of the portfolio managers which might be *expected* given the basic variability of the nature of account performance. The numerator (19.95), on the other hand, is a measure of the *actual* variation in the managers' performance. The F ratio, then, is the ratio of actual to expected differences between managers. It exceeds 1.00 in this particular case because more variation is present than would be expected, but the problem is whether the amount by which it exceeds 1.00 is sufficient to provide the department head with the required level of confidence to justify policy decisions. To resolve this problem, intuitive interpretations must give way to more precise probabilities.

The probabilities of any given F have already been computed and placed in tables, a fact already mentioned in the chapter on hypothesis testing. These tables can be used to test the hypothesis that the managers have equal performance by looking up the table value for F in, say, the .05 risk level table. The degrees of freedom of the numerator equals $k - 1$ (3 in the example) and in the denominator equals $N - k$ (56 in the example). In the example, the table value of $F_{3,60}$ is the closest available value and equals 2.18. This is slightly less than $F_{3,56}$ would be, but the difference is quite small, as can be seen by noting that $F_{3,40}$ is 2.23. The department head can now see that the computed F of 1.66 is definitely not large enough to justify the assumption that it is due to anything other than chance. The managers must still be assumed to be equal in performance capability.

TWO-WAY ANALYSIS

The preceding example showed an application of one-way analysis of variance. This stems from the fact that the effect of only one variable (the portfolio manager) was being studied. Suppose that instead of taking this basic approach, the department head requested that his data be classified both by portfolio manager and also by the type of account. This would be an example of two-way analysis of variance. Assume that the accounts are classed as type P, M, or I, where:

$P =$ performance account.
$M =$ moderate, very safe appreciation account.
$I =$ income oriented account.

The department head has 15 accounts from each portfolio manager selected for each type of account and has the average appreciation calculated for each set of portfolios. The data are then presented to him as shown in Table 10–2.

TABLE 10–2

	Manager			
	1	2	3	4
Type of Account	(1)	(2)	(3)	(4)
P..........................	14%	16%	10%	18%
M..........................	8	6	10	8
I..........................	5	6	7	4

This table can be analyzed using analysis of variance techniques, but now the impact of two variables upon the performance of the accounts must be measured, that is, portfolio manager and type of account. This means that the total variability of the data needs to be broken into separate components which will measure the impact of each of the two variables and the amount of chance variation. Letting A stand for the first variable and B stand for the second, we have:

$$SST = SSA + SSB + SSE$$

The technique measures the actual deviation from the grand mean, which occurs in the different account types and also measures the actual deviation which occurs between portfolio managers. By developing the SSE, it provides a measure of the expected amount of deviation. From this information, it is able to develop an F statistic for the first variable (called F_A) as the ratio between the actual deviation between account types and the expected deviation. In similar fashion, it can develop F_B from the actual deviation between portfolio managers divided by the expected deviation. Each of these F's can then be compared to the appropriate table value of F in order to determine whether the difference between account types, portfolio managers, or both is significant.

MEASURING INTERACTION

The two techniques discussed up to this point allowed the department head to evaluate his account types and his portfolio managers, but assumed that there was no relationship between the two, that is, the models assume that the performance of any particular *type* of account will be about the same regardless of which manager handles the portfolios. If this assumption did not in fact represent the true situation, then the one-way and two-way models would produce invalid results. In order to represent the real world more accurately, it is often necessary to use a model which measures the *interaction* of the two variables being studied. In the last example, it is quite possible that one manager may be quite good on the *P* type of accounts but not on others, while another manager has a special capability in handling type *I*.

The idea of interaction is of special interest to the financial analyst, for it indicates the presence of a relationship between the two sets of categories. This relationship may prove valuable in developing theories of company earnings patterns, stock market behavior, and the like. The advantage of using interaction is that it is capable of measuring relationships between *categories,* while correlation can only measure relations between *variables.* In the case of the department head in our example, interactions are interesting for two reasons. First, if they are present, they may have invalidated his earlier one-way and two-way studies, as already described. Second and more important, however, is the fact that if interactions are definitely present, he can specialize his portfolio men by account type and so improve the department's performance. Primarily for this latter reason, he decides to expand his model to include the effect of interaction (*SSI*). Therefore:

$$SST = SSA + SSB + SSI + SSE$$

The same data can be used in this model, but multiple observations (called replications) are required and so the model explicitly uses each account included in the sample. The mathematical development is too complicated to be included here, but the output of the model will be an F_A measuring the effect of the portfolio type, an F_B measuring managers, and an F_I measuring the interaction of account type and manager. A significantly high F for *SSI* would cause the department head to specialize his managers, with a corresponding increase in performance. If *SSI* explained virtually all of the variance and *SSA* and *SSB* had almost no significance, such a specialization could make it irrelevant that an account was, say, type *B,* or that it was assigned to manager three; what *would* be important is that *if* it is type *P, then* it is handled by manager three.

LIMITATIONS AND CONCLUSIONS

Much more complicated models than those presented here are available under the general heading of analysis of variance. The techniques, unfortunately, become increasingly complex. One characteristic common to all of the material considered up to this point, however, is that the techniques are parametric. They assume that the data have normal distribution either because the population which the data represent follows the bell-shaped normal curve or because the observations constitute the means of random samples (the means of random samples are known to be normal if the sample size is sufficiently large). It is important to point out that the techniques formally test whether or not the subgroups are drawn from the same population. This means that F will be significant if it is found that the subgroups differ either in means *or in variance.*

The analysis-of-variance techniques appear to be very sensitive to nonnormality in the data and may give incorrect results if this assumption is violated. If an analyst has reason to suspect that the data are not normal, he does, however, have recourse to several nonparametric analysis-of-variance techniques. One of the best known of these is the Kruskal-Wallis one-way analysis of variance which, as the name implies, considers only problems that have one classification (portfolio managers, for example). Using this approach, only the ranking of the data is needed. All of the observations in the study are ranked from smallest to largest. The analysis then proceeds according to roughly the same line of attack (but with different calculations at certain critical points) that was used in the standard one-way model. The resulting statistic is not an F but rather a χ^2 which can be tested for significance using the table.

In summary, the analysis of variance has been shown to be a set of models which enable the analyst to determine the statistical significance of the differences in the average profit margins of three industries. It can indicate whether the P/E's of six different companies in the same industry are significantly different, although it may be necessary first to transform the data so as to produce a normal distribution. Similar applications are quite easy to locate. In addition, the two-way model permits data which are classified according to two different categories to be evaluated. If stocks are either low, moderate, or high P/E and also have either low, moderate, or high earnings growth, is there a significant difference in the price performance of these stocks as a result of the P/E? As a result of their earnings growth? Using the model which allows for interaction, the question might be: Is the performance of the stocks due to certain *combinations* of P/E and growth? Although the statistical computations may become complex, they can easily be handled by a competent statistician or a computer program. The emphasis in this chapter has not been on the technical execution of one technique, but on how the elementary models of analysis of variance can be applied.

ADDITIONAL READINGS IN ANALYSIS OF VARIANCE

An extensive literature has grown up around the subject of analysis of variance because of its enormous value in the construction and interpretation of scientific experiments. Elementary aspects of the subject are usually included in introductory statistics courses, and advanced features can be as complex as any subject in mathematical statistics. Because of this breadth of difficulty, it is important to select further readings on the basis of a specific purpose, such as a need for additional knowledge on the method of conducting valid investigations, the precise arithmetic steps necessary for a two-way analysis which must be performed, and so forth.

FREUND, JOHN E. *Mathematical Statistics.* Englewood Cliffs, New Jersey: Prentice-Hall Inc., 1962.

This book has one chapter (Chapter 14) on the analysis of variance which is much less difficult than the name of the text might imply. The book as a whole (350 pages) is difficult but has sections which move into mathematical foundations unnecessary for everyday applications. Chapter 14, however, can be read independently of the other material and contains a very clear explanation of the one-way, two-way, and interaction models which provides insight into why each technique works. The chapter requires only a knowledge of Σ notation and subscripts.

BALSLEY, HOWARD L. *Quantitative Research Methods for Business and Economics.* New York: Random House, 1970.

This work discusses the techniques of disciplined research and elementary aspects of a number of models (292 pages). Chapter 1 (32 pages) and Chapter 3 (28 pages) are useful introductions to the concepts of scientific analysis. The analysis of variance section of Chapter 4 (20 pages) shows the calculations necessary for the elementary models by actually printing every calculation required in the example applications.

COCHRAN, WILLIAM B. AND COX, GERTRUDE M. *Experimental Designs.* 2d ed. New York: John Wiley & Sons, 1957.

This work considers the problem of analysis of variance models from an advanced standpoint. The material is well presented but intrinsically difficult because more complicated problems are considered. The text is well worth the effort required if the reader has reason to need an understanding of the deeper aspects of these models.

Chapter

11 Matrix Algebra or

the Mass Manipulation of Data

A matrix is a rectangular array of data. When so arranged, matrices can be added, subtracted, and multiplied by other matrices and a process similar to division called inversion is also possible. The power of handling large quantities of data gives matrices wide application, particularly since simple statements to a computer can result in the mass manipulation of data.

INTRODUCTION

Matrices are a difficult concept to introduce because they are useful in such a diverse set of applications. Presenting only a few of their uses in a brief chapter must give the reader an extremely inadequate picture of their broad field of application. Matrices can be used to summarize data, to express weighted totals, to indicate sets of calculations to be performed on data, and for a number of other applications. They are heavily used in the theory of regression and econometrics, linear programming and multivariate statistics, as well as such diverse areas as engineering, chemistry, and physics. In short, a basic understanding of matrix algebra is a prerequisite for any analyst who ever wishes to undertake serious reading in any of the more sophisticated mathematical models.

The preceding list of the applications of matrices makes the concept of a matrix sound extremely complicated. Actually, this could not be further from the truth, for a matrix is defined as simply being a rectangular array of numbers. In effect, any of the tables used daily by a security analyst could be called a matrix. In the section covering notation, one

TABLE 11–1
Average Annual P/E

Name	1967	1966	1965	1964	1963
Gulf	12.6	11.3	13.5	14.4	12.4
Royal Dutch	10.2	9.3	11.2	12.8	10.6
Standard (California)	11.7	12.9	14.3	14.2	14.1
Standard (New Jersey)	12.1	14.2	17.3	17.2	14.3
Texaco	13.7	13.8	17.1	18.4	15.6

such table was presented as an example of the use of double subscripts. It is reprinted here for convenience as Table 11–1. This table, or matrix, deals with the annual average P/E of a group of international oil stocks. A similar matrix covering oils could be built which would indicate the total market value of each of these stocks in one particular account for each of five years. See Table 11–2.

TABLE 11–2
Account A
(in thousands of dollars)

Name	1967	1966	1965	1964	1963
Gulf	1	1	1	1	1
Royal Dutch	2	2	1	1	1
Standard (California)	3	3	4	3	3
Standard (New Jersey)	5	4	3	2	1
Texaco	4	4	3	3	3

This table provides information which may prove valuable to either the analyst or the portfolio manager, but a similar matrix could just as easily deal with cost, dividends, number of shares, and the like. Continuing with the example as it stands, however, it is logical to consider the same matrix for another account, say account B as shown in Table 11–3.

TABLE 11–3
Account B
(in thousands of dollars)

Name	1967	1966	1965	1964	1963
Gulf	2	2	3	2	1
Royal Dutch	5	5	4	4	4
Standard (California)	6	5	5	3	2
Standard (New Jersey)	8	7	7	6	7
Texaco	4	5	5	6	6

MATRIX ADDITION AND SUBTRACTION

By using matrix algebra, it is possible to find the total market value of all accounts for the oils in each year. The two matrices A and B can simply be added and the result is the matrix T which shows the total. If A and B are the only accounts:

$$T = A + B$$

which merely means add the corresponding elements of $A + B$ and store the total in the proper element of T. The calculation, including the "T" or total matrix would be:

Name	Account A					Account B					Total				
	1967	66	65	64	63	67	66	65	64	63	67	66	65	64	63
Gulf......................	1	1	1	1	1	2	2	3	2	1	3	3	4	3	2
Royal Dutch..........	2	2	1	1	1	5	5	4	4	4	7	7	5	5	5
Standard (Cal.).......	3	3	4	3	3	6	5	5	3	2	9	8	9	6	5
Standard (N.J.).......	5	4	3	2	1	8	7	7	6	7	13	11	10	8	8
Texaco	4	4	3	3	3	4	5	5	6	6	8	9	8	9	9

From the purely mathematical standpoint of the matrix manipulations involved:

$$
\begin{matrix} A \end{matrix} \quad + \quad \begin{matrix} B \end{matrix} \quad = \quad \begin{matrix} T \end{matrix}
$$

$$
\begin{pmatrix} 1 & 1 & 1 & 1 & 1 \\ 2 & 2 & 1 & 1 & 1 \\ 3 & 3 & 4 & 3 & 3 \\ 5 & 4 & 3 & 2 & 1 \\ 4 & 4 & 3 & 3 & 3 \end{pmatrix} + \begin{pmatrix} 2 & 2 & 3 & 2 & 1 \\ 5 & 5 & 4 & 4 & 4 \\ 6 & 5 & 5 & 3 & 2 \\ 8 & 7 & 7 & 6 & 7 \\ 4 & 5 & 5 & 6 & 6 \end{pmatrix} = \begin{pmatrix} 3 & 3 & 4 & 3 & 2 \\ 7 & 7 & 5 & 5 & 5 \\ 9 & 8 & 9 & 6 & 5 \\ 13 & 11 & 10 & 8 & 8 \\ 8 & 9 & 8 & 9 & 9 \end{pmatrix}
$$

This matrix addition permits a large number of calculations to be indicated by a very simple equation. Matrix subtraction accomplishes exactly the same thing, merely being the reverse of addition. To find the value of account A given T and account B, merely write:

$$A = T - B$$

This removes the value of B's holdings from the value of the total holdings T, leaving the value of A, which is known to be the holdings in account A. The equation indicates that the subtraction is to be performed for each and every element, leaving (after all operations have been performed) the matrix A. To portray the actual matrices:

$$
\begin{array}{ccc}
T & - & B & = & A
\end{array}
$$

$$
\begin{pmatrix}
3 & 3 & 4 & 3 & 2 \\
7 & 7 & 5 & 5 & 5 \\
9 & 8 & 9 & 6 & 5 \\
13 & 11 & 10 & 8 & 8 \\
8 & 9 & 8 & 9 & 9
\end{pmatrix}
-
\begin{pmatrix}
2 & 2 & 3 & 2 & 1 \\
5 & 5 & 4 & 4 & 4 \\
6 & 5 & 5 & 3 & 2 \\
8 & 7 & 7 & 6 & 7 \\
4 & 5 & 5 & 6 & 6
\end{pmatrix}
=
\begin{pmatrix}
1 & 1 & 1 & 1 & 1 \\
2 & 2 & 1 & 1 & 1 \\
3 & 3 & 4 & 3 & 3 \\
5 & 4 & 3 & 2 & 1 \\
4 & 4 & 3 & 3 & 3
\end{pmatrix}
$$

Start with the total matrix T	$-$	All of the hold- ings in account B	$=$	All of the remaining holdings, which must be account A.

Many more advanced matrix manipulations have been defined by mathematicians and all are as useful as the simple addition and subtraction operations already shown. Matrix algebra handles masses of numbers as easily as elementary algebra handles single numbers. As a result, it is the natural mathematical technique of business and actually has been used for years without benefit of formal mathematical definition. The importance of the theory has grown, however, since the use of computers has become common because the computer is uniquely adapted to the control and manipulation of subscripted tables, i.e., matrices.

MATRIX MULTIPLICATION

Introduction

Matrix multiplication is actually one of the most common mathematical operations performed by anyone involved in investments. The technique produces what is mathematically called a linear combination or what is popularly termed a "weighted total." For example, suppose a portfolio manager has the analyst's projected growth rates and wishes to find the expected growth of a portfolio which he analyzes. He might write on an analysis pad the following figures:

	Growth Rate		% of Portfolio		
Stock A	5%	×	50%	=	2.50%
Stock B	10%	×	25%	=	2.50%
Stock C	15%	×	25%	=	3.75%
					8.75%

8.75% = expected growth rate of the portfolio.

The figure 8.75% is a weighted total and is therefore a linear combination. Another example is the calculation of the total market value of an account:

	Shares Held		*Price*		
Stock A	400	×	10	=	$ 4,000
Stock B	300	×	15	=	4,500
Stock C	350	×	20	=	7,000
					$15,500

The Nature of the Calculation

Obviously, security analysts and portfolio managers have been using linear combinations for quite some time. At this point, it is possible to introduce matrix multiplication as a simplified notation for what is already being done daily. Using the numbers in the first example:

$$(5, 10, 15) \begin{pmatrix} .50 \\ .25 \\ .25 \end{pmatrix} = (5 \times .50) + (10 \times .25) + (15 \times .25) = 8.75\%$$

Whenever a set of numbers is to be multiplied by a set of numbers, as is the case above, we *define* the result to be the sum of the products, a linear combination, because it is convenient to our purposes. Note that the first number in the row is multiplied by the first number in the column, the second by the second, etc. Also note that the result is the same as in traditional notation, but that the description is simpler. In fact, if we call the analyst's growth estimates E and the diversification of the portfolio D, the entire calculation can be defined by writing:

$$ED = \text{expected growth}$$

Expressing the earlier example of the total market value of an account in matrix notation, we have:

$$(400, 300, 350) \begin{pmatrix} 10 \\ 15 \\ 20 \end{pmatrix} = 15,500$$

Note that the multiplications move in the direction of the arrows — across the rows and down the columns. This sequence produces $(400 \times 10) + (300 \times 15) + (350 \times 20)$, which equals 15,500. This completely defines the mathematical computations to be performed, and therefore defines the solution implicitly.

The real value of matrix notation, however, occurs when larger matrices are used. Carrying the ideas which have already been developed just a little further, it is possible to "mass" linear combinations by using matrix notation. For example:

$$(400, 300, 350) \begin{pmatrix} \overset{Price}{10} & \overset{EPS}{1.10} & \overset{Div'd}{.60} \\ 15 & 1.15 & .55 \\ 20 & 1.20 & .40 \end{pmatrix} = (x, y, z)$$

The matrix of answers (x, y, z) is simply a listing of three numbers in order. Because matrix multiplication is being performed, x, y, and z must be linear combinations. x is found by using the first column of the "blocked" matrix and ignoring the rest of the columns. This gives us:

$$(400, 300, 350) \begin{pmatrix} 10 \\ 15 \\ 20 \end{pmatrix} = x = 15{,}500 = \text{the sum of price times shares, or total market value.}$$

Because y is the second number in the solution, it uses only the second column:

$$(400, 300, 350) \begin{pmatrix} 1.10 \\ 1.15 \\ 1.20 \end{pmatrix} = y = 1{,}205 = \text{total dollar earnings.}$$

And obviously,

$$(400, 300, 350) \begin{pmatrix} .60 \\ .55 \\ .40 \end{pmatrix} = z = 545 = \text{total dollar dividends.}$$

The entire set of calculations can be specified in one matrix equation by agreeing to call the first matrix A, the second D, and the resulting matrix S. This produces:

$$AD = S$$

This can be shown by actually writing the numerical value of each matrix as:

$$(400, 300, 350) \begin{pmatrix} 10 & 1.10 & .60 \\ 15 & 1.15 & .55 \\ 20 & 1.20 & .40 \end{pmatrix} = (15500, 1205, 545)$$

In normal mathematical jargon, a matrix which is only a single row or a single column of numbers is usually called a *vector*, while a "block" of numbers (two or more vectors) is called a *matrix*. Hence:

$$(400, \quad 300, \quad 350)$$

is a vector; and

$$\begin{pmatrix} 10 & 1.10 & .60 \\ 15 & 1.15 & .55 \\ 20 & 1.20 & .40 \end{pmatrix}$$

is a matrix, in which each number in a column is a similar piece of data, but in which no relationship between columns is necessary.

It is useful to press matrix multiplication one step further and examine the multiplication of two full-scale matrices. The matrix which has already been developed will still be called D (for data). Now examine the (400, 300, 350) vector. This represents the number of shares in each of the three stocks which are held in one account. But what if a portfolio manager has six accounts?

| | Account Matrix A | | |
Account	Stock 1	Stock 2	Stock 3
1	400	300	350
2	500	400	400
3	800	700	500
4	700	700	400
5	600	600	500
6	900	800	700

It is possible to define the total market value, total dollar earnings, and total dollar dividends for all six accounts by simply writing:

$$AD = S$$

where S = the matrix of answers. In fact, only one fairly simple statement in a computer program would be required to perform the calculation. The solution would regard the first row of the A matrix as demanding a calculation:

$$(400, 300, 350) \begin{pmatrix} 10 & 1.10 & .60 \\ 15 & 1.15 & .55 \\ 20 & 1.20 & .40 \end{pmatrix} = (s_{11}, s_{12}, s_{13})$$

Where the subscripts of s simply refer to the location of the particular number in the final solution matrix S. s_{13} is the answer stored in row 1 and column 3 of S. This is exactly the same as before, but since there is now a second row, the following calculation is also demanded:

$$(500, 400, 400) \begin{pmatrix} 10 & 1.10 & .60 \\ 15 & 1.15 & .55 \\ 20 & 1.20 & .40 \end{pmatrix} = (s_{21}, s_{22}, s_{23})$$

This answer for the second account is stored in the second row of the solution matrix. The process is repeated for the third row, the fourth row, and so on. The final solution is a matrix having six rows (one for each account) and three columns (one for each desired characteristic of an account).

If all of these results are "blocked" into one array, the result would have the following form:

$$\begin{pmatrix} 400 & 300 & 350 \\ 500 & 400 & 400 \\ 800 & 700 & 500 \\ 700 & 700 & 400 \\ 600 & 600 & 500 \\ 900 & 800 & 700 \end{pmatrix} \begin{pmatrix} 10 & 1.10 & 0.60 \\ 15 & 1.15 & 0.55 \\ 20 & 1.20 & 0.40 \end{pmatrix} = \begin{pmatrix} s_{11} & s_{12} & s_{13} \\ s_{21} & s_{22} & s_{23} \\ s_{31} & s_{32} & s_{33} \\ s_{41} & s_{42} & s_{43} \\ s_{51} & s_{52} & s_{53} \\ s_{61} & s_{62} & s_{63} \end{pmatrix}$$

Actually performing the indicated calculations:

$$\begin{pmatrix} 400 & 300 & 350 \\ 500 & 400 & 400 \\ 800 & 700 & 500 \\ 700 & 700 & 400 \\ 600 & 600 & 500 \\ 900 & 800 & 700 \end{pmatrix} \begin{pmatrix} 10 & 1.10 & 0.60 \\ 15 & 1.15 & 0.55 \\ 20 & 1.20 & 0.40 \end{pmatrix} = \begin{pmatrix} 15,500 & 1,205 & 545 \\ 19,000 & 1,230 & 680 \\ 28,500 & 2,285 & 1,065 \\ 25,500 & 2,055 & 965 \\ 25,000 & 1,950 & 890 \\ 35,000 & 2,750 & 1,260 \end{pmatrix}$$

The meaning of the solution matrix S can be seen more easily if the column and row headings are inserted. Recall that S was computed one row at a time and that for each row a total market value, a total earnings, and a total dividend were calculated and stored in columns one, two, and three, respectively. The results in the first row related to the first account. When the calculations for the second row were performed, they used the number of shares in the second account, and so on through row six. The column and row headings are therefore:

Matrix S

	Total Value	Total Earnings per Share	Total Dividends
Account 1	15,500	1,205	545
Account 2	19,000	1,230	680
Account 3	28,500	2,285	1,065
Account 4	25,500	2,055	965
Account 5	25,000	1,950	890
Account 6	35,000	2,750	1,260

Row and Column Dimensions

Although it is relatively simple to restate a problem in matrix terms, it is very difficult to develop an intuitive feel for the particular operations that are taking place. In order to improve insight in this area, consider the problem of how the dimensions or categories involved in the matrices are affected by the preceding calculation.

Solution Matrix

	Matrix A Stock (shares held)				Matrix D		
	#1	#2	#3		Value	Earnings	Div'd
Account 1	400	300	350	Stock #1	10	1.10	0.60
Account 2	500	400	400	Stock #2	15	1.15	0.55
Account 3	800	700	500	Stock #3	20	1.20	0.40
Account 4	700	700	400				
Account 5	600	600	500				
Account 6	900	800	700				

=

	Matrix S		
	Total Value	Total Earnings	Total Div'd
Account 1	15500	1205	545
Account 2	19000	1230	680
Account 3	28500	2285	1065
Account 4	25500	2055	965
Account 5	25000	1950	890
Account 6	35000	2750	1260

The solution matrix can be seen to have the same row meanings (particular accounts) as the first matrix involved in the multiplication. On the other hand, it has the same column meanings (value, earnings, and dividends) as the second matrix. This will always be the case in any matrix manipulation and explains why the solution matrix will always have the same number of rows as the first matrix and the same number of columns as the second. Also, notice that matrix A has the same column dimensions as the row dimensions in matrix D. This explains why the first matrix in the matrix multiplication must have the same number of columns as the number of rows in the second matrix. It also shows why AD need equal DA.

The next problem quite naturally concerns the meaning of the s_{ij}, the elements in the solution matrix. In order to deal with this question, it is important to first check on what happened to the "stock" category which was present in both of the original matrices. Each of the matrices in the product AD had three stocks, but the solution matrix S did not. This is always the case in matrix multiplications; the "column category" of the first matrix which is also the "row category" of the second matrix disappears in the solution matrix because all of the numbers referring to it are added into a single number (a weighted total). In the example, every number (s_{ij}) in the solution is a weighted total of all of the stocks involved in the calculation. Since every s_{ij} is a linear combination of stocks, all of the data concerning individual stocks are destroyed. It has been built into one or another of the various totals and therefore disappears as a separate category. For example, the first indicated calculation in the problem produces $s_{1,1}$:

$$
\begin{array}{c}
\textit{Stock} \\
\begin{array}{ccc} 1 & 2 & 3 \end{array} \\
\text{Account 1} \quad (400, \ 300, \ 350)
\end{array}
\qquad
\begin{array}{c}
\textit{Price} \\
\textit{(or value)} \\[4pt]
\text{Stock } \begin{array}{c} 1 \\ 2 \\ 3 \end{array}
\begin{pmatrix} 10 \\ 15 \\ 20 \end{pmatrix} = s_{1,1} = 15{,}500 = \begin{array}{l}\text{price (or} \\ \text{value) of} \\ \text{Account 1.}\end{array}
\end{array}
$$

From what has been said about dimensions, $s_{1,1}$ can be seen to be the "price" of "Account 1." This does not include data on stocks because the data were used to calculate the value of the account.

The applications of even the basic technique of matrix multiplication to problems in the investment industry are almost unlimited. Using matrices, extremely elaborate computational schemes can be defined in a single statement and then performed by a statistical assistant or by the computer. One very important application of matrix multiplication is the "operator matrix."

Operator Matrices

Matrix multiplication, then, can be used to produce a large number of linear combinations in a single operation. In fact, in the example just presented it is entirely possible to regard the matrix A in the equation:

$$S = AD$$

as an "operator" which changes the data related to particular stocks into data related to particular accounts. It "maps" the data *from* stocks *to* accounts. Alternatively, the matrix D can be regarded as an operator on the data in matrix A. This concept of a matrix as an operator can be illustrated more clearly in the following example.

Assume that an analyst has data on a number of accounts indicating for each account the annual capital appreciation plus dividends received. He wishes to calculate the *cumulative* gain from investment in each account, i.e., the total amount of increase in the value of the account from the first year to any other year. His data appear as follows in Table 11–4.

TABLE 11–4
Annual Return in the Analyst's Accounts
(expressed in percent)

			Account		
Year	A	B	C	D	E
1	5	3	4	4	6
2	3	3	2	3	4
3	7	5	8	9	5
4	4	4	5	4	3
5	5	6	6	7	4

The analyst wishes to convert the annual gains into cumulative gains, so that (for example) the row showing year 3 will show the total gain of each account from year 1 through year 3. Since each row now shows the results for only one year, the matrix needs to be converted into a matrix of "running totals." He can specify the calculations required by defining the following "operator" matrix:

$$\begin{pmatrix} 1 & 0 & 0 & 0 & 0 \\ 1 & 1 & 0 & 0 & 0 \\ 1 & 1 & 1 & 0 & 0 \\ 1 & 1 & 1 & 1 & 0 \\ 1 & 1 & 1 & 1 & 1 \end{pmatrix}$$

This matrix will perform the desired accumulation when multiplied by the account matrix. In fact, like any operator matrix, it was especially selected precisely *because* it performs the desired operation. Calling the account matrix X and the operator matrix C, the desired result is obtained by performing the matrix multiplication CX. In order to check to see if this actually works, we can define S to be the solution, and:

$$
\begin{array}{ccc}
C & X & S \\
\begin{pmatrix} 1 & 0 & 0 & 0 & 0 \\ 1 & 1 & 0 & 0 & 0 \\ 1 & 1 & 1 & 0 & 0 \\ 1 & 1 & 1 & 1 & 0 \\ 1 & 1 & 1 & 1 & 1 \end{pmatrix}
&
\begin{pmatrix} 5 & 3 & 4 & 4 & 6 \\ 3 & 3 & 2 & 3 & 4 \\ 7 & 5 & 8 & 9 & 5 \\ 4 & 4 & 5 & 4 & 3 \\ 5 & 6 & 6 & 7 & 4 \end{pmatrix}
=
\begin{pmatrix} 5 & 3 & 4 & 4 & 6 \\ 8 & 6 & 6 & 7 & 10 \\ 15 & 11 & 14 & 16 & 15 \\ 19 & 15 & 19 & 20 & 18 \\ 24 & 21 & 25 & 27 & 22 \end{pmatrix}
\end{array}
$$

showing that the specified calculations do actually produce the desired running totals as columns showing the progressive enhancement of the accounts. This use of matrices as operators is often quite useful, as matrices can be constructed which will specify moving averages, the change from an earlier time period, that the data should be led or lagged some number of time periods, etc.

The most interesting single operator, however, is useful because it does nothing. For example:

$$
\begin{pmatrix} 1 & 0 & 0 & 0 & 0 \\ 0 & 1 & 0 & 0 & 0 \\ 0 & 0 & 1 & 0 & 0 \\ 0 & 0 & 0 & 1 & 0 \\ 0 & 0 & 0 & 0 & 1 \end{pmatrix}
\begin{pmatrix} 5 & 3 & 4 & 4 & 6 \\ 3 & 3 & 2 & 3 & 4 \\ 7 & 5 & 8 & 9 & 5 \\ 4 & 4 & 5 & 4 & 3 \\ 5 & 6 & 6 & 7 & 4 \end{pmatrix}
=
\begin{pmatrix} 5 & 3 & 4 & 4 & 6 \\ 3 & 3 & 2 & 3 & 4 \\ 7 & 5 & 8 & 9 & 5 \\ 4 & 4 & 5 & 4 & 3 \\ 5 & 6 & 6 & 7 & 4 \end{pmatrix}
$$

A matrix with ones in the diagonal from top left to bottom right and zeros everywhere else can be seen to have no effect on the data. Because of this unique feature, it is given a special name, the "identity" matrix, and the special symbol "I." The most interesting point about I is its relationship to the number 1. In normal (or "scalar") algebra, $(1)(x) = x$. This means that "1" times any number leaves that number unchanged. Since this is precisely the same relation that I has to matrices, we can conclude that I is to matrix algebra what 1 is to everyday algebra.

DIVISION AND MATRICES

Introduction

The discussion of I in the preceding section would be purely academic if I wasn't vital in matrix division. Actually, matrix division *per se* is not permitted, but something very similar can be done which has roughly the same effect. A statement such as:

$$AX = C$$
$$X = C \div A$$

is not permitted in matrix algebra for the simple reason that it does not produce the correct answer. Fortunately, however, a study of elementary algebra will lead to the development of an approach which will work in place of division. Recall that if an equation such as:

$$5x = 10$$

is encountered, solving for x required isolating x on one side of the equation. For example,

$$5x = 10$$
$$(1/5)(5x) = (1/5)(10)$$
$$x = 2$$

In matrix algebra, $AX = C$ is an entire *system* of linear equations, and the entire system (even if it is 100 equations in 100 different unknowns) can be solved if X can be isolated on one side of the equation. But it is not legitimate to divide both sides of this equation by A, and so a similar operation must be defined which will accomplish the same thing. Returning to algebra for a moment:

$$5x = 10$$
$$(1/5)(5x) = (1/5)(10) \quad \text{This equation is equivalent to:}$$

$$(5)^{-1}(5x) = (5)^{-1}(10)$$
$$x = 2$$

Using letters instead of numbers for the same operation:

$$(a)^{-1}(ax) = (a)^{-1}(c)$$
$$(a^{-1}a)x = (a)^{-1}(c)$$
$$1x = (a)^{-1}(c)$$
$$x = c/a$$

Therefore, multiplying by a^{-1} (called "a inverse") accomplishes the same thing as dividing by a. For example, multiplying by 5^{-1} is the same as dividing by 5. Generalizing from everyday algebra to matrix algebra, we can say that if a matrix A^{-1} (called "A inverse") could be found, it would be possible to *multiply* both sides of the equation by A^{-1} and isolate X. In other words, it would be possible to solve a simultaneous system of linear equations of any size.

Mathematically, it is possible to say that if A^{-1} were known,

$$AX = C$$

could be multiplied by A^{-1}, producing:

$$A^{-1}AX = A^{-1}C$$

but $A^{-1}A$ is equal to I just as $(5^{-1})(5) = (1/5)(5) = 1$. This means that the above equation can be restated as:

$$IX = A^{-1}C$$

The I is formed from $A^{-1}A$, which was in turn formed by premultiplying both members of the equation by A^{-1}. This premultiplication explains why $A^{-1}C$ is present. It has already been shown that I times any matrix leaves that matrix unchanged. IX is comparable to the expression $1x$ in simple algebra. Just as $1x$ can be written as x, IX can be written as simply X. It is therefore possible to rewrite the above equation as:

$$X = A^{-1}C$$

Since the goal in solving a set of equations is to isolate the unknowns, this final equation which has X alone on one side of the equal sign must be the solution to the system of equations. What set of linear equations does this manipulation solve? Since no particular set of numbers for A or C has been mentioned, multiplying both sides of the matrix equation by A^{-1} will solve any system of linear equations whatever, providing the analyst can find the actual numerical value of A^{-1} in the particular problem that he is evaluating. Notice that $A^{-1}C$ represents the solution and is *not* the same as CA^{-1}.

The Nature of Inversion

Actually, a technique for finding the inverse of almost any square matrix exists and is called, understandably enough, matrix inversion. As a result of this, inverses can be used to solve a broad number of problems in which equations are involved. The technique is actually very simple, and an example of the inversion of a 3 by 3 matrix is included in the addendum to this chapter for reference (the technique applies to square matrices regardless of size).

We wish to perform the set of calculations which will produce the inverse to this matrix:

$$\begin{pmatrix} 1 & 2 & 3 \\ 2 & 4 & 5 \\ 3 & 5 & 6 \end{pmatrix}$$

In order to do this, we put this matrix (call it "A") up against the I matrix (the identity matrix). This produces the following new matrix (called $[A \mid I]$):

$$\begin{pmatrix} 1 & 2 & 3 \\ 2 & 4 & 5 \\ 3 & 5 & 6 \end{pmatrix} \begin{array}{ccc} 1 & 0 & 0 \\ 0 & 1 & 0 \\ 0 & 0 & 1 \end{array}$$

Now, the objective is to perform a set of calculations on this matrix which will change the *A* half into the identity matrix. The *I* half of the matrix will serve as an "accounting system," recording all of the calculations which were necessary to change *A* into *I*:

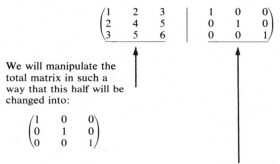

We will manipulate the total matrix in such a way that this half will be changed into:

$$\begin{pmatrix} 1 & 0 & 0 \\ 0 & 1 & 0 \\ 0 & 0 & 1 \end{pmatrix}$$

As a result of our efforts to change the first half of the matrix, this half will be "carried along." In other words, it also will be altered. The changes which take place in this half "record" the manipulations which were necessary to convert the other half into the identity matrix.

Now that the goal has been defined, the obvious question is why any-one would *want* to change *A* to *I* and record the operations used to make this change. This question can be answered by returning for a moment to ordinary algebra. In algebra, it has been shown that $a^{-1} = 1/a$ and also that $(1/a)(a) = 1$. It follows that $(a^{-1})(a) = 1$. Now the comparable matrix algebra statement would be $A^{-1}A = I$ and, in fact, this relationship has already been seen to be true. Now it is possible to carry the argument a step further by using the concept of an "operator" matrix, which has al-ready been discussed. We know that the statement

$$A^{-1}A = I$$

makes sense and is really only an extension of ordinary algebra. We also know that any matrix used in matrix multiplication can be regarded as an "operator matrix." It follows that A^{-1} can be regarded as an operator which changes *A* into *I*. Now this result is really interesting, for it says that the set of all of the operations which are required to change A into I must necessarily be the matrix A^{-1}. If A is therefore manipulated in such a way that it is changed into I, then these calculations considered as a whole must be A^{-1}. *And if these manipulations are recorded, then the record must be A^{-1}* when all calculations are completed.

Reviewing what the above paragraph means, and relating it to the matrix $[A \mid I]$, we have stated that the goal of matrix inversion is to change A into I, *while I records the changes.* We now know that the recorded changes must by definition be A^{-1}. After the manipulations have been completed, it follows that $[A \mid I]$ will have been changed into $[I \mid A^{-1}]$. Since A^{-1} is the desired result and has many useful applications, the manipulations have proven themselves to be valuable.

SYSTEMS OF EQUATIONS

In fact, the rationale for the matrix inverse provides a direct insight into the nature of systems of equations. A system of linear equations can be written as:

$$AX = B$$

The study of inversion has shown that the set of weights A^{-1} can be regarded as a single "operator" which may be applied to AX, producing $A^{-1}AX$. Since this expression equals X, the operator A^{-1} can be seen to be the set of weights which "unscrambles" the x's. Given a set of equations, each equation can be regarded as a "mix" of x's which have been "scrambled" into a total. For example, the first of the following equations shows a scrambling of x_1, x_2, and x_3 into a "mix" which totals "6":

$$1x_1 + 2x_2 + 3x_3 = 6$$
$$2x_1 + 4x_2 + 5x_3 = 11$$
$$3x_1 + 5x_2 + 6x_3 = 14$$

Using A^{-1} on the set of equations will "separate" the x values into:

$$1x_1 + 0 \quad + 0 \quad = -2$$
$$0 \quad + 1x_2 + 0 \quad = 3$$
$$0 \quad + 0 \quad + 1x_3 = -1$$

This is obviously an operation "unscrambling" mixes to locate the "pure" value of the x's.

In a system of equations, then, each of the mixes has a value b which it equals. The operator A^{-1} applied to these values B produces the values of the unmixed x's. In other words, A^{-1} applied to both sides of the equation $AX = B$ unscrambles both sides. This raises the interesting question of how the x's got scrambled in the first place. In the equation $AX = B$, A can be regarded as an operator which has *already* mixed the x's and their values. From this perspective, A^{-1} can be viewed as a specially constructed operator which "undoes" the mixing already performed by A. A cake is a mix of flour, sugar, shortening, etc. If an analyst is given the price of cakes, he knows the total of the mixes and needs to use A^{-1} to unscramble the mix and find the price of the flour, sugar, and shortening. But the baker, who started with flour, sugar, and shortening in the first place, used his recipe (A) to determine how the ingredients were to be mixed. A moves from flour to cakes; but given cakes, A^{-1} is needed to get back to the price of flour. If no one ever needed to argue from the value of mixes of quantities to the values of the quantities themselves, solutions to systems of equations would not be needed. But a high percentage of the problems of the analyst involve the evaluation of very scrambled items indeed, and the solution of equations is tailored to his needs.

APPLICATIONS OF EQUATIONS

The role of matrices in the concrete problem of finding the solution to a set of equations can only be shown by presenting a concrete example. Most business applications of this problem arise from the use of the simultaneous equation methods in econometrics, but a realistic problem in this area would be so complicated that the basic concepts would be obscured. Instead, consider the following (admittedly contrived) example which uses the matrices A and A^{-1}, which have already been discussed.

In this example, there are three products that are generally considered to be extremely poor items to manufacture—buggywhips, widgets, and left-handed wrenches. The simple manufacturing processes required for these products allow no room for innovation and, as a result, any company making any of these products will receive exactly the same profit margin. Only three companies now produce these commodities, but each of the three companies is actively engaged in the production of all three items. Each company reports its sales by product, producing the matrix shown in Table 11–5.

TABLE 11–5
Net Sales
(millions of $)

Company	Buggywhips	Widgets	Wrenches	Total
A	1	2	3	6
B	2	4	5	11
C	3	5	6	14

In their annual reports, the three companies show that their profits are $.1 million, $.3 million, and $.3 million, respectively. No company will indicate the profitability of any of its products. The problem, naturally, is to find the profit margin of all three products.

Let:

$$x_1 = \text{the profit margin on buggywhips.}$$
$$x_2 = \text{the profit margin on widgets.}$$
$$x_3 = \text{the profit margin on left-handed wrenches.}$$

Then:

For Company A: $1 million (x_1) + $2 million (x_2) + $3 million (x_3) = $.1 million profit.
For Company B: $2 million (x_1) + $4 million (x_2) + $5 million (x_3) = $.3 million profit.
For Company C: $3 million (x_1) + $5 million (x_2) + $6 million (x_3) = $.3 million profit.

This can be expressed in matrix terms as:

$$AX = B$$

Or:

$$\begin{pmatrix} 1 & 2 & 3 \\ 2 & 4 & 5 \\ 3 & 5 & 6 \end{pmatrix} \begin{pmatrix} x_1 \\ x_2 \\ x_3 \end{pmatrix} = \begin{pmatrix} .1 \\ .3 \\ .3 \end{pmatrix}$$

It is known that

$$AX = B$$

is the same as

$$A^{-1}AX = A^{-1}B \qquad \text{or} \qquad X = A^{-1}B$$

and finding the value of $A^{-1}B$ will therefore produce the solution for X. The value of A^{-1} for the matrix in this example is calculated in the addendum to this chapter and found to be:

$$\begin{pmatrix} 1 & -3 & 2 \\ -3 & 3 & -1 \\ 2 & -1 & 0 \end{pmatrix}$$

The numerical value of $X = A^{-1}B$ is therefore:

$$X = \begin{pmatrix} 1 & -3 & 2 \\ -3 & 3 & -1 \\ 2 & -1 & 0 \end{pmatrix} \begin{pmatrix} .1 \\ .3 \\ .3 \end{pmatrix}$$

Determining the value of each particular x_i at this point is simply a problem in matrix multiplication. Actually performing the indicated calculations produces:

$$\begin{pmatrix} 1 & -3 & 2 \\ -3 & 3 & -1 \\ 2 & -1 & 0 \end{pmatrix} \begin{pmatrix} .1 \\ .3 \\ .3 \end{pmatrix} = \begin{pmatrix} -.2 \\ .3 \\ -.1 \end{pmatrix}$$

This establishes that $X = (-.2, .3, -.1)$. By writing X in its original, non-matrix form, it is possible to state the same result in more familiar terms:

$$x_1 = -.2 = a -20\% \text{ margin on buggywhips.}$$
$$x_2 = .3 = a \quad 30\% \text{ margin on widgets.}$$
$$x_3 = -.1 = a -10\% \text{ margin on wrenches.}$$

Widgets can now be seen to be the only profitable product. The profit margins can be substituted back into the original equations in order to determine whether they do, in fact, explain each company's total profits.

$$1x_1 + 2x_2 + 3x_3 = (1)(-.2) + (2)(.3) + (3)(-.1) = -2 + 6 - 3 = \$.1 \text{ million}$$
$$2x_1 + 4x_2 + 5x_3 = (2)(-.2) + (4)(.3) + (5)(-.1) = -4 + 12 - 5 = \$.3 \text{ million}$$
$$3x_1 + 5x_2 + 6x_3 = (3)(-.2) + (5)(.3) + (6)(-.1) = -6 + 15 - 6 = \$.3 \text{ million}$$

The calculated margins of the three products therefore produce exactly the same company profits that were originally taken from the annual reports.

If this example appears to be rather removed from practical analysis, consider taking five large chemical companies and breaking their sales into industrial chemicals, agricultural chemicals, plastics, synthetic fibers, and liquid gases. The sales breakdown of five companies into product areas is a system of equations. By setting each company's sales breakdown equal to its overall earnings, the margin of each product area can be determined, assuming that all of the companies are equally profitable in each of the product lines. This assumption, of course, will not be true, but it is frequently interesting to examine what the situation would be if it *were* true. For example, it can give practical answers if the assumption is approximately true. Taking another approach, economics indicates that the assumption of equal margins will become more true as time passes due to the action of competitive pressures. The equations would therefore provide some indication of where competition would force margins to move assuming that each company retains its current profitability. Unrealistic results for product profitability would mean that it would be unrealistic to extrapolate the current relative profitability of the companies.

Another possible treatment of the assumption of equal margins stems from comparing actual results to the predicted results from the equations. If, for example, reporting requirements were changed so that margins on individual products would be reported by each company, then the deviation of a company's margin from the margin assuming equal profitability could be a fruitful departure for financial probing. Even without the reporting requirements, this approach can be very useful whenever an analyst has a good "feel" for a company's current margins.

The use of systems of equations is certainly not restricted to a consideration of profit margins. With known rates of return on various products, the total amount of capital invested by each company in each product area can be analyzed. If the number of stores in each of five regions of the country are known for each of five national grocery chains, the profitability of the regions can be examined. If four companies manufacture one commodity but each firm uses a combination of four production processes, the value of each process can be analyzed. The use of systems of equations for these purposes only provides insight for further analysis because the assumption of equal results by each company in each product or market is not fully met. Nevertheless, the approach may have some value in explaining variables which are normally available only as part of a company's overall structure.

CONCLUSION

Matrix algebra is the fundamental language of a very high percentage of the mathematical work being done today. It occurs frequently in articles in both academic and professional journals, and its use can be expected to increase very rapidly. Matrix addition, subtraction, multiplication, and inversion are just as important to modern mathematics as addition, subtraction, multiplication, and division are to everyday arithmetic.

Despite its power in complicated applications, however, matrix algebra is often used in normal business applications, and its use in standard analytic procedure will increase. Matrix addition and subtraction can be applied daily to data relating to accounts, companies, industries, and so forth. Matrix multiplication can be used whenever weighted totals or accumulated multiplications are needed. Inversion permits systems of equations to be solved and has a large number of more advanced applications.

Another very important value in understanding matrices is the fact that they are extensively used in more sophisticated mathematical and statistical applications. Matrix algebra is particularly important in the theory of multiple regression, linear programming, and the multivariate techniques such as component analysis, factor analysis, discriminant analysis, canonical correlation, and latent structure analysis. Very few structural, organizing principles which have the power to guide man's thought have ever been discovered. The matrix qualifies as one of these concepts, for it has the ability to control the complicated relationships found in applications ranging from simple tables to the frontier of current thought.

ADDITIONAL READINGS IN MATRIX ALGEBRA

Matrix algebra is included as a preparatory chapter or as an appendix in almost all modern texts covering quantitative techniques. Unfortunately, these chapters almost invariably treat the same aspects of the subject. The mathematical theory of matrices, on the other hand, catapults the reader almost immediately into some of the most advanced features of current quantitative and scientific thought. Since the problems in effectively understanding matrices usually stem from a feeling that the various calculations are just so much meaningless number smashing, the following list emphasizes applications or books which provide some intuitive insight into the calculations.

CHENERY, HOLLIS B. AND CLARK, PAUL G. *Interindustry Economics.* New York: John Wiley & Sons, Inc., 1959.
This book discusses the nature of economic input-output analysis (336 pages). The subject is inherently interesting to any analyst and the material is well presented in this book. It is listed here because input-output analysis is one of the simplest and yet most valuable applications of matrices, especially matrix inversion.

SPRINGER, C. H., HERLIHY, R. E., AND BEGGS, R. I. *Probabilistic Models,* Vol. 4. Homewood, Illinois: Richard D. Irwin, Inc., 1965.
This work discusses two interesting applications of matrices. In Chapter 3 (31 pages), markov processes are described and translated into a matrix formulation. Markov chains are an interesting extension of basic probability theory where events are permitted to be dependent upon the immediately preceding event. The theory has direct application to brand switching, inventory control, etc., but is included here only as an example which may clarify the use of matrices. Chapter 7 (47 pages) discusses decision models, and shows in simple terms the relationship between matrices and the decision trees used in probability theory. Both chapters are written in a nontechnical, rather satirical style and constitute light reading which is surprisingly painless.

YAMANE, TARO. *Mathematics for Economists.* 2d ed. Englewood Cliffs, New Jersey: Prentice-Hall, Inc., 1968.
This work contains a 210-page section on matrices which can be consulted when detailed information on computational procedures or mathematical relationships is required.

ADDENDUM TO CHAPTER 11

The preceding chapter presented the rationale behind matrix inversion but did not discuss the technique by which the actual inverse of a particular matrix can be found. This technique is usually performed by a computer and therefore need not be committed to memory in all of its step-by-step detail. Nevertheless, it is valuable to understand the general process by which the inverse is found because it points out with great clarity the relationship between A, A^{-1}, and I. It also shows how matrices can be viewed as operators and how operations can be performed on matrices.

The following paragraphs therefore present the steps which invert a given matrix. The material is intended only to show a "flow" of changes in the matrix which eventually produce the desired result. It is *not* intended to serve as a training course in professional matrix inversion. One additional point should be made before the process is described. Not all matrices have an inverse. On occasion, a matrix will be encountered for which the inverse is not defined. Such a matrix is called "singular" and is seldom encountered in practical applications.

The technique of matrix inversion converts A into A^{-1} by converting $[A \mid I]$ into $[I \mid A^{-1}]$, as discussed in the body of the chapter. This is done in a step-by-step fashion by repeatedly applying operations on the matrix until the desired result is achieved. The next question, naturally, is what the nature of these operations might be.

First, it is legal to divide any row of the matrix by any number.

Second, it is legal to add or subtract a multiple of any row from any other row.

These two operations can be used to systematically change A to I in the following manner:

Start the conversion process at the upper left corner of the matrix. We know that the first element must be made to be a 1 if it is to agree with the corresponding element in an identity matrix. Since it already is 1, we can move to the second step.

$$\begin{pmatrix} 1 & 2 & 3 & 1 & 0 & 0 \\ 2 & 4 & 5 & 0 & 1 & 0 \\ 3 & 5 & 6 & 0 & 0 & 1 \end{pmatrix}$$

Now it is necessary to convert the remainder of the first column to make it agree with the first column of an identity matrix. In other words, convert $\begin{pmatrix} 1 \\ 2 \\ 3 \end{pmatrix}$ into $\begin{pmatrix} 1 \\ 0 \\ 0 \end{pmatrix}$:

This element must be
changed to a 0. In
order to legally reduce
it to a 0, subtract———————→
2 times row one from
row two producing the
following matrix.

$$\begin{pmatrix} 1 & 2 & 3 & 1 & 0 & 0 \\ 2 & 4 & 5 & 0 & 1 & 0 \\ 3 & 5 & 6 & 0 & 0 & 1 \end{pmatrix}$$

O.K.
O.K.

This element needs to be———————→
a 0. In order to legally
reduce it to a 0, subtract
3 times row one from row
three.

$$\begin{pmatrix} 1 & 2 & 3 & 1 & 0 & 0 \\ 0 & 0 & -1 & -2 & 1 & 0 \\ 3 & 5 & 6 & 0 & 0 & 1 \end{pmatrix}$$

$$\left(\begin{array}{ccc|ccc} 1 & 2 & 3 & 1 & 0 & 0 \\ 0 & 0 & -1 & -2 & 1 & 0 \\ 0 & -1 & -3 & -3 & 0 & 1 \end{array}\right)$$

One column of this side
now looks like the identity
matrix.

Note that one column
of this side has been
"carried along" quite
naturally in the
course of the cal-
culations.

At this point, the first column has the desired form — it is the same as the
first column of an identity matrix. This was done by first changing the
proper row (row one in this case) into a "1" and then subtracting a multiple of that row from the other rows in order to produce the needed zeros.
The next step is to continue this process for another column. Choosing
column three, we have:

$$\begin{pmatrix} 1 & 2 & 3 & 1 & 0 & 0 \\ 0 & 0 & -1 & -2 & 1 & 0 \\ 0 & -1 & -3 & -3 & 0 & 1 \end{pmatrix}$$

The −3 must be changed into a 1.
We therefore multiply the row by
−1/3.

The −1 must be———————→
changed to a 0.
This can be done
by adding row
three to row two.

$$\begin{pmatrix} 1 & 2 & 3 & 1 & 0 & 0 \\ 0 & 0 & -1 & -2 & 1 & 0 \\ 0 & 1/3 & 1 & 1 & 0 & -1/3 \end{pmatrix}$$

The 3 needs to be changed to a 0.
We subtract 3 times row three
from row one.

$$\begin{pmatrix} 1 & 2 & 3 & 1 & 0 & 0 \\ 0 & 1/3 & 0 & -1 & 1 & -1/3 \\ 0 & 1/3 & 1 & 1 & 0 & -1/3 \end{pmatrix}$$

$$\begin{pmatrix} 1 & 1 & 0 & -2 & 0 & 1 \\ 0 & 1/3 & 0 & -1 & 1 & -1/3 \\ 0 & 1/3 & 1 & 1 & 0 & -1/3 \end{pmatrix}$$

Columns one and three are now the same as columns one and three of the identity matrix. We therefore attack another column, and only column two remains:

The 1/3 must be changed to a 1. We therefore multiply row two by 3.

$$\begin{pmatrix} 1 & 1 & 0 & -2 & 0 & 1 \\ 0 & 1/3 & 0 & -1 & 1 & -1/3 \\ 0 & 1/3 & 1 & 1 & 0 & 1/3 \end{pmatrix}$$

The 1 in the second column must be changed to a 0. We therefore subtract row two from row one.

$$\begin{pmatrix} 1 & 1 & 0 & -2 & 0 & 1 \\ 0 & 1 & 0 & -3 & 3 & -1 \\ 0 & 1/3 & 1 & 1 & 0 & -1/3 \end{pmatrix}$$

The 1/3 must be changed to a 0. We subtract 1/3 times row two from row three.

$$\begin{pmatrix} 1 & 0 & 0 & 1 & -3 & +2 \\ 0 & 1 & 0 & -3 & 3 & -1 \\ 0 & 1/3 & 1 & 1 & 0 & -1/3 \end{pmatrix}$$

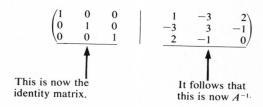

$$\begin{pmatrix} 1 & 0 & 0 \\ 0 & 1 & 0 \\ 0 & 0 & 1 \end{pmatrix} \quad \begin{pmatrix} 1 & -3 & 2 \\ -3 & 3 & -1 \\ 2 & -1 & 0 \end{pmatrix}$$

This is now the identity matrix.

It follows that this is now A^{-1}.

Chapter

12 Multiple Linear Regression or Using a Number of Variables to Predict the Unknown

Extending linear regression, which has been considered previously, multiple regression permits the prediction of an unknown variable that depends on not one but on several other known variables. The approach is similar, being based on past observations and assuming some basis for the relationships between the variables. Each of the independent variables is provided a weight depending on its contribution to determining the dependent variable. In addition to an equation describing the relationships between the dependent variable and the weighted independent variables, the technique provides coefficients of correlation that measure the relationships between any two variables and a coefficient of determination that describes the explanatory power of all of the independent variables. Moreover, the technique can provide confidence tests for the significance of the weights and for the predictions provided by the overall equation representing the relationship. Examples are given for presenting and understanding all of this information in one equation. Partial correlation and several other extensions of the tool are discussed briefly.

INTRODUCTION

Expanding the Regression Concept

Multiple regression is one of the most valuable techniques available to the financial analyst because it permits a number of variables to be used to find a prediction of some unknown variable. For example, the growth rate, debt to equity ratio, and yield of stocks might be used to predict the stocks' *P/E*. Multiple regression is simply an extension of simple regression, which has already been discussed. In simple regression, the analyst can find an equation of the form $y = a + bx$ which describes (more or less) the relationship between the two variables which are being studied. Applications for the two-variable case are often encountered, but quite frequently the financial manager has reason to believe that the value of y is heavily influenced by more than one thing. In this case y is a function of more than one x. Actually, in the extremely complicated financial world, $y = f(x_1, x_2, \ldots x_n)$ is almost always a model significantly superior to $y = f(x)$.

The most logical extension of simple regression, therefore, is multiple regression. Instead of using x to locate or "retrieve" the value for y, it is possible to use $x_1, x_2, \ldots x_n$. The mathematical technique is more complicated, but the concepts involved are essentially the same. The analyst still is attempting to discover the particular linear function that will predict or describe y. A number of past observations of the x's and of y are still required before the model can provide meaningful information. The model still provides an equation as an answer, and the equation can still be used in the same way. The similarity in form between the two equations can be seen by the following examples:

$$y + 10 + 0.8x \qquad\qquad y = -0.10 + 0.6x_1 + 0.4x_2$$

Note from the examples that the use of subscripts makes the expression simpler than using completely different letters. Subscripts are used extensively in multiple linear regression, as could be expected from what was said in the section on notation about simplification when many variables are introduced.

What multiple regression does, in effect, is to state that, since y is related to several x's, it is reasonable simply to add the values of the x's in order to get the value of y. It goes one step further, however, "adjusting" each x before adding the adjusted figures. The "adjustment" is a weight applied to each variable, and the real purpose of the model is to select the "best" weights to use in the equation, which produces, naturally, the "best" such equation.

In mathematical notation, any variable with a zero subscript is defined to equal the number "1." For example, x_0 by definition equals 1. In a regression equation such as $y = b_1x_0 + b_2x_1 + b_3x_2 + b_4x_3$, the b's represent the particular weights chosen by the model, and as can easily be seen, the weighted x's are then added to "retrieve" the value of y.

The next question is how the model treats the qualitative idea of "best" in mathematical terms. Regression uses the data which are provided by the analyst concerning the values of y which occurred given certain values for the x's. It evaluates the weights (the b_i) which could have been used for the x's in order to predict the values of y. The set of weights which would have produced the *predictions* of y closest to the *actual* values of y is then selected. As a result, the equation produced is the linear combination of the x's that most accurately predicted all of the values of y which were provided as input to the model. The equation might therefore be expected to produce about the same quality of predictions for new values of y. If anyone could graph the equation (in four-dimensional space because there are four variables), he would find that it is the straight line that "bisects" or "best fits" the "swarm" of data points which were input to the model. This is analogous to the way that $y = a + bx$ "fits" the points in a scatter diagram in two dimensions.

An Example

The principles of regression can be understood much more easily if they are presented within the framework of a concrete example. The following problem was therefore fabricated in such a way that the results appear to be reasonable. It is important to remember, however, that the example is not the result of actual data. Extending the example which was used in the chapter on simple regression, let:

$y = P/E$ of any stock being analyzed.
$x_1 = $ Growth rate of the stock's earnings.
$x_2 = 1 - $ the debt to equity ratio of the company. (Simply called debt/ equity in the chapter.)
$x_3 = $ The yield of the stock.

The equation that this study would produce would have the form:

$$y = b_1 x_0 + b_2 x_1 + b_3 x_2 + b_4 x_3$$

(Note: Recall that $x_0 = 1$ by definition.)

The objective of the analyst is to study the relationship between: (1) the growth rate, debt/equity ratio, and yield of stocks; and (2) the P/E which the market is willing to assign given any stock's values in these three areas. Naturally, an analyst would not undertake this analysis if he did not already feel that x_1, x_2, and x_3 were factors which were, in fact, involved in the determination of the price-earnings ratios of stocks.

Input Requirements

In order to be able to utilize the multiple regression model, the researcher obviously needs to provide a certain amount of data as input. In the case of this particular example, the data consist of the P/E, growth rate, debt/equity ratio, and yield of a number of stocks. It is obvious that it would not be sufficient to provide only one stock, for this would be equivalent to providing only one point for a scatter diagram. It would be impossible to draw the best line "fitting" only one point. In fact, since two points are needed to draw a line on a plane representing two variables, it is reasonable to expect that when the study has a surface representing four variables at least four points will be needed. In the example, this would mean at least four stocks.

Actually, however, more stocks than this are needed for a valid study, for the points must form a "swarm" having at least some "scatter" around the regression line. In the most primitive terms possible, the regression line is supposed to be a mathematical expression representing general, broad relationships in the data, and enough observations must be present to allow the relationships to become recognizable and to be subjected to statistical examination. The minimum number of observations (stocks, in this case) must exceed the number of variables in the study, but as many observations as possible should be used because each additional observation increases the reliability of the results and the accuracy of any future predictions that might be made.

THE CORRELATION MATRIX

The Nature of the Matrix Elements

In the section on simple regression, r was used to describe the degree of relationship between the two variables. It ranged between -1.00 and $+1.00$, with 0.0 showing no relationship and ± 1.00 showing perfect positive or negative correlation. The r statistic is retained in multiple regression but is expanded a bit because multiple regression involves more than two variables. Nevertheless, *any pair* of variables can have a coefficient of correlation, so that what develops is a *matrix* of r's, called the *correlation matrix*.

In order to understand the correlation matrix, it is necessary to identify uniquely the two variables to which each r relates. Using subscripts for this purpose, let:

Subscript		Variable
1	=	y
2	=	x_1
3	=	x_2
4	=	x_3

In this notation, $r_{1,2}$ would be the correlation coefficient of the variables y and x_1; $r_{3,4}$ would deal with x_2 and x_3. It is now possible to present a hypothetical matrix of the r_{ij} which might result from the study of P/E's:

$$\begin{array}{llll}
r_{1,1} = 1.00 & r_{1,2} = .99 & r_{1,3} = .95 & r_{1,4} = .96 \\
r_{2,1} = .99 & r_{2,2} = 1.00 & r_{2,3} = .93 & r_{2,4} = .93 \\
r_{3,1} = .95 & r_{3,2} = .93 & r_{3,3} = 1.00 & r_{3,4} = .98 \\
r_{4,1} = .96 & r_{4,2} = .93 & r_{4,3} = .98 & r_{4,4} = 1.00
\end{array}$$

Each of the values in this matrix is a simple correlation coefficient and has exactly the same interpretation as in simple regression. For example, $r_{3,1} = .95$ is the correlation coefficient for variables 3 and 1, and .95 is precisely the same value for r that would be obtained if a simple regression was run for these two variables without any consideration of the other variables whatsoever.

THE STRUCTURE OF THE MATRIX

This array points out several interesting facts. First, the correlation of a variable to itself is 1.00. This is reasonable, for if the value of a variable is known, its value can then be predicted with perfect accuracy. Since the main diagonal of the matrix is the correlation between variables 1 and 1, 2 and 2, etc., this diagonal is all ones. Second, $r_{1,2} = r_{2,1}$, and $r_{3,4} = r_{4,3}$, and so forth. This means that the upper right triangle of the matrix equals the lower left triangle. Third, since the meaning of each r_{ij} is fixed by its location in the matrix, the coefficients can be presented without showing the variables with which they deal. The first row deals with the first variable and the first column also deals with the first variable, etc. The coefficient in the second row and the third column is, obviously, the value of $r_{2,3}$. The correlation matrix can therefore be written as:

$$\begin{pmatrix}
1.00 & .99 & .95 & .96 \\
.99 & 1.00 & .93 & .93 \\
.95 & .93 & 1.00 & .98 \\
.96 & .93 & .98 & 1.00
\end{pmatrix}$$

And since the upper right triangle equals the lower left triangle, the correlation matrix R is frequently written as:

$$\begin{pmatrix}
1.00 & .99 & .95 & .96 \\
 & 1.00 & .93 & .93 \\
 & & 1.00 & .98 \\
 & & & 1.00
\end{pmatrix}$$

without the loss of any information.

The R matrix provides a table of the results of a number of simple regressions even before the *real* multiple regression is begun. Interpreting this particular R in terms of the variables used in the example, it can be seen that the relationships are high in every case, but that the "yield" variable has the lowest relationship to P/E and that the worst relationships are found in growth to debt/equity ratio and growth to yield. The results of the study are already interesting, for it begins to look like growth may be a being-unto-itself which is more closely tied to the P/E than to any other variable. But this is as far as "r" can go. To proceed, the analyst needs a measure of the "explanatory power" of *all* of the x's, not just one at a time.

THE COEFFICIENT OF DETERMINATION

R^2, the coefficient of determination, serves the purpose of measuring the extent to which all the x's taken as a whole serve as an "explanation" of y. Its meaning is the same as in simple regression, for it still measures the percentage by which the overall fluctuation in y can be removed (or "predicted") by the use of the regression equation. The R^2 statistic has a direct interpretation as the percentage of y's variation which is eliminated (or "explained") by the values of the x_i variables. If the regression equation is the result of a simple regression, it measures the explanatory power of x; but if the equation is a *multiple* regression, it measures the total explanatory power of *all* of the x_i. If $R^2 = .95$, then 95% of y's movement could be eliminated by the regression equation. R^2 obviously is a very useful measure of the value of the regression, and its chief drawback is that its ability to provide a synopsis of the results has caused it to be used as a *sole* indication of the results without regard for other aspects of a regression study. R^2 is a key measure of the value of the equation which the model produces, but it should be used in conjunction with other statistical results provided by the technique.

The coefficient of determination, R^2, is frequently presented with subscripts to indicate the particular variables included in the model. The dependent variable y (the variable being predicted), is the first subscript, and is followed by the x's (independent variables). The y is separated from the independent variables by a period (or sometimes by a comma). Hence, $R^2_{1.234}$ would be a way of writing the coefficient of determination in our example of P/E ratios. Alternative ways of expressing R^2 are fairly numerous — $R^2_{y.123}$ meaning R^2 for y *given* x_1, x_2, and x_3 is one possibility, another is $R^2_{y.x_1x_2x_3}$, which is clearer but is somewhat cumbersome.

Reviewing, it can be seen that R^2 is a kind of a "percentage" measure which indicates the proportion of the fluctuations or "scatter" in y which can be explained by the changes which occurred in x_i. If y goes all over the chart, but x_i is the only reason for this wandering, x_i "explains" *all* of y's movement and the index is 100% (expressed as $R^2 = 1.00$). If a study were conducted which initially involved ten independent variables and an equation using only three of the x_i were finally selected, the resulting R^2 might be $R^2_{y.345} = .87$, which would be an 87% "explanation" of y by the variables x_3, x_4, and x_5. If all of the x_i explained absolutely none of the fluctuation in y, then R^2 would equal 0.00. The subscript notation used for R^2 can also be applied to the standard error, giving $s_{y.123}$, meaning the "expected" miss in the predictions of the equation, i.e., the size of the "channel" in the scatter diagram which showed y predicted by x_1, x_2, and x_3. As a specific example, a $s_{y.123} = .12$ would normally mean that the predicted value of y missed the actual value of y by .12 or less about 68% of the time.

A MEASURE OF THE VALUE OF *b*

In statistics, almost everything is a "give or take a little" type of problem. For example, when the statistical idea of the "probability of missing" was applied to the problem of predicting y, the concept of the standard error proved to be helpful. Statisticians openly accept the limitations of the regression model as a predictor. In effect, the technique produces an equation which is itself a model of the actual relationships found in the real world. Because of the inherent limitations in any consideration of data having a random element, the equation may not be the absolutely correct equation even if the relationship in the real world satisfies all of the assumptions of the model. The problem is that in an equation like $y = a + bx$, the technique is estimating the actual value of b which describes the situation in the real world, and this estimate may well be wrong. However, it is possible to determine statistically how *likely* it is to be wrong.

Recall from algebra that in the equation $y = a + bx$, the b is the weight given the predicting variable. Geometrically, it is the "slope" of the line which best describes the data in a scatter diagram. It tells us how much "extra y" is received for each "extra x" that is put into the equation. The amount of error in the coefficient of x (b, in other words) can be measured by a statistic called $\hat{\sigma}_b$ (the standard error of the coefficient). The "σ" is a familiar symbol which is always related to the measurement of variation. It indicates what type of measure this new statistic is, a "give or take this amount or less about 68% of the time" type of number. The b, of course, indicates that it is the variability of b that is being measured. The $\wedge$ (hat) indicates that the $\hat{\sigma}_b$ is an estimate of the true condition in the real world.

As a concrete illustration of this statistic, assume that $\hat{\sigma}_b$ is .03 for the coefficient (b_1) of x_1 and the actual value of b is .85. The regression model appears to have generated an equation which describes the "real world" relationship very well, for it appears that the .85 value is accurate within about .03. In the example of regression which is being used in this chapter, x_1 is the earnings growth rate of a company. A value of 8 for x_1 would mean an 8% annual rate of growth. The coefficient (b_1) of .85 would therefore mean .85 of the 8 could be added to the P/E of the company. The value of $\hat{\sigma}_b$ shows that the .85 could be as low as .82 or as high as .88. This range is fairly narrow, which justifies the conclusion that the equation is valuable. Instead of .03, if the model showed that $\hat{\sigma}_b = .65$, the true value of b_1 would be anywhere between .85 ± .65 (this is a [.20 − 1.50] range). The predictions of the model would obviously be far less accurate, for a 1% increase in the growth of a company could increase its P/E by anything between .20 P/E multiples and 1.50 P/E multiples.

The $\hat{\sigma}_b$ statistic can actually be used in a much more precise way by calling upon the t statistic discussed in the chapter on hypothesis testing. It is possible to compute a value for t in simple regression by the following formula:

$$t = \frac{b}{\hat{\sigma}_b}$$

where $\hat{\sigma}_b$ is equal to:

$$\sqrt{\frac{\frac{\Sigma(y - \hat{y})^2}{n - 2}}{\Sigma x^2 - (\Sigma x)^2/n}}$$

In multiple regression, a t can be computed for each b_i being estimated. As in the earlier chapter, the calculated value of t is of no direct benefit to the analyst. By using the t table with $n - 2$ degrees of freedom, however, it is possible to accept or reject the null hypothesis that $b_i = 0.0$ at any desired level of confidence. If it cannot be shown by this test that b_i is not equal to zero, then the variable x_i (growth rate, for instance) must still be assumed to have no relationship to the item being predicted (P/E, in this case). This is because of the fact that a $b_i = 0.0$ means that an increase in growth will add 0.0 to the value of the P/E. If all changes in the growth rate have a zero impact on the P/E, the two variables are obviously not related. Using t to reject the null hypothesis that $b_i = 0.0$ is therefore a statistical method to establish with some confidence the fact that a relationship exists.

After the t associated with any given variable x_i and its coefficient b_i has been found, it can be compared to the table value of t (found by using $n - 2$ d.f. and the desired risk level). If the calculated t exceeds the value of t in the table, then the value of b_i cannot be explained by chance alone. The only alternative explanation is that, say, growth (x_1) does affect the value of P/E (y). If this is found to be true for all of the variables x_i, then the regression equation can reasonably be expected to produce better predictions than would result from simply guessing the value of y without referring to the values of the predicting variables x_i.

It is also possible to compute confidence limits for b_i using the t statistic. Confidence limits are a range or an interval within which a value might be expected, say, 95% of the time. Since b is estimated by the model and therefore may be subject to error stemming from chance variation, it is frequently valuable to provide an interval within which the true value of b_i in the real world can be expected to fall. This interval is $b_i \pm$ (the value of $\hat{\sigma}_b$ times the table value of t at $x - 2$ d.f. and the desired risk level).

CONFIDENCE INTERVAL FOR PREDICTIONS

The true value of b_i in the real world is often called β_i, in which case b_i is said to be an estimate of β_i. The confidence interval for b_i is therefore the interval which is expected to contain β_i 95% of the time. The idea of a confidence interval, a range within which a number can reasonably be expected to fall, is a useful concept to apply to the predictions of the value of y which are provided by a regression equation. The regression provides a value for y which can be used as a prediction of y assuming certain values for the x_i in the equation. But the accuracy of this prediction is certainly not indicated in the single value for y which the equation produces. In the example, a predicted P/E of 17.0 for a stock does not indicate whether the actual P/E can be expected to be between 16.9 and 17.1 or between 14.0 and 20.0. It would be much more valuable if the model provided an interval within which y could be expected to fall 95% of the time. The single value of y (such as $P/E = 17.0$) would be the midpoint of this interval, but the "spread" of the interval would serve as an indication of the value of the prediction.

Multiple regression provides this information, and the results are once again found by the use of the t statistic. The value of the interval is the predicted value of y (which is $\hat{y}$) $\pm$ the table value of t (with $n - 2$ d.f. and the desired risk level) times $\hat{\sigma}_{\bar{y}}$ (which is called the standard error of y). The mathematical calculations need not be discussed here, for the important point is that the confidence interval is more valuable in predictions than the single estimated value for y which is produced by the regression equation.

AN EXAMPLE OF APPLICATION

A study of some hypothetical regression output may show the relationships between the various statistical measures that have been discussed. An example of a simple regression is:

$x =$ growth rate.
$y = P/E$.
$y = a + bx$.

where the model found:

$a = .7$ P/E multiples.

$b = .85$ of one P/E to be added for each 1% annual growth.

$\hat{\sigma}_b = .03$ so b may be off by .03 P/E's.

$s_{1,2} = .12$ so the actual y may be .12 or so off from our estimate.

$r_{1,2} = .99$, so the correlation is extremely high.

$R_{1,2}^2 = .97$, so x "explains" 97% of y (not exactly equal to the square of r due to the fact that r was rounded).

Rearranging:

$$P/E = .7 + (.85)(\text{growth rate}); \qquad R^2 = .97$$
$$(.03)$$
$$s_{1,2} = .12$$

Extending these results to multiple regression, each x will have a coefficient, so that each will have a $\hat{\sigma}_b$. Writing one possible multiple regression in the rearranged style:

$$P/E = 10 + .60 \text{ growth} + .40 \text{ debt/equity}; \qquad R_{y.12}^2 = .99$$
$$(.07) \qquad\qquad (.10)$$
$$s_{y.12} = .09$$

Interpreting this regression, we see that the x_i explain almost all of the P/E because $R^2 = .99$ (and 1.00 is perfect). If growth rate and debt/equity are zero, the P/E is 10. It is obviously unlikely that the two variables will be zero, however, and so a certain amount of additional P/E must be given for each unit of increase in the growth rate or debt/equity. How much should be added? The total P/E is given .60 P/E's for every unit of increase of growth and .40 P/E's for every unit of increase in the debt to equity measure which is being used. These are the coefficients (b_i) in the equation.

What was gained by going from a simple (growth, P/E) regression to a multiple regression? By including debt/equity in the explanation of P/E's behavior, the model increased R^2 to 99% from 97% and so achieved a slightly better explanation. In addition, the "scatter" around the predicted values for y (the P/E) dropped from .12 to .09, thus permitting a more accurate prediction of y.

If adding the debt/equity ratio to the simple regression (thus making the study a multiple regression) added a reasonable amount of information to the study, what impact would adding the yield have? Including yield in this particular study added only 0.001 to R^2 and reduced the standard error by only .0009. In effect, this eliminates yield from this hypothetical study due to a lack of confidence in the existence of a correlation, although more precise reasons for dropping yield can be developed using partial correlation as discussed in the next section. As a result of rejecting this variable, the analyst would conclude that the "best" explanation of the P/E ratio is found by the use of growth and the debt/equity ratio. In other words, P/E is best described as a function of the growth rate and debt/equity. And if this particular function is used, the regression indicates that it is not statistically useful to include the yield at all as a predictor of the value of a stock's P/E.

PARTIAL CORRELATION

The extremely valuable results which have been achieved in the last four hundred years or so as a result of the use of the scientific method can, to a very large extent, be ascribed to the concept of the "controlled experiment." The scientist attempts to eliminate the influence of all aspects of his problem except the particular variables with which he is dealing in order to obtain reliable measurements and so provide a firm foundation for his conclusions. As an example, a physicist rolling a ball down a slope would not be expected to conduct his experiment on an extremely windy day unless he specifically wished to include the effects of wind as a factor in his experiment. Unfortunately, the basis of this scientific method, the *controlled* experiment, is not available to the investment analyst. Businessmen and economists attempting to analyze their problems scientifically are not able to control outside influences and as a result are forced to accept analyses which suffer from a great deal of unavoidable imprecision.

It would certainly be useful to be able to calculate the relationship between two items in a scientifically controlled environment, but this is impossible. The analyst, however, does have an alternative at his disposal. It is possible to determine statistically the relationship between, say, P/E and growth as it *would* have been *if* the price-earnings ratio had not been affected by an outside influence of, say, yield. In effect, the variable which constitutes the outside influence is controlled statistically instead of by the physical design of the experiment. The variable which is statistically controlled is in effect eliminated from the correlation under consideration by the nature of the statistical technique. This technique is called partial correlation.

The symbol for a partial correlation is familiar from previous applications. The correlation coefficient r is used, but it now has subscripts attached in such a way that the meaning is clearly distinguishable from a standard correlation coefficient. The only new aspect of the notation for partial correlation is the location of a period in the subscripts. All variables which are in front of the dot are included in the correlation, while all items after the dot are (in a certain statistical sense) held constant. And so, if $r_{12.4} = .88$, variables number 1 and 2 are correlated to a fairly high degree if variable number 4 is not allowed to influence the study. Another example would be $r_{y1.2} = .95$, indicating that y and the first x have a very high relationship if the second x is not allowed to interfere with the investment analyst's "experiment."

Returning to our example, the two independent variables growth and debt/equity were used to predict P/E:

$$r_{y1.2} = .91$$

This statistic shows the correlation between P/E and growth, net of the impact of the debt/equity ratio. In other words, the technique of partial correlation has held the debt/equity ratio constant and then measured the correlation between the two variables being considered, P/E and growth in this case.

Partial correlation permits one variable to be held constant in the statistical sense because the analyst is unable to hold it constant in the real world. The correlation which results from this removal of an unwanted factor need not be the same as the simple correlation. In fact, if the factor being removed *does* have an impact on the apparent relationship, the "adjusted" correlation will *necessarily* vary from the simple one. The simple correlation of P/E to growth is .99, but the correlation net of the variations induced by the debt/equity ratio is .91. This indicates that some of the variations in debt/equity are causing both P/E and growth to react, and this tendency for both variables to react to a common cause quite naturally forces them to appear to be more highly related than is actually the case.

The impact of unwanted changes in an extraneous variable is shown even more graphically in $r_{y2.1} = .71$. This is the correlation of P/E to the debt/equity ratio net of the impact of growth. This value is .71, down from .96 for the simple correlation coefficient for P/E and debt/equity. This indicates that a great deal of the apparent relationship between P/E and debt/equity actually stems from the fact that both are sensitive to changes in the value of another variable—the growth rate.

The partial correlation coefficients are computed from the simple correlation coefficients through the use of a fairly simple formula and are automatically provided by most regression programs.

REGRESSION AND SYSTEMS OF EQUATIONS

In the chapter covering matrix algebra, a number of examples of possible applications of simultaneous equations were presented. It was indicated at that time that the fundamental importance of systems of equations to the financial analyst stemmed from their applications in econometrics. As a result, the applications actually presented had a somewhat forced appearance. The discussion of multiple regression makes it possible to expand significantly upon the uses of systems of equations in two ways.

First, the particular systems which the econometricians must solve by matrix algebra are almost inevitably developed by the use of regression theory. Assume, for example, that an economist developed five equations which dealt with five particular economic variables. If any of these equations were derived from observed data, it is almost certain that regression technique had been used to discover the numerical value of the coefficients in the equation. Regression, in other words, is used to discover the relations between the five variables, and the solution to the resulting system of equations is the econometric model of the interrelated variables.

This approach is an important expansion of the value of regression to the financial analyst because he is also concerned with predicting entire sets of variables at one time. The analyst specializing in a particular industry, for example, needs to predict a number of variables relating to that industry. Using this approach, he can statistically develop the system which will provide the entire set of desired estimates. He would proceed by first defining the variables that needed to be determined and then decide upon the set of variables that are related to the unknowns. He then would be in a position to gather historical data on all of the variables in the study, run regression studies to develop a set of predicting equations, and then solve the system that was discovered through regression technique.

The second way in which regression expands the use of equations relates to the particular examples which were presented in the matrix algebra chapter. Consider, for example, the case of five chemical companies manufacturing products in each of five broad product classifications. The use of a system of equations breaks down when six chemical companies are being considered because there must be exactly as many equations as unknowns. An analyst might be tempted to choose five of the companies and solve their equations, then choose another five and solve, and so forth for all combinations of the six companies. This would produce six estimates for the profit margin of each product line, and these estimates could be averaged to produce a single estimate for each product.

This approach appears to have some merit, and the degree of similarity of the profit margin of any given product for different sets of companies would provide some measure of the reliability of the "average" profit margin for that product which would be computed after all of the systems of equations were solved. The problem with this approach is that if, say, 30 companies were involved, 142,506 systems of equations would need to be solved. Since this is impractical, regression can be used to accomplish the same purpose.

Regression provides the "best" single estimate of the profit margin of each product line when the number of observations (companies) exceeds the number of variables (products). This stems from the fact that regression estimates the coefficients of the predicting equation, and in this application these coefficients are the profit margins of the various product lines. In effect, it provides a shortcut to averaging all of the estimates that would be produced from all of the systems of equations which could be developed from the data and produces the single estimate for each variable which most closely approximates the known total. As a result, an equation is produced which can be used to predict the total (overall profit margin), and which estimates the magnitude of each variable which provides that prediction (the particular profit margin of each product). In addition, an estimate of the reliability of each profit margin is provided. The presence of more equations than variables actually enhances the information available to the analyst, for he can then use regression technique instead of algebra and so gain the use of statistical tests of the value of the estimates. This approach can be applied to any of the examples in the chapter on matrix algebra as well as to an extremely large number of other problems frequently encountered by analysts.

ADDITIONAL TOPICS IN REGRESSION

Multiple regression actually includes a broad variety of additional techniques which are too complex to be treated in detail here. A brief statement of some of the more commonly used extensions is presented so that the analyst will be able to recognize the approaches taken either in journal articles which he may encounter or in the results of studies undertaken by his firm's quantitative analysts.

Statistical Tests of r

The correlation coefficient, r, is a statistic which is used to estimate the actual relationship between the variables being studied. The actual relationship in the real world is called ρ (rho) and r may incorrectly estimate ρ because of sampling error. If this happens, the analyst would maintain that a relationship was present when in fact it was not. The *possibility* of this occurring is unavoidable, but it is possible to determine the *probability* of error, that is, it is possible to test r at a given level of confidence to see if a relationship does in fact exist (to see if ρ is not zero). A t test is used for this purpose, and the result might be, for example, that one can be 95% confident that the two variables are related.

The Use of F Tests

The analysis of variance can be applied to multiple regression. In this technique, a value for F is computed for each independent variable in the equation. This *F* indicates whether or not the analyst can be confident (at some specified level, say, 90%) that the variable being predicted is in fact dependent upon the value of the given independent variable. Obviously, if the test shows that this level of confidence is not present, then the variable should not be used as a predictor. It is important to note that this technique tests the significance of the independent variable *net of the impact* of the other variables. This means that it tests the significance of the correlation which is measured by the *partial correlation coefficients*. It may be that a predictor with a high correlation coefficient may be completely insignificant when considered in combination with other predictors. This type of result can seldom be seen by a direct traditional analysis of the data and may be useful to the analyst in rejecting relationships as invalid which on the surface appear to be quite real.

Stepwise Regression

The ability to use the *F* test to determine the confidence which can be placed upon the value of any predicting variable is the basis for a powerful extension of regression technique. Stepwise regression permits the analyst to start with a large number of variables which might have predictive value and then use the model to select the particular variables which appear to provide the best prediction.

Using this technique, for example, an analyst might select ten variables which could conceivably influence the price-earnings ratio of stocks and present the values of these variables for a large number of stocks to the model. Stepwise regression would then proceed by calculating the *F* for each of the ten variables. This, of course, is a measure of the significance of each variable as a predictor of *P/E* ratios. If any of the variables are significant, the *most* significant one is used to produce a regression equation. Next, the significance of the variables is *recalculated* to determine their predictive value *given* that the current regression equation is used. If a significant improvement can be achieved by including another variable in the equation, the best variable is selected and the regression equation is recalculated to include the new predictor.

The technique proceeds by simply evaluating the variables and adding them into the predicting equation if it is desirable to do so. The one exception to this rather straightforward process stems from the fact that whenever a new variable is included in a regression equation, it is possible that the significance of other predictors already present may decline substantially. For example, assume that the growth rate of earnings was related to the percentage of earnings retained after dividends and the *P/E* ratio was related to the accumulation of earning assets in any given company. What would happen if the stepwise regression procedure at the first step used the growth rate as a predictor and at the second step added the percent of earnings retained as a second predictor? The significance of the growth rate would decline substantially because a high proportion of its predictive power would now be transferred to the variable just added to the equation. If this loss of explanatory value is so large that the growth rate variable is no longer significant, the regression equation is obviously unsatisfactory.

Stepwise regression solves this problem by checking all of the variables in the equation after a new variable has been added in order to be certain that they remain significant. Insignificant variables are systematically ejected from the equation before any attempt is made to enter any new variable. Once the equation is corrected, the process of evaluating and inserting additional variables is resumed.

The model can be seen to proceed in a stepwise manner, evaluating possible predictors, inserting the best of these into the equation, removing variables in the equation that may have become insignificant, and then returning to the evaluation and insertion of new variables. The process is completed when all of the significant variables that have been presented to the model have been included in the regression equation, and all of the insignificant variables have been excluded. The model will automatically evaluate the variables presented by the analyst and select those most useful in predictions. This entire process is performed in one computer run without any need for additional information at any intermediate step. In effect, the analyst inputs the set of all possible predictors, and the model outputs the most useful regression equation. In addition, all of the statistical information associated with a standard regression is automatically provided *for each step* executed in the procedure.

Nonparametric Correlation

The techniques which have been described in this chapter are parametric; they assume a normal distribution. In a number of cases, this assumption may be severely violated. If so, nonparametric methods for computing correlation coefficients and partial correlation coefficients are available, complete with statistical tests for their significance. Unfortunately, however, the prediction equation cannot be produced by nonparametric methods because these techniques are based upon ranking the data instead of using the actual numerical values.

Nonlinear Regression

The regression equation which has been considered in this chapter is linear (i.e., straight line). Curvilinear (curved line) regressions are possible, however. It is possible, for example, to present the logarithms of a variable to the model instead of the variable itself. The computations used by the model remain exactly the same, but the resulting regression equation is a linear equation in the log of the variable — which is obviously nonlinear in terms of the variable *itself*. It is possible to use the square of a variable, the cosine of a variable, the product of two variables, etc., to produce regression equations. These changes in the original variables are called transformations, and the output of the regression model is still linear in terms of the transformed variables. It is only nonlinear in terms of the original variables.

A truly nonlinear regression (i.e., one which is nonlinear in terms of the coefficients being estimated) is seldom encountered in actual practice. Joint regression occurs when the variable being predicted is a function of two or more other variables which cannot be separated, that is, $y = f(x_1, x_2, \ldots x_n)$ but is not a function of the form $y = f_1(x_1) + f_2(x_2) + \ldots, f_n(x_n)$. In this case, the equation which describes the behavior of y as, say, x_1 changes will itself change for each of the different values of x_2. This shifting of values produces a sticky statistical problem which is complicated even when the set of observations is very large.

More Advanced Models

The development of econometrics has substantially changed regression theory. It has been found that the probabilistic interpretation of regression results is very limited when studies relate to economic variables. As a result, more powerful techniques which overcome at least some of the shortcomings of the standard method have been and are currently being developed. The problem is that the regression model assumes a number of things about the data that may in certain applications not be realistic. If the assumptions are not strictly met, the statistical characteristics of the results will not be strictly valid in a probabilistic sense. If the assumptions are seriously violated, the output can be seriously misleading. These assumptions assert that the x_i are not random variables (although y, the variable being predicted, is random), that the amount by which the regression equation "misses" the actual observations can be described by a normal distribution and is not affected by the value of any of the x_i, that the different observations are unrelated, and so forth. Obviously, in practical financial applications assumptions such as these will almost never be completely met. The results of the model must therefore always be taken with a grain of salt, and econometric models can be valuable in determining whether an assumption is seriously violated. In certain cases, econometrics provides models which can be used when certain assumptions of the basic "least squares" regression model are not met.

SUMMARY

Multiple regression has been shown to be a technique by which an analyst can explore the relationship between variables in a fairly precise quantitative manner. In addition, if variables are shown to be related, a regression equation can be used to assist in the prediction of future values. The model requires past observations of the variables involved in order to have sufficient information to be able to make reasonable assertions, and it is best to have many more observations than variables. The variables which might be chosen as input to the model are selected, of course, because some theoretical consideration leads the analyst to suspect that a relationship exists. The output of the model has been described in some detail, but it is always related to the measurement of the relationships, predictions which can be made on the basis of these relationships, or the accuracy of these predictions.

ADDITIONAL READINGS IN REGRESSION

Regression is another topic which has received attention on all levels of mathematical sophistication. Simple regression is included in most introductory statistics courses and (probably because of the intriguing visual characteristics of the scatter diagram) can be found in almost all journals. Multiple regression is almost invariably treated in the elementary statistics texts even though the instructors never seem to have time to include it in the course. On the other hand, variations of the basic regression model or advanced consideration of the probabilistic meaning of the statistical tests usually included with the basic analysis have filled a number of advanced texts.

The reason for the remarkable volume of material available in this area undoubtedly stems from the practical nature of the regression technique. Properly used, it can provide concrete predictions for real world values and also indicates the accuracy of those predictions. The literature is simply an extended analysis of the meaning of the phrase "properly used."

KLEIN, LAWRENCE R. *An Introduction to Econometrics.* Englewood Cliffs, New Jersey: Prentice-Hall, Inc., 1962.

This work is an extremely readable, essentially verbal, statement of the particular economic problems to which econometric methods have been applied (270 pages). The particular econometric techniques which are discussed are only very minor variations of simple and multiple regression. The text is therefore very valuable as an introduction to actual applications of regression analysis. The emphasis throughout the work is on finding the set of variables which will predict the unknown variable and then setting up the predicting equation. The solution of the equation, (finding the actual numerical value of the coefficients) by actually performing the regression analysis is never discussed. The material is an excellent introductory presentation of the interaction of statistical with economic theory and should be read by every financial analyst.

DUESENBURY, ED. J. S.; FROMAN, G.; KLEIN, L. R.; AND KUH, E. *The Brookings Quarterly Econometric Model of the United States.* Chicago: Rand McNally & Co., 1965.

This book is a collection of regressions performed in order to predict various economic variables (738 pages). The chapters can be read independently, and each is an example of the process by which practical applications of regression are performed. The actual results of the studies are included, but the mathematical characteristics of the regression technique are not discussed. Since the use of regression by financial analysts is naturally more oriented toward the methodology of its application than toward its statistical characteristics, an examination of a few chapters from this book can substantially expand the reader's concept of the power of the statistical method.

CHOU, YA-LUN. *Statistical Analysis.* New York: Holt, Rinehart and Winston, Inc., 1969.

This book is a standard elementary statistics textbook (736 pages). Chapters 19 and 20 (78 pages) present a reasonably clear statement of the method of calculating regressions and their associated statistical tests. The chief value of this material to a financial analyst would be its use as a handbook which can clarify the meaning of various statistics included in computer output which he might receive or articles which he might read.

EZEKIAL, MORDECAI AND FOX, KARL A. *Methods of Correlation and Regression Analysis.* 2d ed. New York: John Wiley & Sons, Inc., 1941.

This work provides an excellent presentation of both the elementary and somewhat more advanced aspects of regression (477 pages). The material is well illustrated with practical examples, and the calculations needed for any given technique are shown in detail. A great deal of verbal discussion on method and on the nature of each technique is included, adding significantly to the reader's intuitive understanding of the models. The first 347 pages provide practical techniques which can assist the analyst in everyday regression studies. The remaining material includes a discussion of joint regression, measuring correlation when the predictor is qualitative, and regression when a system of equations is being estimated.

DRAPER, N. R. AND SMITH, H. *Applied Regression Analysis.* New York: John Wiley & Sons, Inc., 1966.

This work is a somewhat more advanced presentation. It is helpful to an analyst already familiar with regression theory because it includes a number of variations in technique (such as dummy variables) which increase the range of applications without altering the computational aspects of the model itself.

JOHNSTON, J. *Econometric Methods.* New York: McGraw-Hill Book Company, 1963.

This book discusses regression theory from an advanced standpoint (296 pages). The first part of the book covers the standard multiple regression model, and the second covers various modifications to the model which can be made when certain assumptions of the basic model do not apply. A knowledge of the simpler aspects of matrix algebra is required, but the material can be read and understood if a knowledge of the more powerful models is needed.

LATANÉ, HENRY A. AND TUTTLE, DONALD L. *Security Analysis and Portfolio Management.* New York: The Ronald Press Company, 1970.
This book covers a very broad variety of investment topics with an unusually high degree of clarity (732 pages). The diverse set of investment problems are covered within the context of a single methodological framework which nevertheless remains remarkably free of dogmatic fealty to particular applications of models. The framework recommended is very flexible and can easily be used by practitioners without forcing their established techniques to be abandoned. Although the recommended methodology is quantitative, the presentation is verbal.
Regression and correlation are discussed in Chapter Nine (29 pages), but other chapters are very useful as follow-up reading to the presentation of other quantitative tools. Chapter Eight (33 pages) discusses applications of the mathematics of finance and also elementary statistics. Chapters 18 and 19 discuss the applications of probability theory to security analysis (53 pages), and Chapters 23 and 26 cover risk and the portfolio model problem (65 pages). The breadth of quantitative applications in the book make it difficult to decide where it should be listed in this book, and the choice of the regression chapter is purely arbitrary. If time limits the reader to only one selection from the list of additional readings, this book is the logical choice for the investment analyst or portfolio manager.

Chapter

13 Linear Programming or How to Get the Best Answer within Established Limitations

Linear Programming is designed to review a large number of combinations of data and from these select the best combination possible when the selection is affected by a number of restrictions. The definitions of the restrictions are critical, because they must not preclude an answer nor may they permit an infinite number of answers. Properly stated, however, they can present a problem to a computer that can rapidly consider all aspects of a complex problem. The answer will not only be the combination that maximizes the requirements but also provides the cost of selecting a less satisfactory combination.

USING LINEAR PROGRAMMING TO FIND THE BEST MIX

Linear Programming (LP) is an "optimizing" model, and its output is a maximization of all of the possibilities which the analyst presents to the technique. If he presents 45 alternatives, LP selects for him the "best" one. Actually, an infinite number of alternatives are given to the black box, and the best of all possible results is automatically returned. This capability obviously makes LP a useful tool, and it may profitably be used on any problem which the technique will accept. The problem is that the computations used inside the model restrict the type of problem which it can solve. In other words, not every infinite set of possible solutions can be given to an LP model in the expectation of finding the "best" result. In order to understand the type of problem that LP is capable of maximizing, the following example of a legitimate application is given.

199

Assume that a portfolio manager has just received $100,000 cash and must now invest these funds in one or more of the 20 stocks which the research department currently has on the buy list. Naturally, he wishes to obtain the "best possible" return (defined as income plus capital appreciation) on this particular account's investment capital. As a result of a report distributed throughout the portfolio section, he knows the analysts' estimates for the expected return of all 20 stocks during the next year and has no further information upon which to gauge the investment desirability of any of the issues. Obviously, the portfolio manager can purchase an infinite number of possible "mixes" of the 20 stocks, and he must attempt to select the best of these mixes. LP is capable of doing this precise thing: given all possible "mixes" of anything, it selects the best. In this particular, very simple example, both the analyst and the LP would choose to invest all funds in the one stock having the highest return because no consideration of diversification, risk, dividend yield, etc., has been included in the definition of the problem.

From the above example, it can be seen that an attempt to find a use for LP is actually an attempt to locate a problem which involves finding the *best mix* of a number of items. Such problems are very frequent in business because the essential nature of an executive decision is the balancing of simultaneous resources, problems, or objectives. For example, the production man who is responsible for three products at the same time has to produce a "mix" of the three which will prove to be most profitable to the company. The inventory manager with a $200,000 limit on total inventory value must decide upon the best "mix" of supplies to carry if sales losses from unfillable orders are to be minimized. The baker must use the best mix of ingredients in a cake in order to have a saleable product and still keep costs at a minimum. The department manager must decide upon the best mix of personnel in each particular section in order to emphasize output from the most profitable areas of his department and so maximize total output. Obviously, uses for linear programming are very widespread because they deal with the complex "balancing" problems which are encountered daily in business.

In the investment area, what is the best mix of stocks to maximize return on invested capital? What mix of stocks will minimize the total price-earnings ratio in the account? If a relative value approach is being used by the research department, how can the portfolio manager maximize the relative performance of his accounts? In economics, how can the mix of production among the various industries be altered in such a way that total profit could be maximized for a given level of Gross National Product? How do capacity limitations restrict this level of profit? Certainly, other applications can easily be found.

In most, if not all, of the above examples, the solution is obvious.

Buy the stock with the highest return, buy the stock with the best relative value, place all personnel on the most profitable project, etc. Why bother with LP when the answer is obvious? Because the obvious answer is not realistic. The portfolio manager buying only one stock would not be diversifying the risk, and the department manager placing all men on one project would not get all of his jobs done. Any businessman operating in the real world is subject to a large number of restrictions, or constraints. His decision concerning the best mix is usually sharply restricted; it cannot exceed certain bounds.

In the real world, the number of rules which cannot be broken is in most cases very large. For example, the production manager may have two assembly lines having given capacities, a limited number of people assigned to him, five unfilled emergency orders on one particular product, a distributor supply requirement on a marginal product, and so forth. A portfolio manager may have a diversification requirement imposed by the investment committee, a dividend yield requirement on the total portfolio imposed by the client, a yield requirement on each stock in the account imposed by policy, a risk limit stemming from a top-level policy decision, four stocks that cannot be sold for tax reasons, client-requested purchases which must be made, and so forth.

It is the presence of numerous constraints "clouding" the situation which forces the businessman to accept "reasonable" solutions instead of optimum solutions. But LP can consider all such limitations and still produce the single mix which is the best of all possible mixes. This is its usefulness. It is more realistic than human decisions in many cases because it can consider all of the very real aspects of the situation and still produce the best solution. At the same time, the solution still is fundamentally the result of human analysis because the businessman always determines precisely what is to be maximized and what constraints really deal with the particular problem being presented to the model.

Actually, the businessman defines precisely what the best solution really is, and the computer determines the answer which the description implies. Once an analyst defines the problem for the LP run, he also defines a specific solution at the same time. The problem is that the solution is concealed; it is uniquely determined but as yet is not known by the analyst. LP simply reveals the value which this previously specified number has, and therefore it is only a "searching" process methodically hunting for the particular value which will satisfy the specifications laid out by the businessman. LP, more than any other mathematical model in common use in business today, fits the analogy of the file clerk searching file cabinets for a requested memo. When the particular memo is located, it is given to the executive, and it is the memo called for even though the contents may not have been known ahead of time. LP retrieves numbers, and these numbers are the precise ones called for by the analyst defining the problem, even though the "contents" of these items were not known before the model was used. LP, in effect, is simply a retrieval system for numbers.

AN EXAMPLE OF USAGE

Assume for a moment that a portfolio manager has just received a new account which currently consists of only $100,000 cash. The portfolio man has an LP computer program available and also has a statistician who can help him prepare the input data. The manager knows that there are only five stocks currently on the buy list, and he is looking for the amount of money which he should place in each issue ($0 invested in a particular stock being possible). This definitely is a "mix" type of problem, and so he first takes a look at the nature of the mix with which he is concerned.

First, he decides that he wants the mix which will give him the best overall return on the account's investment for the next, say, five years. He is trying to find:

$$\$x_1 \text{ of stock A}$$
$$\$x_2 \text{ of stock B}$$
$$\$x_3 \text{ of stock C}$$
$$\$x_4 \text{ of stock D}$$
$$\$x_5 \text{ of stock E}$$

and he is going to use the percentage rate of return on each of these five stocks to determine the mix. Call r_i the rate of return for stock i. Then $r_1 x_1$ would stand for the total annual dollar return from stock A. Similarly, it is possible to form this term for stock B, C, etc.; and the total of the dollar returns from each stock in the portfolio will equal the total return from the portfolio as a whole. It is therefore legitimate simply to add the five terms together in order to find the total return, and the total return is the quantity to be maximized.

As a result of the analysis of portfolio return, the LP model is asked to maximize:

$$r_1 x_1 + r_2 x_2 + r_3 x_3 + r_4 x_4 + r_5 x_5$$

where r_i is the expected annual rate of return for stock i, say, 8% on Widgets, Inc. Each x_i is the total number of dollars which should be invested in stock i. The rates of return (r_i) are known because they are provided by the research department, but the amounts to be purchased (x_i) are not known. Determining their value is the reason for using the LP model.

This does not involve a great deal of mathematics, for only two changes in notation have been made. The item which is unknown has been given the name x_i, and the returns have been called r_i. The total return on the portfolio has then been stated in terms of r_i times the amount that is invested in each stock. The "r and x" expression is only another way of expressing the total return of the portfolio, total return being the sum of the returns on each stock that we buy. The difficult part of this procedure, of course, is not the mathematical expression itself but the problem of casting the particular nonmathematical problem into the quantitative mode which is necessary if the LP model is to be used.

With the item which is to be maximized fully defined (its technical name is "objective function"), the next logical step for the portfolio manager is to list the restrictions to which he is subject in his investment of these particular assets. For example:

1. The total portfolio yield must exceed 4%.
2. The total portfolio P/E must be less than 16.
3. The total portfolio risk must be less than 10% possible loss for the coming year (using the analysts' estimated figures).
4. No more than 40% of the portfolio may be invested in any one stock.
5. The total investment must be $100,000.
6. A negative amount of stock cannot be purchased.

The last two constraints are obvious, but the computer cannot detect through intuition even the simplest limitations. After the list of limitations has been completed, the manager and his statistician then convert the constraints into their mathematical representation so that it will be possible to prepare their input:

1. The total portfolio yield must exceed 4% of $100,000 or $4,000. By placing y_i = yield on stock i, the term $y_i x_i$ equals the annual dividend return in dollars for stock i. Because the portfolio return equals the sum of the $y_i x_i$, the statistician can write:

$$y_1 x_1 + y_2 x_2 + y_3 x_3 + y_4 x_4 + y_5 x_5 \geqslant \$4,000$$

2. By defining m_i as the P/E multiple for stock i, the term $m_i x_i$ equals the value of stock i weighted by its P/E. The sum of these terms is the weighted value of the entire portfolio, that is, (P/E) times $(100,000)$. It is possible to write:

$$m_1 x_1 + m_2 x_2 + m_3 x_3 + m_4 x_4 + m_5 x_5 \leqslant 1,600,000$$

3. Setting v_i equal to the variation, or downside risk in stock i given a market down, say 15%, the term $v_i x_i$ stands for the risk-weighted commitment to stock i. The sum of these terms equals the total

dollar risk in the portfolio as estimated by the research analysts. This can be written as:

$$v_1x_1 + v_2x_2 + v_3x_3 + v_4x_4 + v_5x_5 \leq \$10,000$$

4. Since each x_i (each stock) must be less than 40% of $100,000, in other words, $40,000, we have:

$$x_1 \leq \$40,000$$
$$x_2 \leq \$40,000$$
$$x_3 \leq \$40,000$$
$$x_4 \leq \$40,000$$
$$x_5 \leq \$40,000$$

5. Because the total investment in all five stocks must not exceed $100,000:

$$x_1 + x_2 + x_3 + x_4 + x_5 \leq \$100,000$$

6. Because only a positive amount of stock can be purchased in this account:

$$x_1 \geq 0 \qquad x_2 \geq 0 \qquad x_3 \geq 0 \qquad x_4 \geq 0 \qquad x_5 \geq 0$$

With this quantitative description, the problem can be presented to LP, and the result will be a precise statement of the number of dollars to be invested in each of the five stocks. In addition, the model will provide the total return on the portfolio, given that the investments were made in the way recommended.

FORMULATING OBJECTIVES AND CONSTRAINTS

From what has already been said about the nature of linear programming, it can be seen that the most difficult part of the model is actually nonquantitative in nature. The major problem in establishing an LP model is the managerial problem of specifying the objective which is to be maximized and the limitations which are present in the real world as constraints upon the set of acceptable solutions. This selection of a desirable characteristic (objective) and real world restrictions are obviously not mathematical in nature, for mathematics is concerned neither with desires nor with real world conditions. Mathematics only manipulates symbols; managers must see to it that those symbols represent his desires and his reality.

The portfolio model which has been used as an example of LP shows this principle very clearly. As already presented, the model has been given the objective of maximizing the expected total return on the portfolio over the next five years. The "desired characteristic" was chosen because of a decision by the portfolio manager, not because of any mathematical consideration. The expected return over the next one year could have been chosen just as easily. In fact, the objective does not need to relate to "return" at all. An income-oriented account may have an objective of maximizing current income subject to constraint of a "satisfactory" total return. If a portfolio manager accepts present value theory for stock valuation, the objective might be the maximum present value of the future dividend stream of the stocks available for investment. If relative value is the favored approach, the estimated deviation from "equilibrium" or "normal relative to the current structure of the market" might be chosen as the characteristic to be maximized. A very conservative manager might choose to minimize the downside potential of the account or possibly maximize the probability that the account will not decline. The choice of objectives is at the discretion of the manager, not the model, as these alternatives show. The LP technique will produce the portfolio most "desired" only after the manager has defined what he regards as "desirable," and different objectives produce different portfolios when using LP. This is realistic, for it is a well-established financial principle that different stocks suit different investor needs.

The constraints are also entirely under the control of the manager constructing the model. They can be realistic or unrealistic, depending upon the validity of his personal view of real-world conditions. LP will not violate his constraints under any circumstance, and he can choose to limit risk or to limit the minimum level of plant before depreciation. The model will accept both requirements as valid even though requiring some minimum level of plant before depreciation is a "strange" specification at best. The mathematical technique does not judge the constraints or "second guess" the manager; it simply produces the most desirable portfolio. The value of that portfolio is a function of the value of the manager, not the value of LP.

Constructing reasonable constraints can be a difficult matter, however, for the specifications must be firmly grounded in financial theory. Two major types of constraints can be applied to the portfolio example. First, limits must be placed on any portfolio as a result of the manager's knowledge of sound portfolio theory. Second, limits must be placed on particular portfolios to represent their individual needs and peculiarities. Examples of general constraints are limits on P/E, limits on risk, and limits requiring diversification. Examples of individual constraints are limits requiring a minimum level of yield, limits treating capital gains taxes, and limits restricting the sale of family-owned businesses.

Even though many constraints are general in nature, the precise level chosen for the constraints can be tailored to the needs of individual accounts. For example, the constraint limiting maximum acceptable possible loss may be set at 10% for the conservative account and at 20% for a more aggressive portfolio. Relaxing the level of this restriction in more risk-oriented accounts permits the model to purchase more high-return stocks before having to "worry" about satisfying the risk requirement. This permits the selection of a portfolio which has a higher estimated return but nevertheless does not go beyond the (now less severe) risk limitation of the (now more aggressive) investor. Relaxing the level of any constraint will usually result in a higher return (or more of the desired characteristic, however that might be defined). In fact, the only time that "loosening" a constraint will *not* raise the return is when the constraint was already so loose that it did not restrict the selection of the best portfolio in the first place.

The return on the portfolio can be seen to be heavily dependent upon the constraints. If a high yield is required, the LP model must examine only the possible portfolios that produce the necessary immediate income. This naturally eliminates from consideration a number of portfolios that have a high return. The result is a lower expected return on a portfolio that is constrained by a high yield requirement. The same line of thought applies equally well to very restrictive diversification or risk requirements, or to any constraint whatsoever. For this reason, care must be taken to assure the necessity of each constraint and to set each constraint at the most relaxed level possible. Failure to do this will reduce the desirability of the portfolio by requiring it to conform to a "nonsense" restriction.

All of the observations in this section point to one very important fact. The *value* of a mathematical model is not grounded in the *mathematics;* it is based upon the manager's ability to specify conditions in the real world. Mathematics merely points out the logical results of these specifications which must be realistic *given* that the original description of the world was realistic. If, for example, the original estimates of the return on each stock were "miserable," it is logical that the results of the LP portfolio that maximizes these "miserable" return estimates will not be outstanding. Since the LP model is usually run on a computer, this is an example of the fact that "computer selected" stocks are really selected by the criteria given to the computer by investment men and can produce results only as good as the theory used to build the model.

RELATIONSHIP TO SYSTEMS OF EQUATIONS

The constraints which limit the various mixes which the LP model can consider have a very interesting relationship to the "screening" aspects of equations discussed in the section on functions. Recall that an equation such as:

$$Cost = 10 + 0.8 \text{ (Production)}$$

can be regarded as a mathematical way of screening out a number of inadmissible or undesirable pairs of (Production, Cost) values. A combination like (Production = 10, Cost = 8.2), for example, would no longer be possible. This "rule" for valid combinations is very similar to the "constraint" in LP which states that certain values are not permitted. In the example of an LP application, the first constraint was:

$$\Sigma(y_i x_i) \geq \$4{,}000; \quad y_i = \text{yield}$$

This statement requires that whatever the maximum solution of $\Sigma(y_i x_i)$ might be, the set of stocks purchased (the x_i) must have a total yield of $4,000 or greater. The constraint therefore "screens" a number of x_i combinations out of the set of possible solutions.

The nature of this use of inequalities as screens can clearly be seen if graphs are used to "picture" the various possible combinations. In order to use graphs, return for a moment to the two-variable case of Production and Cost, and assume that instead of an equality the following was known:

$$C \geq 10 + 0.8P$$

The graph would look like Figure 13–1, where any C in the shaded

FIGURE 13–1

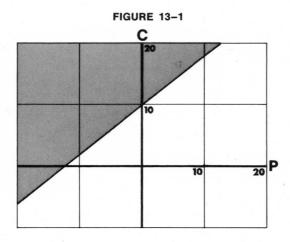

region is still acceptable because it would be greater than $10 + 0.8P$. The line which forms the lower boundary is, of course, the equation $C = 10 + 0.8P$. If we consider the inequality

$$C \leq 10 + 0.8P$$

the graph would look like Figure 13–2.

FIGURE 13–2

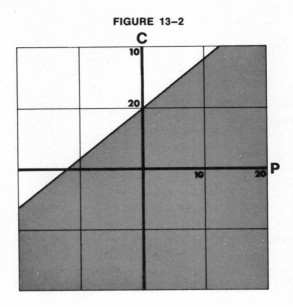

This shows that the other set of C values pass this inequality. The only set passing *both* inequalities is the set of (C, P) pairs which satisfy the *equation $C = 10 + 0.8P$*. This is reasonable, for if:

$$C \geqslant 10 + 0.8P$$

and

$$C \leqslant 10 + 0.8P$$

are both true, the obvious conclusion is that $C = 10 + 0.8P$, and this is graphed as the straight line, with all points above or below the line screened out.

Returning to the LP constraints, $\Sigma(y_i x_i) \geqslant \$4,000$ can be seen to screen a number of x_i combinations out of the solution in the same way as the graph screened certain Cost values; that is, the inequality sets up a "wall" in the solution space of x_i values. All x_i combinations on one side of the wall are excluded. If a number of constraints are introduced, a number of "walls" will "box in" the set of valid combinations of the x_i. This "boxing in" can be illustrated in the two-dimensional case by the graph in Figure 13–3.

FIGURE 13–3

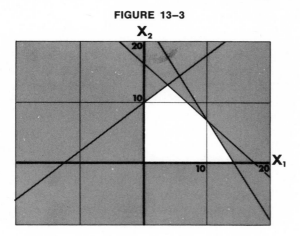

The unshaded area represents the set of possible solutions which do not violate any constraint. Mathematicians have spent a great deal of time examining the characteristics of this set, and the proof that LP will work depends on these qualities. Only a few points are of interest here, however.

The most important point that can be seen from this graphic presentation is the fact that once the analyst "boxes in" the permitted solutions, the LP solution technique (called an algorithm) can examine the set of possible combinations and locate the "best."

The second conclusion which is evident from the discussion is that it is quite possible to specify a number of constraints which screen the set of possible solutions so thoroughly that no solution is possible at all. In this case, no possible mix can be constructed which will satisfy all of the requirements, and the problem is said to be "infeasible." An example of an infeasible set of requirements might be a $P/E \leq 10$, a yield $\geq 10\%$, and a growth rate $\geq 25\%$ per year. In this case, the model need not select the best of many alternatives, for it could not locate even a single stock which could pass these constraints.

A third concept which can be related to the graphic interpretation of LP is the problem of an "unbounded" solution. If the analyst formulates the problem in such a way that the set of acceptable solutions is not "boxed in" completely, the model will be unable to evaluate all of the alternatives and no optimum solution can be found. An example of an unbounded problem might be the selection of an optimum portfolio with no limit on the number of dollars which could be invested. LP would simply start buying stocks and never stop.

THE APPROACH USED IN LP SOLUTIONS

The mathematical techniques (algorithms) used for the solution of LP problems are numerous, but the original approach, called the "simplex" algorithm, is still the most useful method if the general nature of the calculation of the solution is to be shown. Understanding a few of the features of the simplex method is important to the analyst for several reasons. It makes the formulation of the problem simpler because the requirements of the model are more fully known. It shows the close relationship between LP and matrix algebra (especially the solution of linear equations). Most important, however, is the fact that a knowledge of the *structure* of LP will permit the analyst to utilize additional features of the *output* of LP.

The portfolio problem introduced earlier in the chapter is somewhat too complicated to use as an example in which the actual computations are shown, and so an artificially simple problem is substituted for clarity. (It is understood throughout that all x_i must be ≥ 0):

$$\max z = 5x_1 + 3x_2$$

where:

x_1 is a stock with an expected appreciation plus dividend of \$5
x_2 is a stock with an expected appreciation plus dividend of \$3

subject to:

$4x_1 + 2x_2 \leq 10$ Total market value $\leq$ \$10; stock x_1 is selling for \$4 and stock x_2 is selling for \$2.

$2x_1 + 2x_2 \leq 8$ Downside loss potential $\leq$ \$8; stock x_1 may decline \$2 in a bad market, stock x_2 may also decline by \$2.

Although it is unlikely that a portfolio manager will ever consider the problem of constructing a portfolio when only two possible investments are available and those stocks are selling at prices of \$4 and \$2, the numbers should serve fairly well as simple examples in the calculations.

First, note that each of the inequalities could be turned into an equality by adding a slack variable. That is, since $4x_1 + 2x_2$ must be less than 10 by *some amount*, adding a variable which is equal to that amount will turn the inequality into an equation:

$$4x_1 + 2x_2 + x_3 = 10$$

where x_3 stands for the unknown amount by which the actual market value of the stocks in the account ($4x_1 + 2x_2$) falls short of the maximum possible value of the account's stocks (10).

Similarly:

$$2x_1 + 2x_2 + x_4 = 8$$

where x_4 stands for the unknown amount by which the account's risk ($2x_1 + 2x_2$) falls short of the maximum risk permitted (8).

Reviewing, x_3 and x_4 are called slack variables and are introduced solely for the purpose of converting the system of inequalities into a system of equations. As a result, the problem can now be written as:

$$\text{Max } z = 5x_1 + 3x_2 + 0x_3 + 0x_4$$

subject to:

$$\begin{aligned} 4x_1 + 2x_2 + x_3 \quad\;\; &= 10 \\ 2x_1 + 2x_2 \quad\quad + x_4 &= \;\,8 \end{aligned}$$

Or in matrix terms:

$$\max z = CX$$

Subject to:

$$AX = B$$

Where:

$$C = (5 \quad 3 \quad 0 \quad 0)$$

$$A = \begin{pmatrix} 4 & 2 & 1 & 0 \\ 2 & 2 & 0 & 1 \end{pmatrix}$$

$$X = \begin{pmatrix} x_1 \\ x_2 \\ x_3 \\ x_4 \end{pmatrix}$$

$$B = \begin{pmatrix} 10 \\ 8 \end{pmatrix}$$

It is not necessary to memorize each step in the solution procedure of an LP problem, but the following paragraphs indicate the general approach used in finding the solution and can be used as a general guide to the "flow" of the model as it moves methodically toward the optimum result.

The simplex method takes the problem as defined, including the slack variables, and arranges the data into Tableau 1.

TABLEAU 1

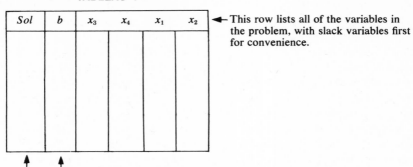

Sol	b	x_3	x_4	x_1	x_2

◄— This row lists all of the variables in the problem, with slack variables first for convenience.

└This column simply records the value of b, the level of the constraints.

This column is reserved for the variables which are currently favored — stocks being purchased, in the example. If these stocks are evaluated later in the analysis and found to be inferior, new stocks will be inserted here. The column heading "Sol" is an abbreviation of "Solution," indicating that the variables listed in the column are the variables currently providing the "solution" to the problem.

Filling out this table and including a few extra features, we have Tableau 2.

TABLEAU 2

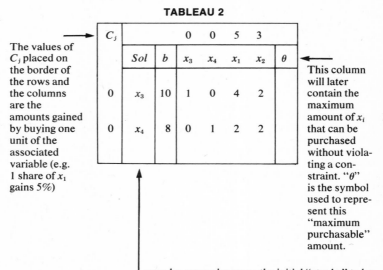

The values of C_j placed on the border of the rows and the columns are the amounts gained by buying one unit of the associated variable (e.g. 1 share of x_1 gains 5%)

C_j			0	0	5	3	
	Sol	b	x_3	x_4	x_1	x_2	θ
0	x_3	10	1	0	4	2	
0	x_4	8	0	1	2	2	

This column will later contain the maximum amount of x_i that can be purchased without violating a constraint. "θ" is the symbol used to represent this "maximum purchasable" amount.

x_3 and x_4 were chosen as the initial "stocks" to be evaluated because they are the slack variables and the algorithm always starts with slack variables. They will be evaluated and replaced with superior alternatives later.

All of the data so far has simply been a rearrangement of information in the original problem. The next logical question is how the method determines whether a different stock (x_1 or x_2 in this case) is superior to the current "stocks" (x_3 and x_4 in this case). In order to answer this question, we need to analyze what happens when such a substitution is made. First, the new stock produces a return on the portfolio. Second, the purchase forces the sale of an existing stock and consequently the loss of the return which the stock sold was providing to the portfolio. This is the indirect cost of adding a variable — of switching stocks. Portfolio managers are familiar with this idea, for they would not expect to be able to add all of the return on a purchased stock to the account return without first removing the return of the stock which was sold to finance the new purchase. This lost return on the stock sold to finance the purchase is the "indirect cost" of the switch. Let $z_j =$ *the indirect cost* of adding one share of stock j to the portfolio. The tableau already has c_j, which is *the direct gain* from adding one share of stock j. It follows that $c_j - z_j$ is the *net gain* of adding one share of stock j. Tableau 3, then, is the full simplex tableau.

TABLEAU 3

c_j			0	0	5	3	
	Sol	b	x_3	x_4	x_1	x_2	θ
0	x_3	10	1	0	4	2	
0	x_4	8	0	1	2	2	
	z_j	0	0	0	0	0	
	$c_j - z_j$	0	0	0	5	3	

z_j is the indirect cost of purchasing one unit of j. It stems from having to sell one unit of a stock in the "Sol" column. It is computed as the total of the products of the c_i of stocks purchased and the corresponding table entry a_{ij}. $(\Sigma_i(c_i a_{ij}))$

$c_j - z_j$ is the net gain from purchasing one share of stock j. The c_j is the gross gain from adding one unit of the stock, and the z_j is the "expense" of having to sell one unit of a stock to "make room" for the purchase. A positive $c_j - z_j$ shows an attractive "switch."

The $c_j - z_j$ row shows the amount by which the purchase of one share of any stock would change the value of the portfolio. The stock which would most increase the value of the portfolio as a whole if one share were purchased is a logical one to buy. In the example, this is x_1, with a $c_j - z_j$ of 5.

HOW MUCH OF A GOOD THING

This leaves the problems of how much of x_1 should be purchased and which stock should be sold to make room for the acquisition. This is the function of the θ column. Without going into detail, we will simply define θ_i as being the value of b_i divided by the value of the selected x (called x_k) in the appropriate row. This can most easily be explained by Tableau 4.

TABLEAU 4

c_j

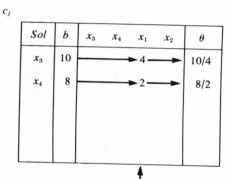

Sol	b	x_3	x_4	x_1	x_2	θ
x_3	10			→4→		10/4
x_4	8			→2→		8/2

x_1 has already been selected for purchase because it had the highest net benefit (highest $c_j - z_j$).

The smallest value of θ is then chosen, and that is the row to be removed (the stock to be sold). The value of θ is the number of shares of stock purchased, $2\frac{1}{2}$ shares of x_1 in this case. The total gain from the switch is $(c_j - z_j)(\theta)$. It is the value gained for one share purchased $(c_j - z_j)$ times the number of shares acquired (θ).

PERFORMING THE SWITCH

At this point, the stock to be purchased has been chosen (the column x_1) and the stock to be sold has been found (the row x_3). The next question is how the tableau can be altered in such a way that it will reflect this switch. Fortunately, it is possible to use a technique which has already been explained for this purpose — matrix inversion. All that needs to be done is to change the selected column to a column of the identity matrix (I) (see Tableau 5).

TABLEAU 5

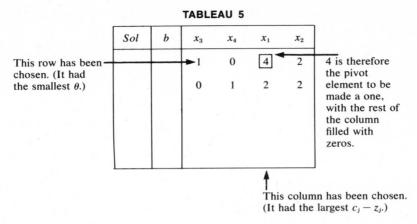

This row has been chosen. (It had the smallest θ.)

		x_3	x_4	x_1	x_2
		1	0	4	2
		0	1	2	2

Sol   *b*

4 is therefore the pivot element to be made a one, with the rest of the column filled with zeros.

This column has been chosen. (It had the largest $c_j - z_j$.)

In order to change this column into a column of the identity matrix, the "4" is changed to a "1" by multiplying the entire row by a suitable number (1/4) just as in inversion. (10 1 0 4 2) becomes (5/2 1/4 0 1 1/2). In addition, all other numbers in the x_1 column must be made equal to zero. The "2" must therefore be made a zero by adding a multiple (−2) of the first row to the second. This is also the same type of operation as is found in inversion, and Tableau 6 is the resulting tableau.

TABLEAU 6

Note that x_1 has replaced x_3 in the solution.

Sol	*b*	x_3	x_4	x_1	x_2
x_1	5/2	1/4	0	1	1/2
x_4	3	−1/2	1	0	1

Note that x_1 is now part of the identity matrix.

This is the new table, and the model proceeds by evaluating these stocks, locating possible switches (positive $c_j - z_j$ values), and bringing them into the solution one by one. Each switch which is made is called an iteration, and the model interates until no positive $c_j - z_j$ values can be found — until no net gain can be achieved by switching stocks. Note, however, that when each switch is being evaluated, *all of the constraints* are considered and never violated. When all iterations are completed, not one share of stock could be switched without lowering the portfolio's expected return.

SHADOW PRICES

One of the greatest side benefits of a knowledge of the nature of the simplex algorithm is a knowledge of the nature of the $c_j - z_j$. These are net gains when the iterations are being performed, but once an optimum solution is reached they are all zero or negative (this is the *definition* of optimum). A negative gain is a cost, so that the $c_j - z_j$ tells the analyst the *cost* of each of his constraints and the cost of each variable not in the optimum solution.

The cost information provided by the LP model is frequently called "shadow prices." In the portfolio application of linear programming, typical constraints are yield, P/E, risk, and a restriction on the amount which can be invested in each industry. Each constraint will have a shadow price representing the cost of not relaxing the constraint. For example, assume that the optimum portfolio has an expected return of 12% and is constrained to a yield $\geq 4\%$. Assume further that the shadow price of the yield constraint is 2. This means that the total return on the portfolio could be increased by 2% if the required yield were relaxed by one unit (from 4% to 3%). This shadow price therefore provides a precise measure of the "cost" in lost return which results from the presence of the constraint.

Each constraint has a shadow price, and the same interpretation that was given to the cost of "yield" can be given to any constraint. If, for example, the "risk" constraint were set at 10% of current market value, and had a shadow price of 3, relaxing the risk level to 11% would increase the expected performance by 3%. In the case of restrictions on investment in each industry, there would be one constraint for each industry. Each industry would therefore have a shadow price representing the loss in performance which results from being unable to purchase more stocks in that industry. This information can be of great value in revising the diversification limits on portfolios because it pinpoints the restrictions which are too costly to performance.

In many problems, some of the constraints will be found to have a shadow price of zero. This obviously means that relaxing the constraint by a small amount will not affect the return on the portfolio. The only possible explanation of this occurrence is that the constraint does not restrict the selection of the optimum portfolio in any way. In other words, a constraint with a zero "cost" is satisfied by the portfolio that would have been selected even if the constraint were not present. The constraint, to put it bluntly, is not constraining. It is a limitation that would have been met automatically even if it had not been present.

The presence of such a constraint does not mean that the problem has been incorrectly stated, because it is usually impossible to determine ahead of time that particular requirements will be met automatically. If the portfolio must yield more than 4%, for example, this constraint must be included in the problem. But if the optimum portfolio selected without regard to yield happens to yield 4.5%, the constraint happens to be unnecessary since it would have been satisfied anyway. In this case, the shadow price of the yield constraint would be zero, but the restriction should nevertheless have been included in the problem because the results could not have been foreseen. One of the advantages of LP is that it informs the user of the restrictions that are met without cost (zero shadow price) as well as the ones that are expensive. This pinpoints the "free benefits" in the problem.

Shadow prices are also provided for the variables in the problem. The interpretation of these cost figures parallels the meaning of the constraint costs. In the portfolio example, the variables (x_i) are the stocks available for purchase. The shadow price of a stock indicates the amount by which the portfolio's return would decline if one unit of the stock were purchased. If, for example, the problem were formulated in terms of the percentage of the account invested in each stock and Widgets Inc. had a shadow price of 0.1, then committing 1% of the account to Widgets would reduce the portfolio return by 0.1%. The cost of every stock is provided, and issues having high shadow prices obviously are candidates for sale if currently held in an account. The stocks actually chosen by the LP model for the portfolio, on the other hand, have a zero shadow price, indicating that their purchase would not lower the optimum return. This is natural, since their purchase is *required* for the optimum return.

The particular meaning of shadow prices will vary depending upon the nature of the LP problem being solved. A linear programming extension of input-output analysis will not have shadow prices expressed in terms of stocks. But all shadow prices of all LP problems have in common the fact that they are the cost of constraints or the cost of forcing the use of an undesirable variable. In every case, the shadow price is the $c_j - z_j$ in the tableau of the optimum solution, and by the definition of "optimum," all shadow prices must restrict the value of the objective (return, in the example) or be zero.

EXTENSIONS OF LINEAR PROGRAMMING

Parametric Programming

The level at which the constraints are set has already been shown to have an impact upon the value of the objective function. In the portfolio problem, relaxing the constraints raised the return. The reason why this relation holds true is that different levels for the constraints produce different variables in the final solution. In the portfolio application, for example, relaxing the yield requirement permitted the purchase of more high return stocks that had a low yield.

The relationship between the levels of the constraints and the solution can be systematically explored by means of parametric programming. The precise manner in which the constraints are to be relaxed is stated mathematically, and the solution variables for a wide range of constraint levels are automatically provided. A simple example of this technique would be to hold all constraints constant except for yield and then study the behavior of a portfolio as the yield requirement is increased from zero to infinity. If there were ten stocks available for investment, the results of the study might show something like Table 13–1.

TABLE 13–1

Return	Yield Between	Purchase
16%	0% and 2.4%	x_4, x_8, x_{10}
14%	2.4% and 2.9%	x_4, x_9, x_{10}
13%	2.9% and 4.3%	x_1, x_4, x_9, x_{10}
9%	4.3% and 5.2%	$x_1, x_3, x_4, x_9, x_{10}$
7%	5.2% and 6.5%	x_1, x_3, x_4, x_8, x_9
—	6.5% up	no feasible solution

The return associated with each of these possible portfolios is also provided. The constraint which is examined, of course, does not necessarily relate to yield; it could refer to the level of acceptable risk just as easily. In fact, it is possible to vary two or more constraints at the same time. The level of the constraints in problems of this type is called a parametric requirements vector, and the problem is called "parametric on the right hand side" or "RHS parametric."

An alternative form of parametric programming is "parametric on the objective function." This technique systematically varies the coefficients in the objective function. In the portfolio model, this would vary the expected returns of the stocks. The results of this type of study show how the portfolio would change as the estimated returns of the stocks were changed.

Integer Programming

This is a special form of linear programming where the values of the variables must be integers. An example of the value of this new type of limitation can easily be found in portfolio analysis. Assume that a portfolio problem has been formulated in such a way that the x_i refer to the number of round lots of stock i that are to be purchased. This is not a substantial change from the original example, where x_i referred to the number of dollars of stock i purchased. By using round lots, the integer requirement that the value of x_i be 0 or 1 or 2 or . . . forces the optimum portfolio to avoid the purchase of odd lots (which, of course, are fractions of round lots).

The solution which is given by integer programming is not necessarily the solution which would result if a normal LP run were made and the results were simply "rounded off" to the nearest round lot. If optimum results are desired, the integer requirement must be built into the structure of the problem itself, not approximated after the model has been applied.

The value of integer programming is far greater than might at first be suspected, for it would be ridiculous to follow a "normal" LP solution requiring the purchase of $1\frac{1}{2}$ plants or the addition of 4.35 employees to the staff. Another invaluable use of the technique can only be mentioned in this chapter. If an integer solution is required and the x_i are also required to be ≤ 1, the only two acceptable solutions for any variable are 0 or 1. This type of model can be used in studies related to optimal selection, for the selected variables are assigned a one and the rejected variables are assigned a zero. If the set of "yes-no," "on-off," or "good-bad" variables must be found subject to a number of real world restrictions, this technique is invaluable.

Examples of this "0–1" model can be found in capital budgeting, personnel selection, and research and development allocations. Applications in investment research have not been extensively explored, but the practical nature of the problems solved by this approach indicates that many problems in this field could be approached in this way. For example, what set of companies deserve coverage by the research department? What set of industries not currently considered should be added? Which industries should be assigned to analyst A? What set of accounts deserve weekly review by the portfolio manager? If only five stocks can be recommended in a meeting, which five should be included?

Nonlinear Programming

The major restriction on linear programming can be deduced from its name. The mathematical expression of the "mix" problem must be stated in the form of linear equations or inequalities. Although a surprisingly large number of problems encountered in practical analysis can be expressed in linear terms, occasionally an optimum "mix" of variables is needed where only nonlinear expressions are available. A number of extremely sophisticated mathematical techniques are available to solve these often highly complicated problems. Problems falling into the nonlinear programming category may arise in the course of mathematical analysis, from attempts to optimize random variables (stochastic programming), from attempts to find optimal solutions when x^2 appears in the problem (quadratic programming), or from an analysis of sequential decision problems (dynamic programming). The simple solution common to all of these problems and available to any practicing analyst is to seek the nearest mathematician.

One important application of nonlinear technique should be pointed out, however. A number of portfolio models have been constructed using quadratic programming. These models attempt to maximize return subject to a risk constraint, where risk is defined to be variance of return (variance is obviously quadratic). The two most important formulations in terms of return and risk are due to Harry M. Markowitz and William F. Sharpe. An excellent nontechnical presentation of the nature of the Markowitz model is available in the article by William J. Baumol, "Mathematical Analysis of Portfolio Selections: Principle and Application," which was printed in the *Financial Analysts Journal,* September–October, 1966, and reprinted in *C.F.A. Readings in Financial Analysis,* Second Edition, Homewood, Illinois: Richard D. Irwin, Inc., 1970. A brief sketch of the approach is appropriate at this point.

The Markowitz model asserts that the objective of the investor is to maximize return subject to some limit on the uncertainty associated with the resulting portfolio. He then asserts that this uncertainty can be more or less approximated by a normal distribution which describes the probability of each level of return possible for the portfolio. As the variance of this distribution becomes greater, the investor is more uncertain of any given level of return.

The portfolio's distribution is considered to be a function of the distribution of each security in the portfolio and of the extent to which the price movements of these securities are correlated. Each stock has a distribution describing its return, and the portfolio's risk is calculated using both these distributions and their correlations. If the price movements of the stocks in a portfolio are highly correlated, then the risk in the portfolio will be greater than would be the case if they were independent of each other. If the stocks are risky (have a high variance), then the portfolio will have a higher risk than would be the case if they had more certain returns. This formulation can be seen to cover a number of traditional investment concepts, for it includes risk in the structure of the problem, associates this risk with riskier companies, and implies that risk can be reduced by purchasing a number of different investments having independent price characteristics.

The advantage to this mathematical definition of risk is that it permits the use of a mathematical model which explicitly considers risk in the optimization process. The model develops the portfolio having minimum risk given some stated level of expected return. By then executing the optimization for a large number of stated returns, a number of portfolios are selected, with each portfolio associated with one risk-return combination. The set of all optimal risk-return combinations is called the "efficient frontier," and all other portfolios are said to be inefficient because a higher return could be gained on a different portfolio without an increase in risk.

One of the major disadvantages of this model is that it requires as input the expected return and variance of every security that is a potential investment and the correlation coefficient of every stock to every other stock. In a 200-company universe, this is over 20,000 estimated values. The Sharpe model reduces the input requirements by expressing the risk of each stock in terms of its correlation to a single market index and then proceeds to develop optimal risk-return portfolios. Other variations in the Markowitz-type approach are numerous.

ADDITIONAL READINGS IN LINEAR PROGRAMMING

The literature on linear programming is surprisingly large considering the youth of the technique. The majority of material, however, deals either with particular applications or with minor modifications which reduce the problems in the computer calculation of solutions in special cases. Examples of applications can be found in virtually any journal, and the following is therefore a list of books which cover the broad aspects of the model.

DORFMAN, ROBERT; SAMUELSON, PAUL A.; AND SOLOW, ROBERT M. *Linear Programming and Economic Analysis.* New York: McGraw-Hill Book Company, 1958.
    This work discusses the applications of the LP model in the field of economics (464 pages). Although the computational features of LP are treated briefly, the emphasis is on the use of the technique when dealing with economic problems. This application orientation makes the work very valuable to the analyst and may modify his thinking concerning both the behavior of economic variables and the range of application of LP. The theory of the firm, the possibilities stemming from input-output analysis, and capital accumulation are among the topics considered.

HADLEY, G. *Linear Programming.* Reading, Massachusetts: Addison Wesley Publishing Company, 1962.
    This book is the rigorous mathematical treatment of the subject (516 pages). It is not as difficult as the phrase "rigorous" usually implies, but a solid understanding of matrix algebra is essential.

LLEWELLYN, ROBERT W. *Linear Programming.* New York: Holt, Rinehart and Winston, Inc., 1964.

This book provides an excellent description of the computational aspects of the model (357 pages). If the algebraic aspects of LP need to be considered, this text exhibits the methods of solution in great detail. A number of solution techniques are examined — simplex, revised simplex, dual method, and primal-dual methods. Modifying the final solution, parametric programming, ranging, and integer programming are explained from the computational standpoint.

LUCE, R. DUNCAN AND RAIFFA, HOWARD. *Games and Decisions.* New York: John Wiley & Sons, Inc., 1957.

This book discusses the various aspects of game theory (which is integrally bound up with the structure of LP). Game theory deals with maximizing return under conditions of conflict, and this obviously means that it treats a very wide range of economic phenomena. Unfortunately, mathematical complexities have so far prevented the useful application of the theory in practical problems. Nevertheless, the conceptual structure of conflict situations can in itself be a rewarding study, and this book is the clearest presentation of that structure that is currently available. The presentation is essentially verbal, but extensive use is made of the notation of mathematics.

MARKOWITZ, HARRY M. *Portfolio Selection.* John Wiley & Sons, Inc., 1959.

This book discusses the foundations of the Markowitz model in detail, emphasizing the formulation of the technique and the concepts from elementary probability theory which are used rather than the mathematical procedures for optimization (340 pages). The treatment includes extended discussions of quantitative concepts, but the treatment is practical and emphasizes the intuitive meaning of the tools described. This work is excellent reading for anyone interested in portfolio theory and is also a fine introduction to the behavior and treatment of random variables.

SHARPE, WILLIAM F. *Portfolio Theory and Capital Markets.* New York: McGraw-Hill Book Company, 1970.

This book is a comprehensive discussion of the portfolio model problems on a nonmathematical basis (302 pages). It is by far the clearest and most useful introduction to the current thought in the fields of portfolio optimization and capital markets. The basic structure of the portfolio problem is covered in the first 76 pages. Capital market equilibrium is discussed in 39 pages, and the balance of the book is devoted to modifications of the basic model and an evaluation of their implications. All of the mathematical aspects are concentrated in five appendixes (79 pages). These are very well written and should be consulted by those readers having an interest in the quantitative technique as well as the quantitative theory.

Chapter
14 The Computer and Programming

Many of the techniques described earlier in this book involve the use of a computer. Although an analyst is not expected to be either a programmer or a computer scientist, an understanding of some of the fundamentals of how a computer works and how it can be used will enable him to use a computer more intelligently. A computer is a complex and flexible machine that is a combination of hardware and programming software. Programs are instructions to the computer telling it what to do and in what order. Special languages such as Fortran and Cobol have been designed to simplify programming by translating the instructions into the computer's machine language. These programs can be designed to perform very complex and repetitious steps with simple instructions. An illustration is given by an elementary program written in Fortran.

NATURE OF THE COMPUTER

The computer is the most powerful tool that has ever been made available to the financial analyst. Without it, only a few of the quantitative techniques described in this book could ever be applied in a practical fashion to complicated problems. Computer science is an extremely broad and highly technical area. This chapter, however, is not designed to be an exhaustive treatment of the nature or use of the computer. It is only an attempt to familiarize the financial analyst with the very basic principles by which a digital computer functions.

The computer is a machine, but it is not like any other type of machine used in business today. A businessman may buy a typewriter if he needs a machine to transfer words neatly from verbal to written form. Or he may buy an adding machine to calculate certain values, graphic devices to provide displays, a machine sorter to organize punchcard decks, and so forth. The computer, however, is a "black box" par excellence; it is a machine which when properly programmed can behave as if it were a typewriter, adding machine, sorter, and the like. The computer, in other words, can be any combination of a number of machines, depending upon the particular program which tells it what to do. In a way, it is possible to say that the computer plus any given program equals a "black box" and that the computer can be as many "black boxes" as there are programs to guide it. Properly instructed, the computer can serve not only as a typewriter, sorter, adding machine, and the like, but also as an entire accounting system, an information system automatically reporting key facts to management, a multiple regression model, a linear programming model, and more. Each program converts the computer into a different type of "black box," and as a result "creates" a new machine. Naturally, the intrinsic value of the computer stems from the combination of the physical computer "hardware" and the instructions which constitute the programming "software"—from the combination of the computer's "labor force" and the programmer's "management."

The functions performed by any computer operating under the instructions of any given program can be divided into the three logical sections of Figure 14–1.

FIGURE 14–1

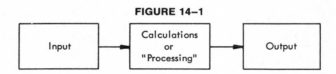

This division of functions can be seen to correspond to the natural requirements of any practical "black box":

1. Something must be put into the box for anything to happen at all.
2. The box must do something to the input or it has no practical value at all.
3. The results of the activity of the box on the input must be reported, or the calculations will be performed but the results will never be known by the researcher.

THE "CALCULATE" OR "PROCESS" FUNCTION

When computers are mentioned in everyday discussions, what is usually meant is the calculation or "thinking" aspect of a computer system. This function is the heart of any computer installation and is performed by the central processing unit (CPU). The simplest way to picture the CPU is to regard it as a "grid" of storage locations. Each storage location is capable of holding a number or letter and all of these locations taken together provide the computer with a "memory." Obviously, this memory is restricted to the number of storage locations present in any given CPU. The important point in working with the computer is to bear in mind that the computer is not capable of processing any information which is not in memory at the time that the calculation is desired, i.e., the computer cannot calculate using numbers that it cannot find in one of its storage locations.

Figure 14–2 shows a hypothetical computer which has only 20 storage locations:

FIGURE 14–2

Second Digit of Storage Location

	0	1	2	3	4	5	6	7	8	9
First Digit of Storage Location 0						2				
1								3		

The illustration shows that only two numbers have been stored in the computer memory (technically called core storage). Location number 5 has the number (2), and the number (3) is stored in location number 17. If the next instruction in the computer program were to add the contents of location number 5 to the contents of location 17 and store the result in location 12, core storage would have the appearance of Figure 14–3 after the instruction was performed:

FIGURE 14–3

	0	1	2	3	4	5	6	7	8	9
0						2				
1			5					3		

All computer instructions are in principle quite similar to the addition instruction just shown. They refer to the contents of storage locations and manipulate those contents in various ways, eventually storing the results of the manipulation in some other storage location. As a result of the nature of this process, all calculations can easily be seen to be completely dependent upon the contents of core storage at the time that the calculation is made.

PROGRAMS

Just as a man with only a memory and no ability to use judgment in relating his memory or experience to practical problems is regarded as having limited value, so the value of the computer would be restricted without a program by which it can process the data in memory. *All* programs are a step-by-step list of instructions which the computer is to perform sequentially. The strength of the computer is that it follows these instructions in the minutest detail, without once deviating from the prescribed rules of operation. The weakness of the computer is its total inability to exercise human judgment on even the most minor matters. Therefore, the programmer is forced to describe his problem in the most precise detail and without even the slightest error or ambiguity.

Once a program has been written and is available to the computer in machine language, the program can be input to the computer at any time. This program can then be used to process whatever data the computer has in core storage. For example, if the program is designed to cause the computer to perform a simple regression analysis, the computer can use this model in connection with one set of data, output the results, and then read in another set of data, proceed by applying the regression model to this set, output the results, and so forth. When all simple regressions have been processed, the computer can then read a linear programming program into core storage, then read in the data for the first LP problem, perform the analysis, output the results, read in the data for the next LP problem, and so on. Putting this into a more concise form, any given program can be designed in such a way that it is capable of handling multiple sets of data, and any computer can execute any number of programs sequentially. Figure 14–4 shows what the core storage of a hypothetical computer might look like just before the program is to be executed.

FIGURE 14–4

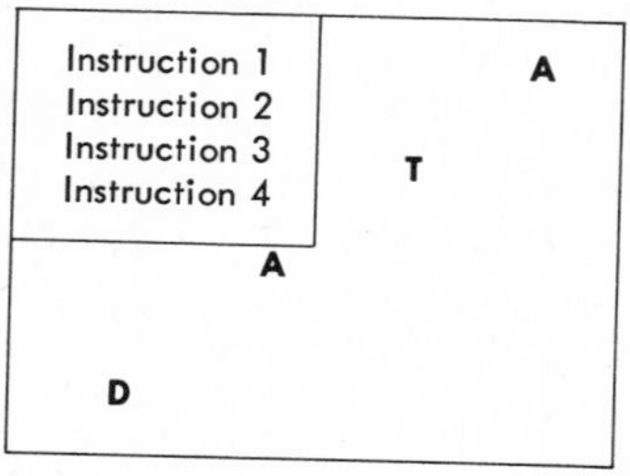

Since any program will always be executed sequentially by a computer, the machine will automatically access instruction one in the section of core which contains the program, perform whatever operation this instruction indicates, then access instruction two, perform this operation, and so on. This process will be continued unless an instruction is encountered which specifically commands a different order of processing or which informs the machine that no additional instructions are present within the program. The above diagram is obviously a simplification for several reasons. First, typical programs having practical application range from 300 to 10,000 or more instructions. Second, the amount of core storage actually occupied by the program depends solely upon the nature of that program. One program may occupy 80% of core while its data occupies only 10%, leaving 10% of core unused. Another program may occupy 10% of core, while its data requires 85%. Core storage, in other words, consists of available storage locations; the computer is completely indifferent to the particular application's choice of storing instructions or data. The only restriction, of course, is the fact that the total of program instructions and data for processing must not exceed the limits of the memory of core.

A DEEPER APPRAISAL OF THE COMPUTER

It is already obvious that working with a computer is much more detailed than is commonly realized. The machine must receive an instruction for every single step of the analysis which is to be performed, and the data must be stored in the computer in a known location or the program would be unable to inform the machine of the specific numbers to be processed. In addition, every single instruction and piece of data must be input to the computer in such a way that it will be present in core storage at the specific time that the application requires it for processing. Finally, the results of the process must be output in some meaningful form. Unfortunately, from the professional programmer's standpoint there is a great deal more to the computer than this. In a digital computer, all contents of core storage must be in binary form. This means that every unit of information made available to the computer must be some arrangement of "1" or "0." This causes no problem if the actual number 0 or 1 is to be processed, but the number 2 must be "rephrased" in such a way that it will consist of an arrangement of 1's or 0's.

The easiest way to explain this new, binary number system is to review the normal, or decimal, system which all investment men use daily. The decimal system gets its name from the number "10," which is the base of the system. In other words, symbols called digits are used to represent all positive whole numbers up to but not including the number 10. These symbols are easily recognized, for they are the numbers "0," "1," "2," "3," "4," "5," "6," "7," "8," and "9." The number 10, however, does not have a unique symbol—it is represented by a combination of the digits "1" and "0." When the digits 1 and 0 are seen together, people automatically recognize it as a symbol for the number ten. But this automatic recognition is more a matter of tradition than mathematics. Mathematically, the concept which is involved could be called "placement value." The fact that the number 1 is placed to the left of the number 0 gives the digit "1" a different meaning. In the decimal system, the meaning is defined as "one set of ten." The 0 is the rightmost digit of the number and its meaning is "zero sets of one." In the decimal number 100, the 1 stands for "one set of ten times ten, or one set of one hundred." The leftmost 0, of course, stands for zero sets of ten, and the rightmost 0 stands for zero sets of one.

As can be seen from these examples, any reasonably large number in the decimal, or base ten, system is actually the sum of the digits involved in the numbers weighted according to the base of the system. Figure 14–5 may make this point clearer.

FIGURE 14–5

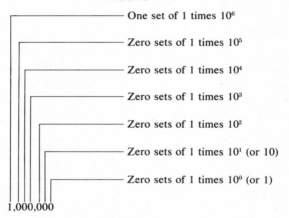

One set of 1 times 10^6

Zero sets of 1 times 10^5

Zero sets of 1 times 10^4

Zero sets of 1 times 10^3

Zero sets of 1 times 10^2

Zero sets of 1 times 10^1 (or 10)

Zero sets of 1 times 10^0 (or 1)

1,000,000

"One million" therefore implies:

$$(1 \cdot 10^6) + (0 \cdot 10^5) + (0 \cdot 10^4) + (0 \cdot 10^3) + (0 \cdot 10^2) + (0 \cdot 10^1)$$
$$+ (0 \cdot 10^0) = 1,000,000$$

In the binary number system, the base of the system is the number "2," and only positive whole numbers less than, but not including, 2 have unique digits identifying them. Obviously, in this case only the numbers "0" and "1" are used as fundamental digits. In order to express larger numbers, the binary system uses the same technique as the more familiar decimal system, assigning a "placement value" to the digits whenever numbers larger than one need to be represented. But since the base of the binary system is 2, the placement value is weighted by 2 instead of by 10, as was the case in the decimal system. For example, in the binary system, the number "2" is represented as 10, meaning one set of 2 and zero sets of 1. The number "3" is represented by the value 11, meaning one set of 2 and one set of 1. The number "4" is represented by the value 100, meaning one set of 2 times 2 and zero sets of 2 and zero sets of 1. Table 14–1 shows the relationship between the structure of the decimal and the binary number systems.

TABLE 14–1

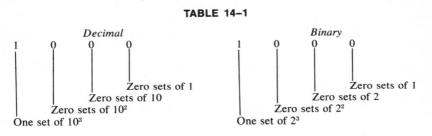

Using the information concerning number systems that has been developed, it is relatively easy to see how any decimal number can have a binary system equivalent. Table 14–2 gives certain selected base ten numbers and the corresponding binary representation.

TABLE 14–2

Decimal Number	Equivalent Binary Number
1	1
2	10
3	11
4	100
5	101
6	110
7	111
8	1000
9	1001
10	1010
25	11001
100	1100100

ASSEMBLERS

When a program is executed on a computer, all of the instructions and all of the data present in core storage are in binary form. In addition, all of the "storage locations" by which the program references the data have "addresses" which are in binary form. In other words, the programmer working solely in machine language would input to the computer only a combination of 1's and 0's for any application. This problem would be so enormous that it would virtually be impossible to use the computer in practical applications if computer scientists had not invented an escape from this mass of detail. The means of escape was, paradoxically, the computer itself. A computer program was written which was capable of receiving as input the programmer's instructions in a humanly intelligible form and provided as output the machine-language binary program. This program, (called an "assembler") permitted programmers to input reasonably intelligible statements to the computer and then converted these statements into the actual program which the computer could at some other time use to process data in an actual application. All modern computers of any reasonable size are now equipped with assembly programs.

The advantages of writing in assembly language instead of machine

FIGURE 14–6

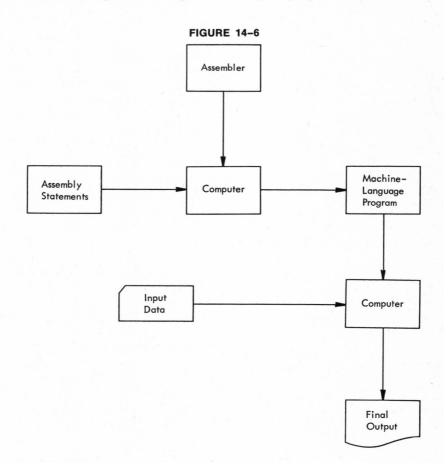

language are threefold. First, the programmer can refer to a storage location by some label which he can choose at will. If, for example, the programmer wishes to refer to a specific number as "X," he can do so in the assembly language and the assembler will automatically assign a storage location for "X" in the program. Second, if the programmer has reason to go to a specific instruction in the program from some other program location, he can easily label any assembly language statement and later write an instruction which goes to that label. The assembler will see to it that the instruction which "branches" to the labeled instruction will go to the correct core location. Third, the various types of instructions which can be processed by the computer can be referenced by alphabetic names which the assembler will automatically convert into their binary equivalent. Figure 14–6 shows how the computer uses the assembly program, assembly language statements, and input data to produce output.

COMPILERS

The binary representation of data and the use of assembly language is actually an area over which the analyst need have little concern. It is included in this chapter only to show the structural means by which the computer solves problems for the analyst. Actually, the advent of compilers makes even assembly language statements too detailed to be considered in depth by anyone other than professional programmers. A compiler is a program by which the computer can write its own machine language program. In other words, computer science has for quite some time already achieved the fabled "self-programming computer." Actually, a compiler is a program which receives as input a number of English-like instructions and then converts these instructions into an assembly language program. The assembly language program is then converted automatically into a machine-language (binary) program. The machine is programming itself in the sense that it is creating a program which it will later use in an actual application, but it is not by any means operating on its own. The machine-language or "object program" performs exactly the same set of operations that are specified by the programmer as input to the compiler. The computer simply handles the majority of the detail work which is necessary to "clean up" the program so that it will be capable of execution by the computer. By using a compiler, it is possible for the programmer to write instructions in a high-level language which the computer can be made to understand, freeing the people who work with the computer from having to deal with the machine's actual characteristics.

Probably the best known compiler language is Fortran. When an investment analyst writes a Fortran program, it is manually keypunched and presented to the computer. The computer first reads the Fortran compiler so that it will be able to understand the Fortran instructions written by the analyst. Next, it reads the Fortran instructions which the analyst has just written and had keypunched. These instructions are frequently referred to as the "source deck." The compiler then converts the source deck into a set of assembly language instructions and turns control over to the assembly program. The assembler then uses the assembly language statements just created by the Fortran compiler as input and converts these into the machine-language program which will be used to process actual data. The machine-language program can then be used to process actual data. The machine-language statements are usually punched on cards by the computer and are referred to as the "object deck." Summarizing the entire process, the computer is not capable of understanding Fortran statements. It has available, however, a Fortran compiler which *can* understand Fortran statements and can translate them into statements which can be used by the assembler to create the machine-language statements which are directly intelligible to the computer itself. The process can be diagrammed as in Figure 14–7.

FIGURE 14–7

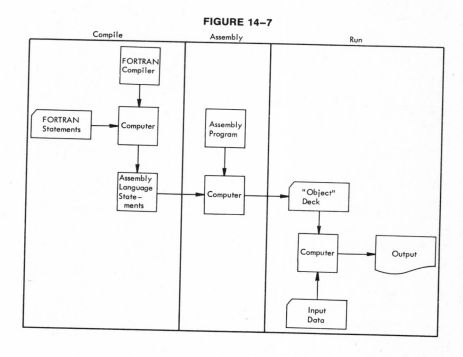

By using Fortran or any other compiler, anyone programming a computer can give specific commands in a language resembling English, or at least mathematical English. Each of these commands is independent of the specific computer language and will usually be translated into a number of machine-language computer instructions. The entire process of going from the Fortran coding sheet (written statements) to the computer output can be handled automatically by the operations division of any moderately large organization, unless the program has an error and must be "debugged." Extensive testing and debugging, however, are inevitable on programs of any magnitude.

A number of compilers or "languages" are available for programming and operate in a manner similar to the Fortran example shown above. All of these languages have essentially the same approach as Fortran, consisting of a set of statements indirectly usable by the computer. The best known high-level languages are Fortran, Cobol, Algol, PL/I, and Basic.

Fortran stands for "Formula Translation" and was designed as a mathematical language which could be used to process rather complicated mathematical problems and then report the results. As a consequence of the motives behind the design, it is very useful in computational programs or programs having extremely complicated logic. However, it is more difficult to use efficiently in problems requiring complicated input-output, editing, or the handling of letters or symbols instead of numbers (called "alphanumeric" data).

Cobol, on the other hand, stands for "Common Business-Oriented Language" and as a result of the motives behind its design is a very powerful tool when the programmer is concerned with the arrangement of the data, editing results to create a businesslike report, speed in input and output of massive amounts of data, and controlling the validity of both the data and the processing. It is, however, much less useful whenever extensive calculations are to be performed or complex logical operations are to be executed on a relatively small amount of data.

Algol is a language which was especially designed for the creation of computational models (called algorithms). As a result, it is perhaps even more powerful than Fortran in the strictly computational aspects of the computer. Unfortunately, it appears to be fairly limited in the nonmathematical portion of computer usage such as input-output.

PL/I is a new language which was specifically designed to synthesize the mathematical capabilities of Fortran with the input-output and editing capabilities of Cobol. As a result, it is very useful on either scientific problems which for some reason require the handling of large amounts of data or for business problems which, due to the growing usage of quantitative techniques, now frequently require rather complicated mathematical manipulations.

Basic is a simplified language which is very similar to Fortran but slightly easier to learn and slightly less flexible.

In addition to these general purpose languages, a number of special purpose programs are available which have certain language characteristics. Several of these are based on decision tables, a concept which unfortunately cannot be explored further because of considerations of space. Other special purpose languages are simulation-oriented, such as GPSS or Simscript, and still others are industry-oriented. From the general languages and the special-purpose languages, programmers can create a number of very general programs, each capable of handling a large number of diverse assignments. These software-packages, or systems, provide the computer user with a kind of middle ground lying between the creation of a large number of small special programs at a high total cost on the one hand and the extreme generalness of the languages on the other.

FLOWCHARTING AND PROGRAM CHARACTERISTICS

The nature of a computer program has already been discussed in moderate detail. For example, it is already known that the program must be in binary machine-language form before it can be processed by a computer, that it must be present in core storage during processing, that it is a step-by-step sequence of instructions which are used by the computer to operate upon data available in core storage and that every single, specific action taken by the computer must be clearly and completely defined in the program instructions. It has also already been shown that a programmer can use a compiler or assembler to allow the computer to relieve him of a large proportion of the detail required to produce the actual instructions required in any particular application. This section is designed to show how a programmer can lay out the step-by-step definition of the program in order to be able to write instructions with a minimum possibility of logical error. It also gives some insight into the types of instructions which the computer is capable of executing. Unfortunately, this section too is an oversimplification, and it is important to remember that the functions which will be included in the following flowcharts are not computer instructions *per se* but rather are logical processes which must first be converted into a number of specific computer instructions before they become intelligible to even a high-level compiler.

A flowchart is a diagram of the sequence by which the various processes to be executed in a program are to be performed. Flowcharts serve the dual purpose of defining the problem to facilitate programming and documenting the program so that a humanly intelligible record of the program's nature will be available if needed at some time in the future. In order to draw even the simplest flowchart, the following symbols need to be defined:

A rectangle is used to represent any operation performed strictly within the CPU and does not involve program control.

A trapezoid is used to represent any operation performed by the CPU which involves input or output.

Using these elementary symbols and showing the flow of processing by arrows, an extremely simple flowchart can be produced, as in Figure 14–8.

FIGURE 14–8

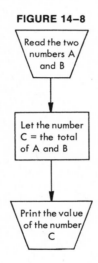

It is now possible to introduce an additional flowchart symbol which has great value in almost all computer applications:

When this symbol is encountered, the computer actually makes a "decision." It can interrogate some computer value and on the basis of the result continue processing *either* in the normal step-by-step procedure *or* branch to some other instruction which is not in the normal instruction sequence. The concept of branching is illustrated in the accompanying flowchart (Figure 14–9) of an extremely simple program which calculates and prints the absolute value of the sum of two numbers:

FIGURE 14–9

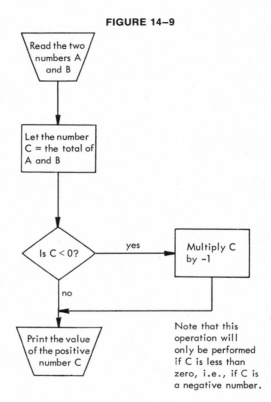

The value of the computer is greatly enhanced by the possibility of branching to alternative "lines" of processing based upon the nature of the data. But the value of the decision capability of the computer goes beyond that of simple branching and includes the concept of a loop. The accompanying flowchart (Figure 14–10) illustrates a program which uses a loop to permit the computer to perform a set of instructions over and over again on different data:

FIGURE 14–10

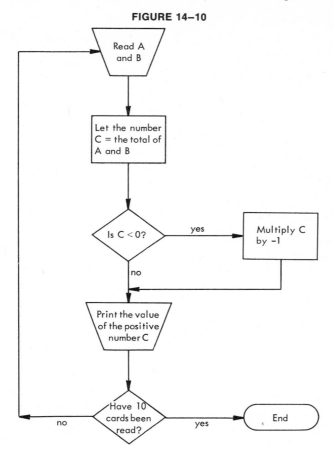

By using loops in various ways, the programmer is able to cause the computer to perform certain sets of instructions many times on slightly different data or, if he wishes, may slightly alter the instructions to be executed inside the loop and so perform an almost identical set of calculations on either the same data or different data. Obviously, processing plus branching and loops when merged into various combinations will permit the computer to handle almost any quantitative problem which can be strictly defined by a fixed procedure of any kind, almost without regard to complexity.

PROGRAMMING IN THE FORTRAN LANGUAGE

Basic Elements

In order to provide a rough understanding of the nature of high-level compiler instructions, it is useful to provide a brief sketch of one language and its characteristics as an example. Fortran is chosen here because it is available on almost all computers and is quantitative in orientation. Two words of caution are necessary before this description. The first is obvious — since this is not a text on programming, the following description is incomplete and will not in any way qualify a reader as a programmer. The second is that the wide variation in the nature of languages makes the use of Fortran as a general example of all compilers a mild distortion of the nature and capability of high-level program statements. This is especially true if "Fortran" and "programming" are mistakenly assumed to be equivalent terms by a reader. All compilers do, however, have some functions in common and, although the forms of the statements and the arrangement of the program's functions may differ, all languages share with Fortran the following four categories of instructions:

1. Input-Output
2. Calculation
3. Control
4. General Purpose

Any analyst with a little knowledge of Fortran and some support from computer specialists is capable of designing and writing his own simple programs. About all that has been said about Fortran up to this point is that it is a compiler which permits the analyst to write a set of statements indirectly understandable by the computer and which can be combined in such a way that a large number of different processes can be defined for computer execution. Unfortunately, the only way that it is possible to move more deeply into the use of this language is simply to jump into the middle of the programming problem and then attempt to slowly dig back out. Accordingly, a complete computer program written in the Fortran language is now presented:

```
         Fortran Program
         READ 1, I, J
         K = I + J
         Print 2, K
       1 FORMAT (I4, I4)
       2 FORMAT (I5)
         END
```

As has already been explained, the computer always processes any program in a step-by-step procedure. In Fortran, this characteristic of the nature of the computer's execution of the generated machine-language program is handled by the following convention. The computer can be assumed to execute the Fortran instructions in order from top to bottom unless an instruction specifically demands that this order of processing be altered (that the computer "branches"). If the above program is used as an example, the statement "READ 1, *I, J*" will be executed first, followed by the statement "*K = I + J.*" This "sequential" system by which the computer's actions "flow" through a program is what is shown diagrammatically in the flowcharts which were explained in the preceding section. In a sense, both the order of statements in a Fortran program and the order of operations in a flowchart are a model of the computer's behavior during the execution of a given program. Both provide a visual representation of the sequence of events, but flowcharts appear to provide a clearer insight into the nature of a procedure and are therefore frequently used to point out graphically the logical structure which is implied in the Fortran program's instructions. The accompanying diagram (Figure 14–11) shows the relationship between the flowchart and the Fortran statements in the example program. On the left is what may be called a "functional" flowchart, which describes the type of processes involved in our example program. The flowchart on the right indicates the corresponding Fortran instruction which permits the computer to execute the required process:

FIGURE 14–11

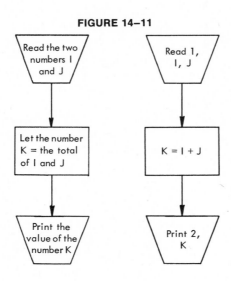

Formats

Continuing our discussion of this very simple program, we see two "format" statements immediately following the print statement in the program listing. Each of the format statements is preceded by a statement number, or label, which permits the program to refer to the particular statement. By using this statement number, the read instruction at the top of the program can easily refer to format statement one, and the print instruction can refer to format two. The use of statement numbers, in other words, enables any Fortran program to establish a kind of inter-statement communications, without which high-level languages such as Fortran would be impossible. In this particular case, statement numbers permit input-output statements to refer to the format statements which describe to the computer the nature of the data being read-in or printed-in.

This formatting procedure is necessary because the computer is unfortunately not able to understand that a number has been given to it until that number has been fully defined, and this definition is the function of the format statement. The computer must be told how many digits are in the number, whether the number has a decimal point, and how many digits are to the right of the decimal point. It must even be told that the number is a number and not a letter.

Needless to say, a large variety of format instructions are possible in the Fortran language, but it is sufficient here simply to indicate that in the sample program the format statement number one defines two numbers of four digits each ($I4$, $I4$) and both of these numbers are integers (they have no decimal point). Format 2 defines one five-digit integer ($I5$). Notice that since the read statement refers to format 1, the computer will read the two numbers which this format described, and the two numbers are *named* in the read statement (I and J). The print statement refers to format 2, which defines one five-digit integer. The print statement lists one number to be printed (the number K). *All numbers in a Fortran program are named in the input-output statement and described more fully in an associated format statement.* In addition, it is worth noting that *any* number which is input to the computer or output from the computer must be "formatted," unless the particular Fortran compiler permits unformatted statements when using tape or disc.

Calculations

The computer treats integers in a way which is completely different from the treatment given numbers which have a decimal point (called "real" numbers). The name which the programmer assigns to any number which is an integer must begin with any of the letters $I, J, K, L, M,$

$N;$ the name assigned to any real number must begin with any of the other letters. In addition, the two types of numbers cannot be "mixed" in the same mathematical statement (although some compilers will allow mixed mode calculations).

Arithmetic statements constitute an extremely large segment of Fortran and present no serious problem to anyone first encountering the language. Fortran simply sets the variable on the left-hand side of the equation equal to the expression on the right-hand side. For example, the statement,

$$C = A + B$$

will cause the computer to set the value of C equal to the sum of the values of A and B. Only three important points need to be kept in mind when writing a Fortran arithmetic statement:

1. Integer numbers and real numbers cannot both be written in the same statement in many compilers.
2. The notation used in Fortran is slightly different from notation which is common in mathematics. The symbol * is used for multiplication; $A*B$ is the same as $(A)(B)$, or $A \times B$, in mathematical notation. Also, ** is used to denote an exponent; $A**2$ is the notation for A^2; $A**3$ is A^3; and so on.
3. A Fortran equation is really an instruction to make the left-hand number equal to the value of the right-hand expression, and it is not a strict mathematical equation. For example, the statement $B = B + 1$ is perfectly legitimate because it instructs the computer to make the new value of B equal to "the value currently in B plus the value of the number 'one.'" It demands that "B" be made one larger than it was. A few examples of simple Fortran arithmetic statements are given below as examples:

Fortran Notation	*Mathematical Notation*
$A = B + C$	$A = B + C$
$A = B**2 + C**2$	$A = B^2 + C^2$
$X = B*(A + C)$	$X = B(A + C)$
$A = A + 1$	-------------------

The last expression is legitimate because it is not a mathematical equation. It is an instruction to make the number called A one greater than it was. If the old A equaled 8, the new A would equal 9.

In more complicated arithmetic statements, many different numbers may be combined by a large number of operations. This immediately raises the question of the order in which various operations are to be performed. In mathematics, for example, $2 + (4 \div 2)$ does not equal $(2 + 4) \div 2$. It is important when calculating to know whether to add or divide first because different answers would be obtained. In Fortran it is important to write the instruction in such a way that the computer will perform the calculations in the correct order for the same reason. Fortunately, this problem is handled in Fortran in almost exactly the same way as in ordinary mathematics. For example, parentheses are used to indicate the order of operation in exactly the same way as normal mathematical statements. In the absence of parentheses, the following priorities, or order of operations, are observed:

1. Exponentiation
2. Multiplication and Division
3. Addition and Subtraction

Therefore the following Fortran statements produce the following corresponding mathematical results:

Fortran Statement	Mathematical Result
$A = B**2*C$	$A = (B^2)(C)$
$A = B + C*D**2$	$A = B + (C)(D^2)$
$A = B/C + D$	$A = \dfrac{B}{C} + D$
$A = B**2/C + D*4.0$	$A = \dfrac{B^2}{C} + 4D$
$A = B**2*2.0 + C$	$A = 2B^2 + C$

If operations have the same priority, they are performed from left to right:

Fortran Statement	Mathematical Result
$A = B*C/D$	$A = \dfrac{BC}{D}$
$A = B + C - D$	$A = (B + C) - D$
$A = B + C - D/E*F$	$A = B + C - \dfrac{D}{E}(F)$
$A = B**2 + C**3 = D*4.0/E$	$A = B^2 + C^3 - \dfrac{4D}{E}$
$A = B*C/D + 4.0 - E$	$A = \dfrac{BC}{D} + 4 - E$

The problem of correctly stating the order of operations is not severe and a little care in the phrasing of the computer statements should eliminate the possibility of error. It is also possible to be very free with the use of parentheses in order to define very clearly the precise sequence of operation. The Fortran language makes no restrictions on parentheses and as many may be used as are desired, even if they are superfluous. In fact, the fluent use of parentheses in formulae is generally regarded as one of the characteristics of the precise programmer.

Program Control

Fortran provides a number of control statements by which the programmer can alter the normal sequential top-to-bottom sequence by which his statements are executed. Only three of these control statements will be considered in this section:

1. The GO TO statement
2. The IF statement
3. The DO statement

The GO TO statement tells the computer to "branch" to a statement which is located somewhere else in the program. Obviously, this branch is unconditional, i.e., the computer is given absolutely no option in the matter and will inevitably branch to the designated statement number.

The IF statement is more useful because it is conditional. It tells the computer to go to a statement which is located somewhere else in the program if, and *only* if, some specific condition is present. The computer is then given the option to "decide" whether or not the branch is to be taken, i.e., whether or not the condition is present. Figure 14–12 shows the syntax involved in the Fortran IF statement and explains the meaning of the various parts of the statement.

FIGURE 14–12

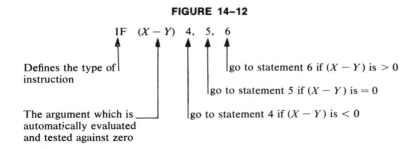

IF $(X - Y)$ 4, 5, 6

Defines the type of instruction

The argument which is automatically evaluated and tested against zero

go to statement 6 if $(X - Y)$ is > 0

go to statement 5 if $(X - Y)$ is $= 0$

go to statement 4 if $(X - Y)$ is < 0

Figure 14–13 shows a flowchart which was used as an example in the section on flowcharts but on the left is an identical flowchart that shows the specific Fortran statements which will enable the computer to execute the specified functions:

FIGURE 14–13

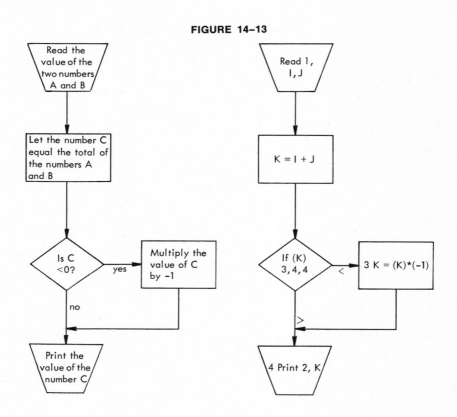

From the above example, it can be seen that the flowchart is a diagram of the following Fortran computer program:

Read 1, *I, J*
$K = I + J$
IF (*K*) 3, 4, 4
3 $K = (K)*(-1)$
4 PRINT 2, *K*
1 FORMAT (*I*4, *I*4)
2 FORMAT (*I*5)
END

This program will add two numbers, just as before. It therefore performs exactly the same function as the first sample program. But because of the conditional branch (the ability of the computer to "decide"), it will multiply all negative values of K by -1 in order to make them positive. In effect, the program produces the absolute value of the sum of any two numbers.

The DO statement greatly adds to the power of Fortran programs by automatically creating a loop wherever the programmer finds one necessary. The DO statement merely specifies the aspects or parameters which define a loop, and the compiler will see to it that the proper set of instructions is repeated the correct number of times. The defining parameters of any loop whether specified by a DO statement or not are as follows:

1. The beginning of the loop must be defined.
2. The end of the loop must be stated.
3. The counter used in the loop must be defined.
4. The number of times that the loop is to be performed must be stated.

The DO statement accomplishes the task of defining these parameters and actually allows even more flexibility, as will become apparent. The syntax of the DO statement is explained by Figure 14–14.

FIGURE 14–14

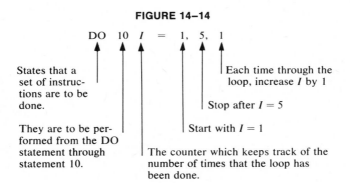

The following examples show several DO statements on the left with a verbal description of the same instruction on the right:

DO 10 $I = 1, 5, 1$ .... Do everything through statement 10 five times, increasing I by one each time the loop is performed.

DO 10 $I = 1, 5$.......................... Same as above. The compiler assumes that the counter is to be increased by one each time the loop is to be performed if no entry is made.

DO 10 $J = 1, 5$.......................... Same as above, except that J will be increased instead of I.

DO 10 $J = 1, 10$......................... Same as above, except that the loop will be performed ten times instead of five.

DO 20 $J = 1, 10$......................... Same as above, except that all statements through statement 20 will be performed for each loop.

Because the DO statement was specifically designed to assist the programmer in creating loops, it is more than reasonable to assume that the example of a loop shown in Figure 14–10 can be programmed more easily using a DO statement than by using the IF statement. The DO statement program corresponding to this flowchart is listed below on the left, and the IF statement program which is capable (though less easily) of performing the same function is stated on the right:

DO 4 $M = 1, 10, 1$	$M = 0$
READ 1, I, J	5 READ 1, I, J
$K = I + J$	$K = I + J$
IF (K) 3, 4, 4	IF (K) 3, 4, 4
3 $K = (K)*(-1)$	3 $K = (K)*(-1)$
4 PRINT 2, K	4 PRINT 2, K
1 FORMAT $(I4, I4)$	1 FORMAT $(I4, I4)$
2 FORMAT $(I5)$	2 FORMAT $(I5)$
END	$M = M + 1$
	IF $(M - 10)$ 5, 6, 6
	6 CONTINUE
	END

The real power of the DO loop, however, is not utilized unless used in connection with subscripted variables. Examining subscripted variables, it is possible to draw on the fairly extensive description of the use of subscripts which has already been given in previous chapters. For example, the most common measure of central tendency is given by the formula $\Sigma X_i/N$, where $i = 1, 2, 3, \ldots N$. Since each of the numbers to be included in the average is defined in computer language as being $X(I)$ and I varies from 1 to N, it is possible to write a program to compute the arithmetic mean *by simply letting the counter of the DO loop be the sub-*

script value and then performing the DO loop ten times. The following section of a program (Table 14–3) should be able to handle the entire problem. The DO loop is boxed.

TABLE 14–3

TOTAL = 0.0 .... Sets the value of $\Sigma X_i = 0.0$

DO 1 I = 1, N..................... Indicates that the addition is to be performed N times.

READ 2, $X(I)$..................... Reads a value for X_i each time through the loop.

1 TOTAL = TOTAL + $X(I)$..... Adds X_i to the total, ΣX_i

DIV = N..................... By the time this statement is reached, the loop is complete and ΣX_i is therefore the sum of all of the X_i which have been read.

AVE = TOTAL/DIV .... Divides ΣX_i by N

PRINT 3, AVE................... Prints the average

Note that the format and end statements are not present because this example is only a program segment, not a complete program.

The first time through the loop, I will be equal to 1, which means that the expression $X(I)$ will mean $X(1)$. The computer will read a card which contains the value of $X(1)$, and then will add this value into the total. Next, the program will loop back and make I equal to 2, which in turn makes $X(I)$ equal to $X(2)$. A card is then read which contains the number $X(2)$, this number is added to the total, and so on. After this process has been performed N times, the program "falls through" the loop and processes the first instruction outside of the loop—in this case dividing the total by N and printing the answer.

The power of the DO loop and subscript combination can be increased even further by the use of doubly subscripted arrays. These arrays are entire tables of numbers which can be represented as, for example, $A(I, J)$. In this notation, I is the row number of the particular element in the table, and J is the column number. The Fortran notation $A(I, J)$ is therefore equivalent to the mathematical notation a_{ij}. It is possible to have one DO loop cause computations to be performed for each row of the table in turn, and within this loop have another DO loop which causes the computations to be performed for each column in turn. Table 14–4 is an example.

TABLE 14–4

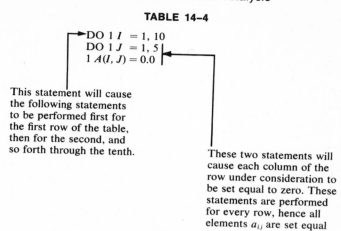

DO 1 I = 1, 10
DO 1 J = 1, 5
1 $A(I, J)$ = 0.0

This statement will cause the following statements to be performed first for the first row of the table, then for the second, and so forth through the tenth.

These two statements will cause each column of the row under consideration to be set equal to zero. These statements are performed for every row, hence all elements a_{ij} are set equal to zero.

The use of nested DO loops is, of course, not restricted to problems involving subscripted arrays, but this is their most important application. The ease provided in processing these arrays is very important, for $A(I, J)$ can be regarded not only as a table of numbers but also as a matrix which can be treated according to matrix algebra (the subject of an earlier chapter).

Program Structure

One additional major concept in the technical aspects of programming needs to be developed. Subroutines are vital to any reasonably complex programming problem, especially in mathematical applications. A subroutine is a set of computer statements which perform a specific function and can be treated as a logical whole. A program can refer to the subroutine whenever the function which the subroutine performs is needed. Any reasonably large program will typically process in the normal sequential fashion but will periodically transfer control to a subroutine when a specific task needs to be performed, then return control to the main line coding until another subroutine is called, and so forth. One of the simplest examples of a subroutine might be a set of instructions which, when given the numeric value of x, returns to the program the value of log x.

From the simplest subroutine to the most complex, the common characteristic of these tools is that they are black boxes. In the simple example just given, the input to the box is x, the output is log x. The input to a complex subroutine might be a large array of data and the output might be a complete multiple correlation analysis. The principle in both cases is the same, and subroutines can easily be seen to be smaller black boxes used by the computer program which is itself a black box from the standpoint of the user. It is even possible for a complex subroutine to utilize or "call" a number of other, more basic subroutines in order to accomplish its function more easily. In fact, in more sophisticated mathematical languages it is even possible for a subroutine to call itself in order to facilitate processing.

The programmer has available a large number of already prepared, or "canned," subroutines and certainly has the option of writing his own subroutines to perform whatever set of functions might be needed. In writing large programs, he will attempt to locate particular functions or operations which are a logical unity and can be reduced to a subroutine. Ideally, the program can be reduced to the sequential processing of routine after routine, leaving no work at all for the main line program. In practical work, however, this is seldom possible, and after all routines have been written a main line program remains to control the order in which the routines are performed. The advantage of this approach is that it "fragments" the problem into a set of clearly defined functions which are connected by a basic skeleton logic. The fundamental, underlying logic therefore becomes much clearer and errors are less frequent. If errors occur, they can usually be seen immediately to have been caused by a certain subroutine. A 30-statement subroutine can then be corrected instead of a 2,000-statement main program. The time-saving can be substantial.

Several basic facts about programming can be gleaned from the discussion of subroutines. First, the problems of program organization make large programs disproportionately more difficult than small ones. A 2,000-statement program is not just ten times more difficult than one with 200 statements, it is an altogether different world. Second, the problem of the programmer is not really one of being certain that every comma is in the right place, as is commonly supposed. Although it is true that attention to detail is important, the characteristic which most distinguishes a good programmer from a mediocre one is the ability to structure the logic of extremely large problems as a whole. Instead of hacking away at the problem one piece at a time, he will view the total problem, break it into its fundamental units, delineate the relationships between these units, code these main line relationships, and then gradually insert the pieces (the subroutines) into their properly defined place within the structured whole.

Although the analyst can write smaller programs using a high-level compiler, he probably will have to rely upon the professional programmer to provide the larger ones. The problems involved in this relationship are basically problems of discovering which results would be valuable and finding ways in which those results can be obtained. This is the subject of the next chapter.

Chapter
15 Computer Usage

With an understanding of how a computer works, some further consideration must be given to how to use this instrument most effectively. A good computer program must be applicable to a real problem and stated in sufficiently general terms so that it can be applied to many similar problems. It is most useful when the problem is repetitive in nature. Because the computer can process data much faster than input can be given the computer or output can be provided, a tradeoff must be reached to balance the time and money spent on proper programming against the speed and cost reduction provided by superior programming. A computer *system* deals not with one problem but the organization of computer output to meet the users' total needs. Establishment of such a system requires defining the structure and organization of the user, defining his needs, and defining the input before the integrated programming can begin. After the system is installed, programs must be modified and updated and computer runs controlled. Only by approaching the computer as an information system rather than a solver of a particular problem can maximum utilization of modern computer technology be achieved.

INTRODUCTION

One of the most common mistakes among people inexperienced with computers is the assumption that the use of the computer is identical with the problem of programming the calculations or internal processing involved in any particular problem. Actually, this is by far the simplest aspect of computer work. The availability of high-level compilers has made both the calculation and logic requirements of any project so simple that more bottlenecks occur in keeping the mathematics correct than in translating the mathematics into a machine workable form. The really difficult portions of any particular computer project can be placed into three categories.

1. Applications and communications.
2. Run time and input-output.
3. Computer systems in the context of business systems.

APPLICATIONS AND COMMUNICATIONS

Highly professional programming has become such a difficult subject that it is almost impossible for programmers to understand fully all aspects of the science. In the little time that is available for self-education, the programmer must deepen his understanding of the characteristics of peripheral devices, the nature of existing compilers, and the more unusual characteristics of the particular machine which he uses. In addition, he must keep aware of the new programming techniques constantly being developed, new languages available, and new programs which may have been made available for public use. He must keep up to date on all business standards and documentation requirements for the company for which he works, the system used by the team running the machine to control the flow of programs, and the management structure used in the programming division to maintain communications and coordination among the programming staff. To make matters worse, the technology in the industry is changing so rapidly that anything that he learns will be obsolete in five years because new machines, new languages and techniques, and new management devices will have completely replaced the ones he spent so much time studying.

The research analyst is in approximately the same situation, for he is responsible for estimates of financial results in several industries which would be taxing even if needed for only one company and access to internal financial records were possible. In addition, the techniques by which he makes his estimates are undergoing a revolutionary change as the quantitative approach becomes more dominant in the investment industry. The requirements for these two different professions of computer science and investments indirectly produce the most significant problem in the application of computer science to the investment field. One man knows the problems which need to be solved and another knows the solution techniques which may be applied to problems in general, but no single person is capable of being acquainted with both the problem and the solution. Because of this, communication difficulties surround every computer project undertaken.

The investment man can state in his technical jargon what needs to be done, but the computer man is not sufficiently acquainted with the investment industry to be able to understand the highly developed terminology used for investment work and so is forced to ask detailed questions.

Unfortunately, these questions appear to an investment analyst to be either highly trivial (such as how many digits go to the right of the decimal point), or completely incomprehensible because they are couched in the *computer* analyst's jargon ("My round-off error can't be helped in any compiler-written program because I can't go beyond 64-bit double-precision in the model 50"). Adding to the confusion is the unfortunate fact that quantitative techniques have already developed to the point where no single person can be an expert in all statistical and mathematical models, and so a three- or four-direction communication confusion results. In this kind of an environment, it is quite possible to have three or four highly skilled individuals involved in a computerization effort and still accomplish nothing because of the lack of direction which stems from an absence of coordination. In many cases, adding more people to the project simply increases this problem and actually *lowers* efficiency.

A knowledge of a few of the basic principles which are known to be requirements of a good computer program may assist the financial analyst in making the initial move to break this communication deadlock. The two keys to any good computer project are applicability and generality. Any computer program must apply to a real problem in investments or it cannot have any value regardless of its cost. But the program must solve reasonably general problems or it will not be used sufficiently to justify its cost. Figure 15–1 is an example of one of the most elementary programs possible on a computer.

FIGURE 15–1

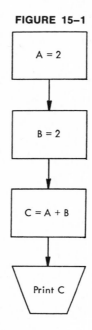

This program would have value only if the sum of two and two were desired. The problem is not sufficiently general because this problem obviously does not occur too frequently and even when it does occur it can be solved without resort to a computer run. Figure 15–2 is substantially superior to the one just analyzed.

FIGURE 15–2

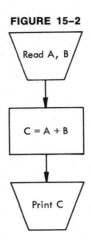

This program will work whenever the sum of any two numbers is desired regardless of what particular numbers are involved. This is a substantial improvement because the problem is encountered much more frequently, but a program could be even more valuable if,

$$C = (A**2)*(B**4)/(A + B)**3$$

were substituted for $C = A + B$. A frequently used complex calculation, in other words, is just as easy for the computer as a frequently used simple one. This produces one of the very basic peculiarities of computer work: *the value of the computer rises as the complexity of the problem increases.* The computer has a very marked tendency to make difficult problems easy. On the other hand, since it requires such specific instructions, it also has a tendency to make simple jobs quite difficult.

By using general variables in the program, a given set of calculations can be performed on different data. This means, for example, that a simple regression can be run on two variables and the program will still apply to another set of two variables related to a completely different investment problem. Another important ingredient in any computer program is repetition. For example, if the sum of five numbers were needed, it would be very easy to use a hand calculator and avoid a computer run. But if this

FIGURE 15–3

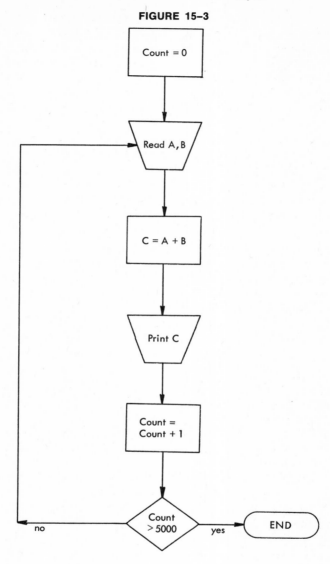

sum were needed on, say, 5,000 different sets of five numbers, the computer becomes substantially more valuable, as shown in Figure 15–3.

Summarizing, for a program to be valuable, it is usually necessary that it be quite general, applying to large numbers of slightly different types of problems. In addition, it is important that the problem to be solved must be encountered repetitively, so that the cost of the program can be allocated to a large number of different sets of data all of which have the same nature.

One of the most common misuses of the computer is the development of a one-time job of moderate complexity. While it is true that an engineer may write a program, run it once, and then throw it away, this approach is seldom valuable in a business environment. The engineer has complicated mathematics built into a simple program with little input-output. As a result, the engineer may save three man-months by using an 80-statement program. The financial man who requests a one-time job typically has need for light mathematics, a moderately difficult program, and rather large input-output. As a result, the analyst may save one man-day with a 200-statement program. It is important to remember that the large cost of a *general* program can be spread over many different computer runs and possibly over a number of fairly diverse applications. But the moderate cost of a program which is used *once* is all applied to the one computer run which results. Once again, the computer has a knack for making the simple difficult and the difficult simple; it can also make the expensive almost free and the moderate cost the highest.

One very interesting point is that this discussion of the reasons why a program has a high value points very strongly toward the use of mathematical models. Mathematical models can be seen to have all of the desirable characteristics of a computer application. They are very general, applying to numerous sets of data and a large number of application areas. They do not go out of date and so require little modification. They can be of use in virtually every industry, allowing the cost to be spread among a number of different companies. In fact, most mathematical models are available as "canned" packages from computer manufacturers and so have very little cost to the user other than the education of the analysts in the characteristics of the program. As will be shown in later sections of this chapter, it is also fortunate that these models have low input-output requirements and that they can be more precisely defined than would ever be possible in a nonmathematical area.

RUN TIME AND INPUT-OUTPUT

The chapter on computer programming divided the computer into three basic functions of input, processing, and output. After making this distinction, the subjects of input and output were promptly eliminated from consideration in the development of the nature of the computer which followed. This distortion, unfortunately, is both necessary and misleading. It is necessary because the processing function of the computer must be fairly well understood before input-output can be discussed. It is misleading because the majority of the purely technical problems in the computer industry stem from input-output difficulties. In other words, if the only problems encountered by programmers were machine-oriented problems, the majority of the programmer's time would be spent treating the input which feeds the computer and constructing the commands which create the output from the computer. (In fact, however, the first section of this chapter shows that the largest problems of the programming function are not technical at all but rather deal with the very human problem of coordination.)

Input-output problems result from three major facts:

1. The computer is substantially slower in inputting raw data and outputting results than it is in actually processing values already present in core.
2. A number of input-output (IO) devices are available and it is necessary to know their characteristics and choose the correct device for each particular application.
3. Input by its very nature means input to the computer *from* human beings. Output means output going *to* human beings. (This statement is only partially true, for the computer is quite capable of generating output and then at a later time using this data as input without any human intervention.) Nevertheless, all data used by computers *initially* comes from people and the final output of any computer project must eventually be given to human beings or the project will not be relevant to human problems.

The fact that the computer is significantly faster when performing internal processing than when reading data or writing results produces a major programming problem. In fact, this difficulty is the reason why this section is called "run time and input-output." The computer in a very simple application might be required to read two numbers, add them together, and print the result. Unfortunately, it takes so much time to read the two numbers that the computer must sit idly waiting for the numbers to be placed in core storage. Depending upon the particular input-output device being used, this may mean that the computer must wait as many as 1,000 seconds for every second that it has data available for processing.

There are a number of sophisticated ways around this problem. The most obvious is simply to develop higher speed IO devices. Unfortunately, computer technology seems to be able to develop faster CPU's (central processing units) more easily than faster IO units, and as a result any gain in input-output speed is quickly offset by newer CPU's which once again widen the disparity. In order to break away from this race in hardware development, programmers have under their own control a number of possibilities:

1. The IO device used in any application must be the fastest practical.
2. While the machine is waiting for data to come in from one IO unit, the program can be designed in such a way that it goes to another IO unit and starts to use input from this alternate source. By properly staggering the input and output commands among a number of units, it may be possible for a programmer to reduce run time substantially.
3. Instead of reading input into only one area in core storage, the programmer may alternately read data into two different areas. The computer can then process area A while information is being read into area B. Hopefully, by the time area A has been finished, area B will be ready for processing. While area B is then being processed, data is read into area A. This process of switching back and forth between input areas is called "input buffering." In effect, the technique allows the computer to perform IO operations and processing at the same time.
4. A number of programs may be placed in core at one time, permitting the computer to process whichever program may have data available at any given time. In actual practice, this "multiprogramming environment" is frequently used, and each program has buffered IO as well.

It would be impossible to describe the variety of input-output devices in any book not essentially devoted to the subject. Nevertheless, it is important to have a speaking acquaintance with the most frequently used types of IO units in order to understand the problems which the programmer may encounter and the impact which these problems have on the development costs and run time which is charged to the investment department.

Data which is to be fed into a computer is technically referred to as a "data set" or a "file." Examples of files might be the assets held in the various portfolios analyzed by the investment division, the analyst's estimates concerning next year's results for all stocks covered by the research department, the historical record of 500 economic time-series, or the financial history of a number of companies frequently analyzed. Any data set can be regarded from a human standpoint as being a stack or pile of information through which he can browse in any manner that he chooses. Unfortunately, however, the computer must access any data set by means of a fixed procedure. If, for example, the analyst's estimates on the companies currently on the recommended list are punched onto cards to be fed into the computer, the computer must access the first card first, then the second, and so on. This means that the cards must be in the proper order (the order expected by the program) if valid results are to be obtained. Most IO devices are designed for the processing of sequential files, but some devices have the ability to permit random access. With random access, the computer is able to select the correct data from the entire data set in any order whatsoever. This means that the computer has the ability to use a "pick and choose" method for accessing information.

The most important IO devices for processing sequential files are card readers, card punches, and magnetic tape. The card reader permits the machine to access at rates as high as 1,000 cards per minute information which has been punched onto cards. The advantage to the card reader is that an analyst can punch virtually any information onto cards and so convert it into a computer readable form. The disadvantage is that the extremely slow speed of the reader causes the computer to spend a very high percentage of its time idly waiting for input to be made available.

Card punches are output devices by which the computer can convert the results of its calculations into punched cards which may then be stored and used later as input. The card punch, however, is even slower than the reader, with the most rapid units operating at about 500 cards per minute. The advantage of the card punch is that it permits the computer to create machine readable output, relieving the analyst from the task of examining printed output and then manually punching the information for use in a later study. The disadvantage, of course, is that the punch is slower than the reader.

Magnetic tape units can be used both for input and output and have the advantage of being substantially more efficient than cards. The fastest tape units are approximately 150 times as fast as the best card readers. The advantage to the use of magnetic tape is its high speed and availability of both input and output. The disadvantage is that the programming of a tape-oriented system is slightly more difficult than when cards are used. A secondary but not inconsiderable value to magnetic tape is the compactness of the data set.

Less important sequential IO devices include the computer console (the control typewriter actually connected to the computer), optical reading devices which are capable of sensing visual characters, punched paper tape, and online terminals which provide a typewriter connected to the computer at a location physically remote from the machine.

The most important random access input-output devices are disc and drum. The use of disc units is slightly slower than tape if the application deals only with a sequential file. However, the random access feature makes it substantially more efficient if the data cannot easily be given to the computer in a simple, well-ordered way. The advantage of disc is therefore its random access capabilities and the ability to store very large data files. The disadvantages are essentially the same as for magnetic tape. The use of a high-speed drum as an input-output device is very efficient, allowing data to be provided to the computer at a very high speed and in a random access environment. Unfortunately, a large amount of data cannot be permanently stored on a high-speed drum in a cost efficient way, so that files must be placed on this unit from other IO devices for any particular application and for only a short period of time.

As a result of the technical characteristics of these input-output devices, the programmer when working on an investment project will prefer sequential files to random access files if possible because of the greater speed. In addition, he will use tape or disc instead of cards at every possible point. He will be willing to read data from cards once, but he will have a strong tendency to try to store it as a permanent file on some other medium, most likely disc. If a high-speed drum is available, he will probably want to load the data file on drum before processing. When the programmer's concern to minimize run time by optimum use of IO hardware is coupled with his design of the actual program using buffering techniques and multiple IO devices, a program having essentially simple logic can easily become very complicated. Because of this fact, the reduction of run time almost inevitably produces an increase in project development cost. If the program's instructions are to be efficient and lower the computer charges, additional time must be spent on the program's development with a corresponding increase in the development cost. Trading off development and efficiency costs by using the "best" level of input-output sophistication is one of the most important decisions in the control of costs on a computer investment project. On one side is the investment man's inherent desire for the flexibility which simplicity in program design produces (and the associated high computer charges). On the other hand is the programmer's almost pathological drive toward the maximum in technological sophistication (with correspondingly high development costs). Unfortunately, the balancing of these opposed positions becomes substantially more complicated when consideration is given to the massive problem of computer systems.

COMPUTER SYSTEMS AND BUSINESS SYSTEMS

Once the rather time-consuming job of learning elementary programming has been completed, the computer can be used to assist the analyst in solving a number of specific problems. Unfortunately, this approach of using the computer on a "one program at a time" basis is only the most elementary of applications. In order to understand how computers are used in business today, it is necessary to undertake the substantially more difficult subject of systems theory and the design and use of the computer system. In this approach, the computer is no longer seen as simply a tool to which various members of the Investment Department occasionally present various isolated problems. Instead, it is seen as the device by which the department's total information requirements can be continuously satisfied in a unified, systematic manner.

In the systems approach, the total investment function is seen as a single operating unit having a definite set of informational needs. The computer programs must, of course, satisfy those needs, but this is not possible if attempted on a program-by-program basis. The needs must be evaluated as a complete, integrated system of requirements, and their resolution must come from a complete, integrated system of computer instructions. This means that, in any really satisfactory computer application to investments, it is not only necessary to have each statement in any given program related to all other such statements but it also is necessary to have all programs interrelated.

This approach of viewing the department as a single unit having information needs and the computer applications as a single unit satisfying those needs is the first aspect of systems theory. The first step, then, is regarding the problems and the solutions in their entirety, in a manner very similar to the way the department head and the computer-applications head regard their operations when undertaking long-range planning. Unfortunately, the second step is more difficult. In actual practice, the two functions are deeply interwoven. The analysts have information needs such as company data or statistical results. They have information output which must be summarized by the computer and then given to the portfolio managers. The managers also receive information concerning their accounts. Their decisions are information output, and so forth. Systems theory in its broadest application refers not to either the investment or the computer function; it refers rather to the analysis of the systematic and interrelated operating unit which results from integrating the two functions in day-to-day operations. The balance of this chapter discusses various aspects of the design of specifically *computer* systems which at least in part satisfy the requirements of *business* systems.

Any computer system is completely dependent upon its data base. This is axiomatic, for although ten related programs may use a single data set (or calculations resulting from this set), no program can ever be designed which pulls numbers out of thin air in order to begin calculations. This implies that all of the solutions which any computer system can provide are constrained by the initial human input, which is then processed and maintained automatically. The second major constraint on the system stems from the output requirements. Since the computer is used to provide information, the nature of the reports needed heavily determines the nature of the system. Because of these two limiting factors, work in computer systems naturally emphasizes a number of input-output principles.

Data should be input to the system only once, and the computer should handle all further manipulations needed. All data which will be needed for any reports must, of course, be input at some time or other, but it is important to avoid the precalculation of data before it is given to the computer. After all, the computer was designed for calculations and it is inefficient to perform them by hand. Output should be tailored to the needs of the user. It should meet his requirements directly, and no further calculations based upon the output should be necessary. In order to avoid inundating the user with output, all reports should be relevant. Going a step beyond this, it is possible to use exception output, i.e., output which is printed only if it is unusual for some reason.

If the analyst has at least a rudimentary understanding of the problems involved in building and operating a computer system, he can utilize the computer more effectively in his work, but more important is the fact that he will more clearly see the nature of his position in the context of the overall effort of the investment research team. The system is built by first analyzing the function and structure of the investment department. Next, the particular information which is needed by each member of the department is strictly defined. The reports are then designed, and their frequency is determined (weekly, monthly, etc.). Once all of the output has been specified, the input which is required to produce the desired results is deduced from the calculations. The most efficient form in which this data can be prepared for the computer is then determined. After all of this has been completed, the actual programs needed to produce the desired results are specified and then designed. The specifications for each program can then be used for the programming (called "coding") of the system. The programs are coded in a logical order which permits portions of the total system to be "phased in" before the total project is complete. Once the system is complete and tested, each program will be heavily related to every other program.

It is important that these design considerations be understood when the investment department undertakes any computer effort. As can easily be seen, the nature of the system makes modification extremely difficult, for a number of programs will be affected. If the definition of the needed information is not complete, additional input may be needed, and this requires a redesign running through the entire length of the system. Errors in specifying calculations are usually less serious because they are often unique to one program, but it may be difficult to detect that an error in definition has occurred if the difference in the results is small. The most important point that can be drawn from the nature of system design is the fact that individual programs cannot be written on a one-at-a-time basis and then combined into an integrated system. A successful computer effort requires a complete definition before the project is undertaken.

Once a system is operational, it must be maintained in an operating environment. This is really two problems. First, the programs must continuously be modified and updated. Second, the computer runs which provide the investment output must be controlled. This control requires the scheduling of machine runs, the orderly distribution of output, and the accurate preparation of input. The input provides the majority of problems. It must be correctly entered on forms in accordance with a strict schedule based on the timing of the machine runs. It is then keypunched, checked for errors, and given to the computer. The majority of difficulties in either the accuracy or the timing of output can almost always be traced to a problem at some point in the input preparation process.

A discussion of computer systems would hardly be complete without some comment concerning time-sharing computer applications (called real-time systems). Any computer having real-time capabilities can be programmed in such a way that it will provide simultaneous service to a number of users working with different programs. For example, one computer owned by an independent computer service company might at any one time be processing the programs of 30 users located in different cities but connected to the CPU by telephone lines and teletype terminals. The CPU would spend a short time on a portion of user A's job, then move to user B's job, and so on. Whenever user A's job requires input or output, the CPU automatically transfers to B's job until A's program is once again ready for processing. Because input-output is so much slower than processing, this feature permits the CPU to process someone else's job instead of simply waiting for data. As a result, the CPU is used much more efficiently, and each user is only charged for the amount of CPU time which was actually spent on his program.

Organizationally, this approach to computer usage produces multiple users sharing the cost of a single computer. This produces two aspects of real-time which are radically different from the investment department's standpoint. First, a company having an investment department may introduce an internal real-time system in which the investment function will participate. Second, the investment department may contract with a time-sharing service bureau to become a user of a computer which is outside the company.

The first alternative, an in-house real-time system, is extremely sophisticated and also extremely complicated. Terminals can be located in the investment department to provide immediate access to all accounting data, statistical output, standard reports, and the like. In addition, any job not efficient in a time-sharing environment can still be processed by the more traditional batch methods if necessary. This type of system provides both the flexibility of real-time terminals and the efficiency of batch processing. Its drawbacks are that it requires a top-management commitment to the implementation of the system, a high degree of coordination between the investment function and the computer function, an extremely high level of software (i.e., systems and programming) expertise, a high cost for design and implementation, and a high cost for computer processing (primarily because of the larger number of applications computerized).

The second alternative, using an outside computer, produces almost the reverse situation. Because the computer company makes available to all users a large number of operational programs, the need for computer sophistication is kept to a minimum. In fact, it is possible to run such an arrangement without even having a programmer, let alone a systems man. Since the investment department is billed only for the time actually used, the computer charges can be kept at a low level. The operating environment is simplified because all data are entered directly on the terminal. No liaison with the in-house computer staff is required.

This time-sharing approach also has drawbacks, however. First, although dollar costs can be kept quite low, the charges will tend to be higher than batch processing on an application-by-application basis. This tendency can become quite pronounced on large jobs. Second, since the programs supplied by the hardware company must be quite general, they cannot be well-integrated into the investment system. If, alternatively, the money is spent to build an integrated system for the time-sharing application, computer usage costs can be much higher than in batch processing. The approach is very limited in input-output. Data entered by hand on the teletype and output is printed at about 120 *words* per minute. Because of the simplified operations, the answers are given in a reduced *lapse*-time, but the fact that the analyst is tied to the slow input-output increases the project's *man*-time, raising costs. It is not possible to utilize a general accounting system on a time-sharing computer. In calculating costs, it is important to note that the charge for time on the terminal is frequently 10–20 times the charge for the CPU time in terms of dollars paid per month. This terminal cost must be coupled with the cost per hour of the analyst tied up at the terminal.

Man-machine conversation can, as the above paragraph shows, be a very expensive approach. This expense, of course, must be weighted carefully against the numerous benefits stemming from the time-sharing environment. One practical approach is to use both computer modes, with each project's individual characteristics determining the computer to be used or whether the computer should be used at all. In general, the time-sharing terminal can be used to gain access to canned programs which can quickly solve small jobs, while the batch mode can be used for the overall system and the large statistical projects. Another, more sophisticated, solution is the use of *remote batch* systems, which have all of the beneficial features of batch processing and in addition allow the use of a remote terminal located in the investment division. This combination permits lower costs and the processing of more complex programs without encountering a high lapse time. If, however, the investment division is quite small, the only option available may be time-sharing, in which case the only decision is whether this approach can be taken on at least a few projects more efficiently than hand methods. This will usually be the case; even if usage is low, only the time used is charged to the investment department.

ADDITIONAL READINGS IN COMPUTER USAGE

NAYLOR, THOMAS H.; BALINTFY, JOSEPH L.; BURDICK, DONALD S; AND CHU, KONG. *Computer Simulation Technique*. New York: John Wiley & Sons, Inc., 1966.

This is a book which will substantially expand anyone's concept concerning the capabilities of the computer and the problems which it can solve (340 pages). The book covers simulation technique, where the computer is programmed to behave as if it were a gas station, or an inventory system, or an economy. The presentation is almost completely verbal, and no knowledge of the computer is assumed. The nature of simulation experiments, examples of possible simulation applications, and several special-purpose simulation languages are discussed at some length. The two chapters on random numbers and probability distributions can be skipped without damaging the presentation if technical aspects of the approach are not needed.

ROSEN, SAUL (Ed). *Programming Systems and Languages*. New York: McGraw-Hill Book Company, 1967.

This book of readings discusses the characteristics of software on a more advanced level than is encountered in the books written to popularize one or another of the various languages available. Fortran, Algol, Cobol, and PL/I are covered in the first 159 pages. The next 202 pages discuss the methods by which compilers operate. List processing and string processing are two advanced techniques in problem solving, and 153 pages are devoted to a description of five languages specializing in these approaches. The remaining 214 pages discuss operating systems, which are the software support systems that provide the computer with the general control environment necessary for particular applications programs to run.

WEINBERG, GERALD M. *PL/I Programming Primer*. New York: McGraw-Hill Book Company, 1966.

This is an excellent introduction to the PL/I language (260 pages). The statements and concepts are introduced in a logical order of increasing complexity and the grammatical aspects of the instructions are subordinated to their actual problem-solving characteristics through the use of applications in the main body of the text.

APPENDIX A – LOGARITHMS

N	0	1	2	3	4	5	6	7	8	9
10	0000	0043	0086	0128	0170	0212	0253	0294	0334	0374
11	0414	0453	0492	0531	0569	0607	0645	0682	0719	0755
12	0792	0828	0864	0899	0934	0969	1004	1038	1072	1106
13	1139	1173	1206	1239	1271	1303	1335	1367	1399	1430
14	1461	1492	1523	1553	1584	1614	1644	1673	1703	1732
15	1761	1790	1818	1847	1875	1903	1931	1959	1987	2014
16	2041	2068	2095	2122	2148	2175	2201	2227	2253	2279
17	2304	2330	2355	2380	2405	2430	2455	2480	2504	2529
18	2553	2577	2601	2625	2648	2672	2695	2718	2742	2765
19	2788	2810	2833	2856	2878	2900	2923	2945	2967	2989
20	3010	3032	3054	3075	3096	3118	3139	3160	3181	3201
21	3222	3243	3263	3284	3304	3324	3345	3365	3385	3404
22	3424	3444	3464	3483	3502	3522	3541	3560	3579	3598
23	3617	3636	3655	3674	3692	3711	3729	3747	3766	3784
24	3802	3820	3838	3856	3874	3892	3909	3927	3945	3962
25	3979	3997	4014	4031	4048	4065	4082	4099	4116	4133
26	4150	4166	4183	4200	4216	4232	4249	4265	4281	4298
27	4314	4330	4346	4362	4378	4393	4409	4425	4440	4456
28	4472	4487	4502	4518	4533	4548	4564	4579	4594	4609
29	4624	4639	4654	4669	4683	4698	1713	4728	4742	4757
30	4771	4786	4800	4814	4829	4843	4857	4871	4886	4900
31	4914	4928	4942	4955	4969	4983	4997	5011	5024	5038
32	5051	5065	5079	5092	5105	5119	5132	5145	5159	5172
33	5185	5198	5211	5224	5237	5250	5263	5276	5289	5302
34	5315	5328	5340	5353	5366	5378	5391	5403	5416	5428
35	5441	5453	5465	5478	5490	5502	5514	5527	5539	5551
36	5563	5575	5587	5599	5611	5623	5635	5647	5658	5670
37	5682	5694	5705	5717	5729	5740	5752	5763	5775	5786
38	5798	5809	5821	5832	5843	5855	5866	5877	5888	5899
39	5911	5922	5933	5944	5955	5966	5977	5988	5999	6010
40	6021	6031	6042	6053	6064	6075	6085	6096	6107	6117
41	6128	6138	6149	6160	6170	6180	6191	6201	6212	6222
42	6232	6243	6253	6263	6274	6284	6294	6304	6314	6325
43	6336	6345	6355	6365	6375	6385	6395	6405	6415	6425
44	6435	6444	6454	6464	6474	6484	6493	6503	6513	6522
45	6532	6542	6551	6561	6571	6580	6590	6599	6609	6618
46	6628	6637	6646	6656	6665	6675	6684	6693	6702	6712
47	6721	6730	6739	6749	6758	6767	6776	6785	6794	6803
48	6812	6821	6830	6839	6848	6857	6866	6875	6884	6893
49	6902	6911	6920	6928	6937	6946	6955	6964	6972	6981
50	6990	6998	7007	7016	7024	7033	7042	7050	7059	7067
51	7076	7084	7093	7101	7110	7118	7126	7135	7143	7152
52	7160	7168	7177	7185	7193	7202	7210	7218	7226	7235
53	7243	7251	7259	7267	7275	7284	7292	7300	7308	7316
54	7324	7332	7340	7348	7356	7364	7372	7380	7388	7396

APPENDIX A (Continued)

N	0	1	2	3	4	5	6	7	8	9
55	7404	7412	7419	7427	7435	7443	7451	7459	7466	7474
56	7482	7490	7497	7505	7513	7520	7528	7536	7543	7551
57	7559	7566	7574	7582	7589	7597	7604	7612	7619	7627
58	7634	7642	7649	7657	7664	7672	7679	7686	7694	7701
59	7709	7716	7723	7731	7738	7745	7752	7760	7767	7774
60	7782	7789	7796	7803	7810	7818	7825	7832	7839	7846
61	7853	7860	7868	7875	7882	7889	7896	7903	7910	7917
62	7924	7931	7938	7945	7952	7959	7966	7973	7980	7987
63	7993	8000	8007	8014	8021	8028	8035	8041	8048	8055
64	8062	8069	8075	8082	8089	8096	8102	8109	8116	8122
65	8129	8136	8142	8149	8156	8162	8169	8176	8182	8189
66	8195	8202	8209	8215	8222	8228	8235	8241	8248	8254
67	8261	8267	8274	8280	8287	8293	8299	8306	8312	8319
68	8325	8331	8338	8344	8351	8357	8363	8370	8376	8382
69	8388	8395	8401	8407	8414	8420	8426	8432	8439	8445
70	8451	8457	8463	8470	8476	8482	8488	8494	8500	8506
71	8513	8519	8525	8531	8537	8543	8549	8555	8561	8567
72	8573	8579	8585	8591	8597	8603	8609	8615	8621	8627
73	8633	8639	8645	8651	8657	8663	8669	8675	8681	8686
74	8692	8698	8704	8710	8716	8722	8727	8733	8739	8745
75	8751	8756	8762	8768	8774	8779	8785	8791	8797	8802
76	8808	8814	8820	8825	8831	8837	8842	8848	8854	8859
77	8865	8871	8876	8882	8887	8893	8899	8904	8910	8915
78	8921	8927	8932	8938	8943	8949	8954	8960	8965	8971
79	8976	8982	8987	8993	8998	9004	9009	9015	9020	9025
80	9031	9036	9042	9047	9053	9058	9063	9069	9074	9079
81	9085	9090	9096	9101	9106	9112	9117	9122	9128	9133
82	9138	9143	9149	9154	9159	9165	9170	9175	9180	9186
83	9191	9196	9201	9206	9212	9217	9222	9227	9232	9238
84	9243	9248	9253	9258	9263	9269	9274	9279	9284	9289
85	9294	9299	9304	9309	9315	9320	9325	9330	9335	9340
86	9345	9350	9355	9360	9365	9370	9375	9380	9385	9390
87	9395	9400	9405	9410	9415	9420	9425	9430	9435	9440
88	9445	9450	9455	9460	9465	9469	9474	9479	9484	9489
89	9494	9499	9504	9509	9513	9518	9523	9528	9533	9538
90	9542	9547	9552	9557	9562	9566	9571	9576	9581	9586
91	9590	9595	9600	9605	9609	9614	9619	9624	9628	9633
92	9638	9643	9647	9652	9657	9661	9666	9671	9675	9680
93	9685	9689	9694	9699	9703	9708	9713	9717	9722	9727
94	9731	9736	9741	9745	9750	9754	9759	9763	9768	9773
95	9777	9782	9786	9791	9795	9800	9805	9809	9814	9818
96	9823	9827	9832	9836	9841	9845	9850	9854	9859	9863
97	9868	9872	9877	9881	9886	9890	9894	9899	9903	9908
98	9912	9917	9921	9926	9930	9934	9939	9943	9948	9952
99	9956	9961	9965	9969	9974	9978	9983	9987	9991	9996

APPENDIX B — PRESENT VALUE AND COMPOUND GROWTH TABLES

TABLE B–1
Future Value of $1

$$F_n = P(1 + r)^n$$

Periods	2%	2½%	3%	4%	5%	6%	8%	10%
1...	1.0200	1.0250	1.0300	1.0400	1.0500	1.0600	1.0800	1.1000
2...	1.0404	1.0506	1.0609	1.0816	1.1025	1.1236	1.1664	1.2100
3...	1.0612	1.0769	1.0927	1.1249	1.1576	1.1910	1.2597	1.3310
4...	1.0824	1.1038	1.1255	1.1699	1.2155	1.2625	1.3605	1.4641
5...	1.1041	1.1314	1.1593	1.2167	1.2763	1.3382	1.4693	1.6105
6...	1.1262	1.1597	1.1941	1.2653	1.3401	1.4185	1.5869	1.7716
7...	1.1487	1.1887	1.2299	1.3159	1.4071	1.5036	1.7138	1.9488
8...	1.1717	1.2184	1.2668	1.3686	1.4775	1.5938	1.8509	2.1436
9...	1.1951	1.2489	1.3048	1.4233	1.5513	1.6895	1.9990	2.3589
10...	1.2190	1.2801	1.3439	1.4802	1.6289	1.7908	2.1589	2.5938
11...	1.2434	1.3121	1.3842	1.5395	1.7103	1.8983	2.3316	2.8532
12...	1.2682	1.3449	1.4258	1.6010	1.7959	2.0122	2.5182	3.1385
13...	1.2936	1.3785	1.4685	1.6651	1.8856	2.1329	2.7196	3.4524
14...	1.3195	1.4130	1.5126	1.7317	1.9799	2.2609	2.9372	3.7976
15...	1.3459	1.4483	1.5580	1.8009	2.0709	2.3966	3.1722	4.1774
16...	1.3728	1.4845	1.6047	1.8730	2.1829	2.5404	3.4259	4.5951
17...	1.4002	1.5216	1.6528	1.9479	2.2920	2.6928	3.7000	5.0545
18...	1.4282	1.5597	1.7024	2.0258	2.4066	2.8543	3.9960	5.5600
19...	1.4568	1.5987	1.7535	2.1068	2.5270	3.0256	4.3157	6.1160
20...	1.4859	1.6386	1.8061	2.1911	2.6533	3.2071	4.6610	6.7276
22...	1.5460	1.7216	1.9161	2.3699	2.9253	3.6035	5.4365	8.1404
24...	1.6084	1.8087	2.0328	2.5633	3.2251	4.0489	6.3412	9.8498
26...	1.6734	1.9003	2.1566	2.7725	3.5557	4.5494	7.3964	11.9183
28...	1.7410	1.9965	2.2879	2.9987	3.9201	5.1117	8.6271	14.4211
30...	1.8114	2.0976	2.4273	3.2434	4.3219	5.7435	10.0627	17.4495
32...	1.8845	2.2038	2.5751	3.5081	4.7649	6.4534	11.7371	21.1140
34...	1.9607	2.3153	2.7319	3.7943	5.2533	7.2510	13.6901	25.5479
36...	2.0399	2.4325	2.8983	4.1039	5.7918	8.1473	15.9682	30.9130
38...	2.1223	2.5557	3.0748	4.4388	6.3855	9.1543	18.6253	37.4047
40...	2.2080	2.6851	3.2620	4.8010	7.0400	10.2857	21.7245	45.2597
42...	2.2972	2.8210	3.4607	5.1928	7.7616	11.5570	25.3395	54.7643
44...	2.3901	2.9638	3.6715	5.6165	8.5572	12.9855	29.5560	66.2648
46...	2.4866	3.1139	3.8950	6.0748	9.4343	14.5905	34.4741	80.1804
48...	2.5871	3.2715	4.1323	6.5705	10.4013	16.3939	40.2106	97.0182
50...	2.6916	3.4371	4.3839	7.1067	11.4674	18.4202	46.9016	117.3920
60...	3.2810	4.3998	5.8916	10.5196	18.6792	32.9877	101.2571	304.4846

Source: Myron J. Gordon and Gordon Shillinglaw, *Accounting: A Management Approach* (4th ed.; Homewood, Ill.: Richard D. Irwin, Inc., 1969), p. 784.

TABLE B-2
Present Value of $1

Years Hence	1%	2%	4%	6%	8%	10%	12%	14%	15%	16%	18%	20%	22%	24%	25%	26%	28%	30%	35%	40%	45%	50%
1	0.990	0.980	0.962	0.943	0.926	0.909	0.893	0.877	0.870	0.862	0.847	0.833	0.820	0.806	0.800	0.794	0.781	0.769	0.741	0.714	0.690	0.667
2	0.980	0.961	0.925	0.890	0.857	0.826	0.797	0.769	0.756	0.743	0.718	0.694	0.672	0.650	0.640	0.630	0.610	0.592	0.549	0.510	0.476	0.444
3	0.971	0.942	0.889	0.840	0.794	0.751	0.712	0.675	0.658	0.641	0.609	0.579	0.551	0.524	0.512	0.500	0.477	0.455	0.406	0.364	0.328	0.296
4	0.961	0.924	0.855	0.792	0.735	0.683	0.636	0.592	0.572	0.552	0.516	0.482	0.451	0.423	0.410	0.397	0.373	0.350	0.301	0.260	0.226	0.198
5	0.951	0.906	0.822	0.747	0.681	0.621	0.567	0.519	0.497	0.476	0.437	0.402	0.370	0.341	0.328	0.315	0.291	0.269	0.223	0.186	0.156	0.132
6	0.942	0.888	0.790	0.705	0.630	0.564	0.507	0.456	0.432	0.410	0.370	0.335	0.303	0.275	0.262	0.250	0.227	0.207	0.165	0.133	0.108	0.088
7	0.933	0.871	0.760	0.665	0.583	0.513	0.452	0.400	0.376	0.354	0.314	0.279	0.249	0.222	0.210	0.198	0.178	0.159	0.122	0.095	0.074	0.059
8	0.923	0.853	0.731	0.627	0.540	0.467	0.404	0.351	0.327	0.305	0.266	0.233	0.204	0.179	0.168	0.157	0.139	0.123	0.091	0.068	0.051	0.039
9	0.914	0.837	0.703	0.592	0.500	0.424	0.361	0.308	0.284	0.263	0.225	0.194	0.167	0.144	0.134	0.125	0.108	0.094	0.067	0.048	0.035	0.026
10	0.905	0.820	0.676	0.558	0.463	0.386	0.322	0.270	0.247	0.227	0.191	0.162	0.137	0.116	0.107	0.099	0.085	0.073	0.050	0.035	0.024	0.017
11	0.896	0.804	0.650	0.527	0.429	0.350	0.287	0.237	0.215	0.195	0.162	0.135	0.112	0.094	0.086	0.079	0.066	0.056	0.037	0.025	0.017	0.012
12	0.887	0.788	0.625	0.497	0.397	0.319	0.257	0.208	0.187	0.168	0.137	0.112	0.092	0.076	0.069	0.062	0.052	0.043	0.027	0.018	0.012	0.008
13	0.879	0.773	0.601	0.469	0.368	0.290	0.229	0.182	0.163	0.145	0.116	0.093	0.075	0.061	0.055	0.050	0.040	0.033	0.020	0.013	0.008	0.005
14	0.870	0.758	0.577	0.442	0.340	0.263	0.205	0.160	0.141	0.125	0.099	0.078	0.062	0.049	0.044	0.039	0.032	0.025	0.015	0.009	0.006	0.003
15	0.861	0.743	0.555	0.417	0.315	0.239	0.183	0.140	0.123	0.108	0.084	0.065	0.051	0.040	0.035	0.031	0.025	0.020	0.011	0.006	0.004	0.002
16	0.853	0.728	0.534	0.394	0.292	0.218	0.163	0.123	0.107	0.093	0.071	0.054	0.042	0.032	0.028	0.025	0.019	0.015	0.008	0.005	0.003	0.002
17	0.844	0.714	0.513	0.371	0.270	0.198	0.146	0.108	0.093	0.080	0.060	0.045	0.034	0.026	0.023	0.020	0.015	0.012	0.006	0.003	0.002	0.001
18	0.836	0.700	0.494	0.350	0.250	0.180	0.130	0.095	0.081	0.069	0.051	0.038	0.028	0.021	0.018	0.016	0.012	0.009	0.005	0.002	0.001	0.001
19	0.828	0.686	0.475	0.331	0.232	0.164	0.116	0.083	0.070	0.060	0.043	0.031	0.023	0.017	0.014	0.012	0.009	0.007	0.003	0.002	0.001	
20	0.820	0.673	0.456	0.312	0.215	0.149	0.104	0.073	0.061	0.051	0.037	0.026	0.019	0.014	0.012	0.010	0.007	0.005	0.002	0.001	0.001	
21	0.811	0.660	0.439	0.294	0.199	0.135	0.093	0.064	0.053	0.044	0.031	0.022	0.015	0.011	0.009	0.008	0.006	0.004	0.002	0.001		
22	0.803	0.647	0.422	0.278	0.184	0.123	0.083	0.056	0.046	0.038	0.026	0.018	0.013	0.009	0.007	0.006	0.004	0.003	0.001	0.001		
23	0.795	0.634	0.406	0.262	0.170	0.112	0.074	0.049	0.040	0.033	0.022	0.015	0.010	0.007	0.006	0.005	0.003	0.002	0.001			
24	0.788	0.622	0.390	0.247	0.158	0.102	0.066	0.043	0.035	0.028	0.019	0.013	0.008	0.006	0.005	0.004	0.003	0.002	0.001			
25	0.780	0.610	0.375	0.233	0.146	0.092	0.059	0.038	0.030	0.024	0.016	0.010	0.007	0.005	0.004	0.003	0.002	0.001	0.001			
26	0.772	0.598	0.361	0.220	0.135	0.084	0.053	0.033	0.026	0.021	0.014	0.009	0.006	0.004	0.003	0.002	0.002	0.001				
27	0.764	0.586	0.347	0.207	0.125	0.076	0.047	0.029	0.023	0.018	0.011	0.007	0.005	0.003	0.002	0.002	0.001	0.001				
28	0.757	0.574	0.333	0.196	0.116	0.069	0.042	0.026	0.020	0.016	0.010	0.006	0.004	0.002	0.002	0.002	0.001	0.001				
29	0.749	0.563	0.321	0.185	0.107	0.063	0.037	0.022	0.017	0.014	0.008	0.005	0.003	0.002	0.002	0.001	0.001	0.001				
30	0.742	0.552	0.308	0.174	0.099	0.057	0.033	0.020	0.015	0.012	0.007	0.004	0.003	0.002	0.001	0.001	0.001	0.001				
40	0.672	0.453	0.208	0.097	0.046	0.022	0.011	0.005	0.004	0.003	0.001	0.001										
50	0.608	0.372	0.141	0.054	0.021	0.009	0.003	0.001	0.001	0.001												

Source: Robert N. Anthony, *Management Accounting: Text and Cases* (4th ed.; Homewood, Ill.: Richard D. Irwin, Inc., 1970), p. 777.

TABLE B-3
Future Value of Annuity of $1 in Arrears

$$F = A\left[\frac{(1 + r)^n - 1}{r}\right]$$

Pe-riods	2%	2½%	3%	4%	5%	6%	8%	10%
1..	1.0000	1.0000	1.0000	1.0000	1.0000	1.0000	1.0000	1.0000
2..	2.0200	2.0250	2.0300	2.0400	2.0500	2.0600	2.0800	2.1000
3..	3.0604	3.0756	3.0909	3.1216	3.1525	3.1836	3.2464	3.3100
4..	4.1216	4.1525	4.1836	4.2465	4.3101	4.3746	4.5061	4.6410
5..	5.2040	5.2563	5.3091	5.4163	5.5256	5.6371	5.8666	6.1051
6..	6.3081	6.3877	6.4684	6.6330	6.8019	6.9753	7.3359	7.7156
7..	7.4343	7.5474	7.6625	7.8983	8.1420	8.3938	8.9228	9.4872
8..	8.5830	8.7361	8.8923	9.2142	9.5491	9.8975	10.6366	11.4360
9..	9.7546	9.9545	10.1591	10.5828	11.0266	11.4913	12.4876	13.5796
10..	10.9497	11.2034	11.4639	12.0061	12.5779	13.1808	14.4866	15.9376
11..	12.1687	12.4835	12.8078	13.4864	14.2068	14.9716	16.6455	18.5314
12..	13.4121	13.7956	14.1920	15.0258	15.9171	16.8699	18.9771	21.3846
13..	14.6803	15.1404	15.6178	16.6268	17.7130	18.8821	21.4953	24.5231
14..	15.9739	16.5190	17.0863	18.2919	19.5986	21.0151	24.2149	27.9755
15..	17.2934	17.9319	18.5989	20.0236	21.5786	23.2760	27.1521	31.7731
16..	18.6393	19.3802	20.1569	21.8245	23.6575	25.6725	30.3243	35.9503
17..	20.0121	20.8647	21.7616	23.6975	25.8404	28.2129	33.7502	40.5456
18..	21.4123	22.3863	23.4144	25.6454	28.1324	30.9057	37.4502	45.6001
19..	22.8406	23.9460	25.1169	27.6712	30.5390	33.7600	41.4463	51.1601
20..	24.2974	25.5447	26.8704	29.7781	33.0660	36.7856	45.7620	57.2761
22..	27.2990	28.8629	30.5368	34.2480	38.5052	43.3923	55.4568	71.4041
24..	30.4219	32.3490	34.4265	39.0826	44.5020	50.8156	66.7648	88.4989
26..	33.6709	36.0117	38.5530	44.3117	51.1135	59.1564	79.9544	109.1835
28..	37.0512	39.8598	42.9309	49.9676	58.4026	68.5281	95.3388	134.2119
30..	40.5681	43.9027	47.5754	56.0849	66.4388	79.0582	113.2832	164.4962
32..	44.2270	48.1503	52.5028	62.7015	75.2988	90.8898	134.2135	201.1402
34..	48.0338	52.6129	57.7302	69.8579	85.0670	104.1838	158.6267	245.4796
36..	51.9944	57.3014	63.2759	77.5983	95.8363	119.1209	187.1021	299.1302
38..	56.1149	62.2273	69.1594	85.9703	107.7095	135.9042	220.3159	364.0475
40..	60.4020	67.4026	75.4013	95.0255	120.7998	154.7620	259.0565	442.5974
42..	64.8622	72.8398	82.0232	104.8196	135.2318	175.9505	304.2435	537.6428
44..	69.5027	78.5523	89.0484	115.4129	151.1430	199.7580	356.9496	652.6478
46..	74.3306	84.5540	96.5015	126.8706	168.6852	226.5081	418.4261	791.8039
48..	79.3535	90.8596	104.4084	139.2632	188.0254	256.5645	490.1322	960.1827
50..	84.5794	97.4843	112.7969	152.6671	209.3480	290.3359	573.7702	1163.9209
60..	114.0515	135.9916	163.0534	237.9907	353.5837	533.1282	1253.2133	3034.8470

NOTE: To convert this table to values of an annuity in advance, take one more period and subtract 1,000.

Source: Myron J. Gordon and Gordon Shillinglaw, *Accounting: A Management Approach* (4th ed.; Homewood, Ill.: Richard D. Irwin, Inc., 1969), p. 785.

TABLE B-4
Present Value of Annuity of $1 in Arrears

$$P_A = A\left[\frac{1 - (1 + r)^{-n}}{r}\right]$$

Periods (n)	1%	1½%	2%	2½%	3%	3½%	4%	4½%	5%	6%	7%
1....	0.9901	0.9852	0.9804	0.9756	0.9709	0.9662	0.9615	0.9569	0.9524	0.9434	0.9346
2....	1.9704	1.9559	1.9416	1.9274	1.9135	1.8997	1.8861	1.8727	1.8594	1.8334	1.8080
3....	2.9410	2.9122	2.8839	2.8560	2.8286	2.8016	2.7751	2.7490	2.7232	2.6730	2.6243
4....	3.9020	3.8544	3.8077	3.7620	3.7171	3.6731	3.6299	3.5875	3.5460	3.4651	3.3872
5....	4.8534	4.7826	4.7135	4.6458	4.5797	4.5151	4.4518	4.3900	4.3295	4.2124	4.1002
6....	5.7955	5.6972	5.6014	5.5081	5.4172	5.3286	5.2421	5.1579	5.0757	4.9173	4.7665
7....	6.7282	6.5982	6.4720	6.3494	6.2303	6.1145	6.0021	5.8927	5.7864	5.5824	5.3893
8....	7.6517	7.4859	7.3255	7.1701	7.0197	6.8740	6.7327	6.5959	6.4632	6.2098	5.9713
9....	8.5660	8.3605	8.1622	7.9709	7.7861	7.6077	7.4353	7.2688	7.1078	6.8017	6.5152
10....	9.4713	9.2222	8.9826	8.7521	8.5302	8.3166	8.1109	7.9127	7.7217	7.3601	7.0236
11....	10.3676	10.0711	9.7868	9.5142	9.2526	9.0016	8.7605	8.5289	8.3064	7.8869	7.4987
12....	11.2551	10.9075	10.5753	10.2578	9.9540	9.6633	9.3851	9.1186	8.8633	8.3838	7.9427
13....	12.1337	11.7315	11.3484	10.9832	10.6350	10.3027	9.9856	9.6829	9.3936	8.8527	8.3577
14....	13.0037	12.5434	12.1062	11.6909	11.2961	10.9205	10.5631	10.2228	9.8986	9.2950	8.7455
15....	13.8651	13.3432	12.8493	12.3814	11.9379	11.5174	11.1184	10.7395	10.3797	9.7122	9.1079
16....	14.7179	14.1313	13.5777	13.0550	12.5611	12.0941	11.6523	11.2340	10.8378	10.1059	9.4466
17....	15.5623	14.9076	14.2919	13.7122	13.1661	12.6513	12.1657	11.7072	11.2741	10.4773	9.7632
18....	16.3983	15.6726	14.9920	14.3534	13.7535	13.1897	12.6593	12.1600	11.6896	10.8276	10.0591
19....	17.2260	16.4262	15.6785	14.9789	14.3238	13.7098	13.1339	12.5933	12.0853	11.1581	10.3356
20....	18.0456	17.1686	16.3514	15.5892	14.8775	14.2124	13.5903	13.0079	12.4622	11.4699	10.5940
21....	18.8570	17.9001	17.0112	16.1845	15.4150	14.6980	14.0292	13.4047	12.8212	11.7640	10.8355
22....	19.6604	18.6208	17.6580	16.7654	15.9369	15.1671	14.4511	13.7844	13.1630	12.0416	11.0612
23....	20.4558	19.3309	18.2922	17.3321	16.4436	15.6204	14.8568	14.1478	13.4886	12.3034	11.2722
24....	21.2434	20.0304	18.9139	17.8850	16.9355	16.0584	15.2470	14.4955	13.7986	12.5504	11.4693
25....	22.0232	20.7196	19.5235	18.4244	17.4131	16.4815	15.6221	14.8282	14.0939	12.7834	11.6536
26....	22.7952	21.3986	20.1210	18.9506	17.8768	16.8904	15.9828	15.1466	14.3752	13.0032	11.8258
27....	23.5596	22.0676	20.7069	19.4640	18.3270	17.2854	16.3296	15.4513	14.6430	13.2105	11.9867
28....	24.3164	22.7267	21.2813	19.9649	18.7641	17.6670	16.6631	15.7429	14.8981	13.4062	12.1371
29....	25.0658	23.3761	21.8444	20.4535	19.1885	18.0358	16.9837	16.0219	15.1411	13.5907	12.2777
30....	25.8077	24.0158	22.3965	20.9303	19.6004	18.3920	17.2920	16.2889	15.3725	13.7648	12.4090
40....	32.8347	29.9158	27.3555	25.1028	23.1148	21.3551	19.7928	18.4016	17.1591	15.0463	13.3317
50....	39.1961	34.9997	31.4236	28.3623	25.7298	23.4556	21.4822	19.7620	18.2559	15.7619	13.8007

Source: Myron J. Gordon and Gordon Shillinglaw, *Accounting: A Management Approach* (4th ed.; Homewood, Ill.: Richard D. Irwin, Inc., 1969), pp. 788-89.

TABLE B-4 (Continued)

8%	10%	12%	14%	15%	16%	18%	20%	22%	24%	25%	26%	28%	30%	40%	50%
0.9259	0.9091	0.893	0.877	0.870	0.862	0.847	0.833	0.820	0.806	0.800	0.794	0.781	0.769	0.714	0.667
1.7833	1.7355	1.690	1.647	1.626	1.605	1.566	1.528	1.492	1.457	1.440	1.424	1.392	1.361	1.224	1.111
2.5771	2.4869	2.402	2.322	2.283	2.246	2.174	2.106	2.042	1.981	1.952	1.923	1.868	1.816	1.589	1.407
3.3121	3.1699	3.037	2.914	2.855	2.798	2.690	2.589	2.494	2.404	2.362	2.320	2.241	2.166	1.849	1.605
3.9927	3.7908	3.605	3.433	3.352	3.274	3.127	2.991	2.864	2.745	2.689	2.635	2.532	2.436	2.035	1.737
4.6229	4.3553	4.111	3.889	3.784	3.685	3.498	3.326	3.167	3.020	2.951	2.885	2.759	2.643	2.168	1.824
5.2064	4.8684	4.564	4.288	4.160	4.039	3.812	3.605	3.416	3.242	3.161	3.083	2.937	2.802	2.263	1.883
5.7466	5.3349	4.968	4.639	4.487	4.344	4.078	3.837	3.619	3.421	3.329	3.241	3.076	2.925	2.331	1.922
6.2469	5.7590	5.328	4.946	4.772	4.607	4.303	4.031	3.786	3.566	3.463	3.366	3.184	3.019	2.379	1.948
6.7101	6.1446	5.650	5.216	5.019	4.833	4.494	4.192	3.923	3.682	3.571	3.465	3.269	3.092	2.414	1.965
7.1390	6.4951	5.988	5.453	5.234	5.029	4.656	4.327	4.035	3.776	3.656	3.544	3.335	3.147	2.438	1.977
7.5361	6.8137	6.194	5.660	5.421	5.197	4.793	4.439	4.127	3.851	3.725	3.606	3.387	3.190	2.456	1.985
7.9038	7.1034	6.424	5.842	5.583	5.342	4.910	4.533	4.203	3.912	3.780	3.656	3.427	3.223	2.468	1.990
8.2442	7.3667	6.628	6.002	5.724	5.468	5.008	4.611	4.265	3.962	3.824	3.695	3.459	3.249	2.477	1.993
8.5595	7.6061	6.811	6.142	5.847	5.575	5.092	4.675	4.315	4.001	3.859	3.726	3.483	3.268	2.484	1.995
8.8514	7.8237	6.974	6.265	5.954	5.669	5.162	4.730	4.357	4.033	3.887	3.751	3.503	3.283	2.489	1.997
9.1216	8.0216	7.120	6.373	6.047	5.749	5.222	4.775	4.391	4.059	3.910	3.771	3.518	3.295	2.492	1.998
9.3719	8.2014	7.250	6.467	6.128	5.818	5.273	4.812	4.419	4.080	3.928	3.786	3.529	3.304	2.494	1.999
9.6036	8.3649	7.366	6.550	6.198	5.877	5.316	4.844	4.442	4.097	3.942	3.799	3.539	3.311	2.496	1.999
9.8181	8.5136	7.469	6.623	6.259	5.929	5.353	4.870	4.460	4.110	3.954	3.808	3.546	3.316	2.497	1.999
10.0168	8.6487	7.562	6.687	6.312	5.973	5.384	4.891	4.476	4.121	3.963	3.816	3.551	3.320	2.498	2.000
10.2007	8.7715	7.645	6.743	6.359	6.011	5.410	4.909	4.488	4.130	3.970	3.822	3.556	3.323	2.498	2.000
10.3711	8.8832	7.718	6.792	6.399	6.044	5.432	4.925	4.499	4.137	3.976	3.827	3.559	3.325	2.499	2.000
10.5288	8.9847	7.784	6.835	6.434	6.073	5.451	4.937	4.507	4.143	3.981	3.831	3.562	3.327	2.499	2.000
10.6748	9.0770	7.843	6.873	6.464	6.097	5.467	4.948	4.514	4.147	3.985	3.834	3.564	3.329	2.499	2.000
10.8100	9.1609	7.896	6.906	6.491	6.118	5.480	4.956	4.520	4.151	3.988	3.837	3.566	3.330	2.500	2.000
10.9352	9.2372	7.943	6.935	6.514	6.136	5.492	4.964	4.524	4.154	3.990	3.839	3.567	3.331	2.500	2.000
11.0511	9.3066	7.984	6.961	6.534	6.152	5.502	4.970	4.528	4.157	3.992	3.840	3.568	3.331	2.500	2.000
11.1584	9.3696	8.022	6.983	6.551	6.166	5.510	4.975	4.531	4.159	3.994	3.841	3.569	3.332	2.500	2.000
11.2578	9.4269	8.055	7.003	6.566	6.177	5.517	4.979	4.534	4.160	3.995	3.842	3.569	3.332	2.500	2.000
11.9246	9.7791	8.244	7.105	6.642	6.234	5.548	4.997	4.544	4.166	3.999	3.846	3.571	3.333	2.500	2.000
12.2335	9.9148	8.304	7.133	6.661	6.246	5.554	4.999	4.545	4.167	4.000	3.846	3.571	3.333	2.500	2.000

NOTE: To convert this table to values of an annuity in advance, take one less period and add 1.0000.

APPENDIX C—PERCENTAGE POINTS OF THE *t* DISTRIBUTION*

(Probabilities refer to the sum of the two-tail areas. For a single tail divide the probability by 2.)

Probability (*P*).

n	·9	·8	·7	·6	·5	·4	·3	·2	·1	·05	·02	·01	·001
1	·158	·325	·510	·727	1·000	1·376	1·963	3·078	6·314	12·706	31·821	63·657	636·619
2	·142	·289	·445	·617	·816	1·061	1·386	1·886	2·920	4·303	6·965	9·925	31·598
3	·137	·277	·424	·584	·765	·978	1·250	1·638	2·353	3·182	4·541	5·841	12·941
4	·134	·271	·414	·569	·741	·941	1·190	1·533	2·132	2·776	3·747	4·604	8·610
5	·132	·267	·408	·559	·727	·920	1·156	1·476	2·015	2·571	3·365	4·032	6·859
6	·131	·265	·404	·553	·718	·906	1·134	1·440	1·943	2·447	3·143	3·707	5·959
7	·130	·263	·402	·549	·711	·896	1·119	1·415	1·895	2·365	2·998	3·499	5·405
8	·130	·262	·399	·546	·706	·889	1·108	1·397	1·860	2·306	2·896	3·355	5·041
9	·129	·261	·398	·543	·703	·883	1·100	1·383	1·833	2·262	2·821	3·250	4·781
10	·129	·260	·397	·542	·700	·879	1·093	1·372	1·812	2·228	2·764	3·169	4·587
11	·129	·260	·396	·540	·697	·876	1·088	1·363	1·796	2·201	2·718	3·106	4·437
12	·128	·259	·395	·539	·695	·873	1·083	1·356	1·782	2·179	2·681	3·055	4·318
13	·128	·259	·394	·538	·694	·870	1·079	1·350	1·771	2·160	2·650	3·012	4·221
14	·128	·258	·393	·537	·692	·868	1·076	1·345	1·761	2·145	2·624	2·977	4·140
15	·128	·258	·393	·536	·691	·866	1·074	1·341	1·753	2·131	2·602	2·947	4·073
16	·128	·258	·392	·535	·690	·865	1·071	1·337	1·746	2·120	2·583	2·921	4·015
17	·128	·257	·392	·534	·689	·863	1·069	1·333	1·740	2·110	2·567	2·898	3·965
18	·127	·257	·392	·534	·688	·862	1·067	1·330	1·734	2·101	2·552	2·878	3·922
19	·127	·257	·391	·533	·688	·861	1·066	1·328	1·729	2·093	2·539	2·861	3·883
20	·127	·257	·391	·533	·687	·860	1·064	1·325	1·725	2·086	2·528	2·845	3·850
21	·127	·257	·391	·532	·686	·859	1·063	1·323	1·721	2·080	2·518	2·831	3·819
22	·127	·256	·390	·532	·686	·858	1·061	1·321	1·717	2·074	2·508	2·819	3·792
23	·127	·256	·390	·532	·685	·858	1·060	1·319	1·714	2·069	2·500	2·807	3·767
24	·127	·256	·390	·531	·685	·857	1·059	1·318	1·711	2·064	2·492	2·797	3·745
25	·127	·256	·390	·531	·684	·856	1·058	1·316	1·708	2·060	2·485	2·787	3·725
26	·127	·256	·390	·531	·684	·856	1·058	1·315	1·706	2·056	2·479	2·779	3·707
27	·127	·256	·389	·531	·684	·855	1·057	1·314	1·703	2·052	2·473	2·771	3·690
28	·127	·256	·389	·530	·683	·855	1·056	1·313	1·701	2·048	2·467	2·763	3·674
29	·127	·256	·389	·530	·683	·854	1·055	1·311	1·699	2·045	2·462	2·756	3·659
30	·127	·256	·389	·530	·683	·854	1·055	1·310	1·697	2·042	2·457	2·750	3·646
40	·126	·255	·388	·529	·681	·851	1·050	1·303	1·684	2·021	2·423	2·704	3·551
60	·126	·254	·387	·527	·679	·848	1·046	1·296	1·671	2·000	2·390	2·660	3·460
120	·126	·254	·386	·526	·677	·845	1·041	1·289	1·658	1·980	2·358	2·617	3·373
∞	·126	·253	·385	·524	·674	·842	1·036	1·282	1·645	1·960	2·326	2·576	3·291

*Appendix C is reprinted from Table III of R. A. Fisher and F. Yates, *Statistical Tables for Biological, Agricultural and Medical Research* published by Oliver & Boyd, Ltd., Edinburgh, by permission of the authors and publishers.

APPENDIX D—PERCENTAGE POINTS OF THE F DISTRIBUTION

(Each entry is the percent point of F which is exceeded by the proportion of values of F listed at the head of its column for degrees of freedom n_1 listed in the major caption and n_2 listed in the stub.)

n_2	$n_1 = 1$			$n_1 = 2$			$n_1 = 3$			$n_1 = 4$			$n_1 = 5$		
	.05	.01	.001	.05	.01	.001	.05	.01	.001	.05	.01	.001	.05	.01	.001
1	161.45	4,052.2	405,284	199.50	4,999.5	500,000	215.71	5,403.3	540,379	224.58	5,624.6	562,500	230.16	5,763.7	576,405
2	18.513	98.503	998.5	19.000	99.000	999.0	19.164	99.166	999.2	19.247	99.249	999.2	19.296	99.299	999.3
3	10.128	34.116	167.5	9.552	30.817	148.5	9.277	29.457	141.1	9.117	28.710	137.1	9.014	28.237	134.6
4	7.709	21.198	74.14	6.944	18.000	61.25	6.591	16.694	56.18	6.388	15.977	53.44	6.256	15.522	51.71
5	6.608	16.258	47.04	5.786	13.274	36.61	5.410	12.060	33.20	5.192	11.392	31.09	5.050	10.967	29.75
6	5.987	13.745	35.51	5.143	10.925	27.00	4.757	9.779	23.70	4.534	9.148	21.90	4.387	8.746	20.81
7	5.591	12.246	29.22	4.737	9.547	21.69	4.347	8.451	18.77	4.120	7.847	17.19	3.972	7.460	16.21
8	5.318	11.259	25.42	4.459	8.649	18.49	4.066	7.591	15.83	3.838	7.006	14.39	3.688	6.632	13.49
9	5.117	10.561	22.86	4.256	8.022	16.39	3.863	6.992	13.90	3.633	6.422	12.56	3.482	6.057	11.71
10	4.965	10.044	21.04	4.103	7.559	14.91	3.708	6.552	12.55	3.478	5.994	11.28	3.326	5.636	10.48
11	4.844	9.646	19.69	3.982	7.206	13.81	3.587	6.217	11.56	3.357	5.668	10.35	3.204	5.316	9.58
12	4.747	9.330	18.64	3.885	6.927	12.97	3.490	5.953	10.80	3.259	5.412	9.63	3.106	5.064	8.89
13	4.667	9.074	17.81	3.806	6.701	12.31	3.410	5.739	10.21	3.179	5.205	9.07	3.025	4.862	8.35
14	4.600	8.862	17.14	3.739	6.515	11.78	3.344	5.564	9.73	3.112	5.035	8.62	2.958	4.695	7.92
15	4.543	8.683	16.59	3.682	6.359	11.34	3.287	5.417	9.34	3.056	4.893	8.25	2.901	4.556	7.57
16	4.494	8.531	16.12	3.634	6.226	10.97	3.239	5.292	9.00	3.007	4.773	7.94	2.852	4.437	7.27
17	4.451	8.400	15.72	3.592	6.112	10.66	3.197	5.185	8.73	2.965	4.669	7.68	2.810	4.336	7.02
18	4.414	8.285	15.38	3.555	6.013	10.39	3.160	5.092	8.49	2.928	4.579	7.46	2.773	4.248	6.81
19	4.381	8.185	15.08	3.522	5.926	10.16	3.127	5.010	8.28	2.895	4.500	7.26	2.740	4.171	6.61
20	4.351	8.096	14.82	3.493	5.849	9.95	3.098	4.938	8.10	2.866	4.431	7.10	2.711	4.103	6.46
21	4.325	8.017	14.59	3.467	5.780	9.77	3.072	4.874	7.94	2.840	4.369	6.95	2.685	4.042	6.32
22	4.301	7.945	14.38	3.443	5.719	9.61	3.049	4.817	7.80	2.817	4.313	6.81	2.661	3.988	6.19
23	4.279	7.881	14.19	3.422	5.664	9.47	3.028	4.765	7.67	2.795	4.264	6.69	2.640	3.939	6.08
24	4.260	7.823	14.03	3.403	5.614	9.34	3.009	4.718	7.55	2.776	4.218	6.59	2.621	3.895	5.98
25	4.242	7.770	13.88	3.385	5.568	9.22	2.991	4.676	7.45	2.759	4.177	6.49	2.603	3.855	5.88
26	4.225	7.721	13.74	3.369	5.526	9.12	2.975	4.637	7.36	2.743	4.140	6.41	2.587	3.818	5.80
27	4.210	7.677	13.61	3.354	5.488	9.02	2.960	4.601	7.27	2.728	4.106	6.33	2.572	3.785	5.73
28	4.196	7.636	13.50	3.340	5.453	8.93	2.947	4.568	7.19	2.714	4.074	6.25	2.558	3.754	5.66
29	4.183	7.598	13.39	3.328	5.421	8.85	2.934	4.538	7.12	2.701	4.045	6.19	2.545	3.725	5.59
30	4.171	7.563	13.29	3.316	5.390	8.77	2.922	4.510	7.05	2.690	4.018	6.12	2.534	3.699	5.53
40	4.085	7.314	12.61	3.232	5.178	8.25	2.839	4.313	6.60	2.606	3.828	5.70	2.450	3.514	5.13
60	4.001	7.077	11.97	3.150	4.977	7.76	2.758	4.126	6.17	2.525	3.649	5.31	2.368	3.339	4.76
120	3.920	6.851	11.38	3.072	4.786	7.31	2.680	3.949	5.79	2.447	3.480	4.95	2.290	3.174	4.42
∞	3.841	6.635	10.83	2.996	4.605	6.91	2.605	3.782	5.42	2.372	3.319	4.62	2.214	3.017	4.10

APPENDIX D (Continued)

n_2	$n_1 = 6$ .05	.01	.001	$n_1 = 8$ .05	.01	.001	$n_1 = 12$ .05	.01	.001	$n_1 = 24$ .05	.01	.001	$n_1 = \infty$ .05	.01	.001
1	233.99	5,859.0	586,937	238.88	5,981.6	598,144	243.91	6,106.3	610,667	249.05	6,234.6	623,497	254.32	6,366.0	636,619
2	19.330	99.332	999.3	19.371	99.374	999.4	19.413	99.416	999.4	19.454	99.458	999.5	19.496	99.501	999.5
3	8.941	27.911	132.8	8.845	27.489	130.6	8.745	27.052	128.3	8.638	26.598	125.9	8.527	26.125	123.5
4	6.163	15.207	50.53	6.041	14.799	49.00	5.912	14.374	47.41	5.774	13.929	45.77	5.628	13.463	44.05
5	4.950	10.672	28.84	4.818	10.289	27.64	4.678	9.888	26.42	4.527	9.467	25.14	4.365	9.020	23.78
6	4.284	8.466	20.03	4.147	8.102	19.03	4.000	7.718	17.99	3.841	7.313	16.89	3.669	6.880	16.75
7	3.866	7.191	15.52	3.726	6.840	14.63	3.575	6.469	13.71	3.410	6.074	12.73	3.230	5.650	11.69
8	3.581	6.371	12.86	3.438	6.029	12.04	3.284	5.667	11.19	3.115	5.279	10.30	2.928	4.859	9.34
9	3.374	5.802	11.13	3.230	5.467	10.37	3.073	5.111	9.57	2.900	4.729	8.72	2.707	4.311	7.81
10	3.217	5.386	9.92	3.072	5.057	9.20	2.913	4.706	8.45	2.737	4.327	7.64	2.538	3.909	6.76
11	3.095	5.069	9.05	2.948	4.745	8.35	2.788	4.397	7.63	2.609	4.021	6.85	2.405	3.602	6.00
12	2.996	4.821	8.38	2.849	4.499	7.71	2.687	4.155	7.00	2.505	3.780	6.25	2.296	3.361	5.42
13	2.915	4.620	7.86	2.767	4.302	7.21	2.604	3.960	6.52	2.420	3.587	5.78	2.206	3.165	4.97
14	2.848	4.456	7.43	2.699	4.140	6.80	2.534	3.800	6.13	2.349	3.427	5.41	2.131	3.004	4.60
15	2.790	4.318	7.09	2.641	4.004	6.47	2.475	3.666	5.81	2.288	3.294	5.10	2.066	2.868	4.31
16	2.741	4.202	6.81	2.591	3.890	6.19	2.425	3.553	5.55	2.235	3.181	4.85	2.010	2.753	4.06
17	2.699	4.102	6.56	2.548	3.791	5.96	2.381	3.455	5.32	2.190	3.083	4.63	1.960	2.653	3.85
18	2.661	4.015	6.35	2.510	3.705	5.76	2.342	3.371	5.13	2.150	2.999	4.45	1.917	2.566	3.67
19	2.628	3.939	6.18	2.477	3.631	5.59	2.308	3.396	4.97	2.114	2.925	4.29	1.878	2.489	3.52
20	2.599	3.871	6.02	2.447	3.564	5.44	2.278	3.231	4.82	2.083	2.859	4.15	1.843	2.421	3.38
21	2.573	3.812	5.88	2.421	3.506	5.31	2.250	3.173	4.70	2.054	2.801	4.03	1.812	2.360	3.26
22	2.549	3.758	5.76	2.397	3.453	5.19	2.226	3.121	4.58	2.028	2.749	3.92	1.783	2.305	3.15
23	2.528	3.710	5.65	2.375	3.406	5.09	2.204	3.074	4.48	2.005	2.702	3.82	1.757	2.256	3.05
24	2.508	3.667	5.55	2.355	3.363	4.99	2.183	3.032	4.39	1.984	2.659	3.74	1.733	2.211	2.97
25	2.490	3.627	5.46	2.337	3.324	4.91	2.165	2.993	4.31	1.964	2.620	3.66	1.711	2.169	2.89
26	2.474	3.591	5.38	2.321	3.288	4.83	2.148	2.958	4.24	1.946	2.585	3.59	1.691	2.132	2.82
27	2.459	3.558	5.31	2.305	3.256	4.76	2.132	2.926	4.17	1.930	2.552	3.52	1.672	2.096	2.75
28	2.445	3.528	5.24	2.291	3.226	4.69	2.118	2.896	4.11	1.915	2.522	3.46	1.654	2.064	2.70
29	2.432	3.499	5.18	2.278	3.198	4.64	2.104	2.869	4.05	1.901	2.495	3.41	1.638	2.034	2.64
30	2.421	3.474	5.12	2.266	3.173	4.58	2.092	2.843	4.00	1.887	2.469	3.36	1.622	2.006	2.59
40	2.336	3.291	4.73	2.180	2.993	4.21	2.004	2.665	3.64	1.793	2.288	3.01	1.509	1.805	2.23
60	2.254	3.119	4.37	2.097	2.823	3.87	1.917	2.496	3.31	1.700	2.115	2.69	1.389	1.601	1.90
120	2.175	2.956	4.04	2.016	2.663	3.55	1.834	2.336	3.02	1.608	1.950	2.40	1.254	1.380	1.56
∞	2.099	2.802	3.74	1.938	2.511	3.27	1.752	2.185	2.74	1.517	1.791	2.13	1.000	1.000	1.00

Source: Frederick E. Croxton and Dudley J. Cowden, *Practical Business Statistics* (2nd ed.; New York: Prentice-Hall, Inc., 1948), pp. 514 and 515. Reprinted by permission of the publisher.

Values of F at the .05 and .01 points were taken, by permission, from Maxine Merrington and Catherine M. Thompson, "New Tables of Statistical Variables," *Biometrika*, Vol. XXXIII, Part 1, pp. 80, 81, 84, and 85. Values of F at the .001 point were taken from Table V of R. A. Fisher and F. Yates, *Statistical Tables for Biological, Agricultural and Medical Research*, Oliver and Boyd, Ltd., Edinburgh, 1938, by permission of the author and publishers. The first reference gives F values to five digits at the .50, .25, .10, .05, .025, .01, and .005 points and for values of n_1, in addition to those shown in the above table. The second reference gives F values to three or more digits at the .20, .05, .01, and .001 points.

APPENDIX E—PERCENTAGE POINTS OF THE χ^2 DISTRIBUTION*

(Each entry is a percent point of χ^2. It is exceeded by the proportion (P) of values of χ^2 listed in the column heading for the number of degrees of freedom (n) given in the stub.)

n.	P=.99	.98	.95	.90	.80	.70	.50	.30	.20	.10	.05	.02	.01
1	.000157	.000628	.00393	.0158	.0642	.148	.455	1.074	1.642	2.706	3.841	5.412	6.635
2	.0201	.0404	.103	.211	.446	.713	1.386	2.408	3.219	4.605	5.991	7.824	9.210
3	.115	.185	.352	.584	1.005	1.424	2.366	3.665	4.642	6.251	7.815	9.837	11.345
4	.297	.429	.711	1.064	1.649	2.195	3.357	4.878	5.989	7.779	9.488	11.668	13.277
5	.554	.752	1.145	1.610	2.343	3.000	4.351	6.064	7.289	9.236	11.070	13.388	15.086
6	.872	1.134	1.635	2.204	3.070	3.828	5.348	7.231	8.558	10.645	12.592	15.033	16.812
7	1.239	1.564	2.167	2.833	3.822	4.671	6.346	8.383	9.803	12.017	14.067	16.622	18.475
8	1.646	2.032	2.733	3.490	4.594	5.527	7.344	9.524	11.030	13.362	15.507	18.168	20.090
9	2.088	2.532	3.325	4.168	5.380	6.393	8.343	10.656	12.242	14.684	16.919	19.679	21.666
10	2.558	3.059	3.940	4.865	6.179	7.267	9.342	11.781	13.442	15.987	18.307	21.161	23.209
11	3.053	3.609	4.575	5.578	6.989	8.148	10.341	12.899	14.631	17.275	19.675	22.618	24.725
12	3.571	4.178	5.226	6.304	7.807	9.034	11.340	14.011	15.812	18.549	21.026	24.054	26.217
13	4.107	4.765	5.892	7.042	8.634	9.926	12.340	15.119	16.985	19.812	22.362	25.472	27.688
14	4.660	5.368	6.571	7.790	9.467	10.821	13.339	16.222	18.151	21.064	23.685	26.873	29.141
15	5.229	5.985	7.261	8.547	10.307	11.721	14.339	17.322	19.311	22.307	24.996	28.259	30.578
16	5.812	6.614	7.962	9.312	11.152	12.624	15.338	18.418	20.465	23.542	26.296	29.633	32.000
17	6.408	7.255	8.672	10.085	12.002	13.531	16.338	19.511	21.615	24.769	27.587	30.995	33.409
18	7.015	7.906	9.390	10.865	12.857	14.440	17.338	20.601	22.760	25.989	28.869	32.346	34.805
19	7.633	8.567	10.117	11.651	13.716	15.352	18.338	21.689	23.900	27.204	30.144	33.687	36.191
20	8.260	9.237	10.851	12.443	14.578	16.266	19.337	22.775	25.038	28.412	31.410	35.020	37.566
21	8.897	9.915	11.591	13.240	15.445	17.182	20.337	23.858	26.171	29.615	32.671	36.343	38.932
22	9.542	10.600	12.338	14.041	16.314	18.101	21.337	24.939	27.301	30.813	33.924	37.659	40.289
23	10.196	11.293	13.091	14.848	17.187	19.021	22.337	26.018	28.429	32.007	35.172	38.968	41.638
24	10.856	11.992	13.848	15.659	18.062	19.943	23.337	27.096	29.553	33.196	36.415	40.270	42.980
25	11.524	12.697	14.611	16.473	18.940	20.867	24.337	28.172	30.675	34.382	37.652	41.566	44.314
26	12.198	13.409	15.379	17.292	19.820	21.792	25.336	29.246	31.795	35.563	38.885	42.856	45.642
27	12.879	14.125	16.151	18.114	20.703	22.719	26.336	30.319	32.912	36.741	40.113	44.140	46.963
28	13.565	14.847	16.928	18.939	21.588	23.647	27.336	31.391	34.027	37.916	41.337	45.419	48.278
29	14.256	15.574	17.708	19.768	22.475	24.577	28.336	32.461	35.139	39.087	42.557	46.693	49.588
30	14.953	16.306	18.493	20.599	23.364	25.508	29.336	33.530	36.250	40.256	43.773	47.962	50.892

For larger values of n, the expression $\sqrt{2\chi^2} - \sqrt{2n-1}$ may be used as a normal deviate with unit variance.

* Reprinted from Table III, pp. 112–13, of R. A. Fisher, *Statistical Methods for Research Workers* (11th ed.), published by Oliver and Boyd, Ltd., Edinburgh, by permission of author and publishers.

Index

277

This book has been set in 10 and 9 point Times Roman leaded 2 points. Chapter numbers and titles are in 16 point Helvetica. The size of the type page is 27 by 45½ picas.